Redefining

Southern

Culture

Mind
and
Identity
in the
Modern
South

Redefining
Southern Culture

James C. Cobb

The

University of

Georgia Press

Athens &

London

Published by the
University of Georgia Press
Athens, Georgia 30602
© 1999 by James C. Cobb
All rights reserved
Designed by Richard Hendel
Set in Monotype Garamond by G&S Typesetters, Inc.
Printed and bound by Maple-Vail
The paper in this book meets the guidelines for
permanence and durability of the Committee on
Production Guidelines for Book Longevity of the
Council on Library Resources.
Printed in the United States of America

03   02   01   00   99   C   5   4   3   2   1
03   02   01   00   99   P   5   4   3   2   1

Library of Congress Cataloging in Publication Data

Cobb, James C. (James Charles), 1947–
Redefining Southern culture : mind and identity
in the modern South / James C. Cobb.
p.   cm.
Includes bibliographical references.
ISBN 0-8203-2111-7 (alk. paper). —
ISBN 0-8203-2139-7 (pbk. : alk. paper)
1. Southern States—History—1865–1951.   2. South-
ern States—History—1951–   3. Southern States—
Intellectual life—1865–   4. Group identity—
Southern States.   5. Regionalism—Southern
States.   6. Social change—Southern States.
7. Industrialization—Southern States.   8. Southern
States—Economic conditions.   I. Title.
F216.C53   1999
975'.04—dc21   98-53758

British Library Cataloging in Publication Data available

To

Will Holmes, Lester Stephens,

and Emory Thomas —

teachers, friends, and colleagues.

Contents

Acknowledgments

A number of my friends and colleagues have published volumes of their essays, and I have generally found them convenient and useful. For me, however, putting together such a book has been a somewhat unsettling experience, because it has raised fears deep within me that what I have already written is more significant than anything I am likely to produce henceforth. (Those who read this volume may well think, "Surely not!") At any rate, I am grateful to Malcolm Call and Karen Orchard of the University of Georgia Press for their interest in publishing a book that fairly screams "midlife crisis!"

As usual, I am indebted to Numan Bartley and Tom Dyer, who, between them, have read practically everything I have written over the years and have never failed to tell me what I needed to hear even if it was not what I wanted to hear. I also want to thank Michael O'Brien for sharing his thoughts with me in conversation and via e-mail. My wife, Lyra Cobb, is both my editor extraordinaire and my best friend. I have been blessed with many good friends over the years. Three of the finest were once my teachers and are now my colleagues. To show my gratitude to them for what they have meant to me over the years, I am dedicating this book to Will Holmes, Lester Stephens, and Emory Thomas.

Finally, I want to express my thanks for permission to reprint the following essays:

"Beyond Planters and Industrialists: A New Perspective on the New South" originally appeared in the February 1988 issue of the *Journal of Southern History*.

"World War II and the Mind of the Modern South" originally appeared in *Remaking Dixie: The Impact of World War II on the American South*, edited by Neil McMillen (1997), and is used by permission of the University Press of Mississippi.

"Does 'Mind' Still Matter? The South, the Nation, and *The Mind of the South*, 1941–1991" originally appeared in the November 1991 issue of the *Journal of Southern History*.

"From Muskogee to Luckenbach: Country Music and the Southernization of America" originally appeared in the *Journal of Popular Culture* (Winter 1982).

Redefining

Southern

Culture

Introduction

For nearly thirty years, I have struggled to understand the impact of what is commonly referred to as "modernization" on
the American South. For many, modernization conjures up
images of high-rise buildings and "high-tech" industry. As
Reinhard Bendix points out, however, modernization is not
such a "modern" phenomenon after all: "The commonsense
of the word 'modern' encompasses the whole era since the
eighteenth century when inventions like the steam engine and
the spinning jenny provided the initial, technical basis for the
industrialization of societies." For most of us, modernization
is easier to describe than it is to define, but we continue to use
the term because, as Bendix puts it, "it tends to wake similar
associations in contemporary readers." This is true primarily
because its history in western Europe and parts of North
America has fostered a widespread conviction that, in addition to its economic ramifications, modernization has some
definite, recurrent social and political consequences. As Bendix explained, "The economic transformation of England coincided with the movement of independence in the American
colonies and the creation of the nation-state in the French revolution. Accordingly, the word 'modern' also wakes associations with the democratization of societies, especially the destruction of inherited privileges and the declaration of equal
rights of citizenship."[1]

For more than a generation of scholars who made it their business to observe the American *South,* the association of modernization with a certain set of social and political advances was borne out dramatically by the experience of the northern industrial states during the late nineteenth and early twentieth centuries. Ultimately, however, their conviction that the industrial North's response to modernization was the norm obliged them to provide some explanation when the South failed to replicate that experience. The search for this explanation spurred a reexamination of the South's history and culture, leading to a virtual consensus that the South's path to modernization had been blocked by the actions of a small, self-serving white minority who ruled with the tacit assent of a huge white majority wallowing in its own ignorance, provincialism, and bigotry.

As I look back, I must confess that I came close to employing this model of "ruling-class" determinism in my first book, *The Selling of the South* (1982), in which I placed most of the blame for a multitude of the region's economic, institutional, social, and environmental problems on the people who fashioned its industrial development policies. By 1984, however, I paid considerably more attention to the broader influences that derived from the region's distinctive place in the national and global economy as I sought to explain "Why the New South Never Became the North." In the ensuing fifteen years, I have flogged this question mercilessly, stressing the need to move the study of modernization in the South out of the shadow of the North's experience and beyond that to divest ourselves entirely of the notion of a fixed, normative model of modernization or modernity.[2]

I have also explored the relationship between modernization and southern life and culture, arguing that the cultural consequences of modernization should be seen as the products of a reciprocal process of adaptation and accommodation. In the South, this process did not destroy the region's cultural identity but continually reshaped and even enriched it, nurturing some of the most notable literary and musical contributions that are associated with southern life. The essays in this collection reflect my efforts not only to come to terms with modernization and its impact on the evolution of the South's cultural identity but to understand the efforts of others to do the same.

The question of the ancestral ties of post-Reconstruction "Redeemer" leaders to the antebellum planter class was a central issue in legitimizing their leadership and that of the "New South" proponents who succeeded them. C. Vann Woodward's challenge to this claim ultimately set him at odds with W. J. Cash, who emphasized the continuities between the "minds" of the Old and New South. The ensuing "Cash v. Woodward" debate dominated the agendas of southern historians for more than a generation. "Beyond Planters and Industrialists: A New Perspective on the New South" analyzes this debate and stresses the need to move beyond it. This essay also affirms a growing sense that the events that truly shaped the destiny of the post-Reconstruction South may have actually come later in what I call the "turning period," which stretched from the Great Migration and World War I through the boll weevil invasion, the Great Depression, the New Deal, and World War II. A growing number of observers now emphasize the impact of World War II on the South, and some even dare to suggest that impact was even greater than that of the Civil War itself. This suggestion is explored in "World War II and the Mind of the Modern South."

As he sensed the inevitability of American involvement in the war in Europe, W. J. Cash fretted about the South's "capacity for adjustment" to the war and to the forces for change that it would likely unloose. "Does 'Mind' Still Matter? The South, the Nation, and *The Mind of the South, 1941–1991*" is an effort to provide some perspective on Cash's remarkable book and the waxing and waning of its influence in response to changes in the South, the nation, and the relationship between the two.

In recent years this changing relationship has often been referred to as the "southernization of America," a phrase carrying the decidedly negative implications of the triumph of a narrow, reactionary, mean-spirited mind-set in American politics, popular culture, and public life. "From Muskogee to Luckenbach: Country Music and the Southernization of America" utilizes changing mass society attitudes toward country music to assess the changing national mood and especially changing attitudes about white southerners and their culture.

"The Blues Is a Lowdown Shakin' Chill" uses the blues as a window into African American culture as it developed in response to emancipation and agricultural modernization in the Yazoo Mississippi Delta during the late nineteenth and early twentieth centuries. It suggests that the blues emerged in tandem with a growing sense of alienation among black workers as they began to sense that neither the anticipated benefits of emancipation nor the full fruits of their labors would ever be theirs to enjoy. This sense of alienation made the message of the blues seem increasingly relevant to white Americans at the end of the twentieth century.

Though country music and the blues seemed to be almost polar opposites, they were actually more closely interrelated than they seemed. The commonalities and contrasts apparent in their distinctive perspectives on southern life became more apparent in the post–Jim Crow era when the "southern way of life" was no longer simply a code phrase for white supremacy and both black and white southerners engaged in fervent efforts to reconfigure their regional identity along nonracial lines. This effort is the subject of "Searching for Southernness: Community and Identity in the Contemporary South."

The struggle with southern identity has been going on for quite a while. In "From 'New South' to 'No South': The Southern Renaissance and the Struggle with Southern Identity," I argue that the first "New South" amounted to a great deal more than a crusade for economic modernization. In fact, it constituted an entirely new regional identity deliberately constructed along the lines of a new national identity. Promising a dynamic economy, but a static racial and political order, the New South identity was a bundle of inconsistency and contradiction. The effort to unravel this bundle provided a central thrust for the Southern Renaissance, a literary and scholarly movement whose participants raised many of the questions that recur throughout this volume.

The concluding essay, "Modernization and the Mind of the South," offers a final mop-up, shoot-the-wounded assault on the classic modernization model traditionally employed to study the South in the years since Reconstruction. It emphasizes several historical, technological, and economic factors that helped to make both modernization and the South's response to it significantly different from what occurred in the northern industrial states.

This essay also stresses the notion of culture as "process," an ongoing cycle of interaction between past and present that sustains the modernizing South's cultural identity as a work in progress rather than fashioning it into a final, finished product. C. Vann Woodward pointed out in 1953 that "from a broader point of view it is not the South but America that is unique among the peoples of the world." In a similar vein, I suggest that as we move into a new century, questions about the South's cultural identity should move beyond a narrowly focused obsession with the issue of southern distinctiveness relative to the rest of the nation. Instead, we should explore larger global commonalities, such as the influence of historical memory or the cultural consequences of modernization in other societies that have shared some of the historical experiences that seemed to set southerners apart from other Americans.[3]

Beyond
Planters
and
Industrialists

A New Perspective on the New South

Agrarian-industrial conflict has been a favorite theme among scholars from a variety of disciplines who have studied the South's history and attempted to diagnose its problems. In the eyes of some, the antebellum South was a premodern agrarian society bludgeoned to submission by a northern industrial behemoth and reduced thereafter to little more than an agricultural colony for the nation's industrial core. Largely discounting this disadvantageous relationship, others saw the postbellum South as its own worst enemy, clinging to discredited, plantation-bred traditions that were wholly incompatible with efforts to build a northern-style industrial economy in the region and to bring it into the nation's social and cultural mainstream as well.[1]

Like other scholars, historians have relied heavily on the agrarian-industrial dynamic in their efforts to measure and to understand continuity and change in the post-Reconstruction South. They have devoted much of their energy to the question of whether agricultural or industrial interests presided over the region after the Civil War and thus shaped its economic, political, and social development according to their own specific interests or priorities. Although it has produced some impressive scholarship, this line of inquiry has overemphasized the social and political distance between planters and industrialists. At the same time, by exaggerating the ability of either group to control its own destiny, much less that of an entire region, this approach has also afforded too little attention to the changing world and national economic context that played a major role in shaping the South's transition from agriculture to industry.

Despite the numerous volumes on the subject that now burden library shelves and university press warehouses, the basic outlines of the planter-industrialist dispute remain roughly where they were in 1951 after the publication of C. Vann Woodward's *Origins of the New South, 1877–1913*. In this influential synthesis and in subsequent writings, Woodward described the postbellum collapse of the planter aristocracy that had led the Old South to renounce its "bourgeois origins." In its place arose a new business and industrial elite, bourgeois to the bone and intent on recasting the South's economy in the image of the North. Woodward's conclusions indicated a fundamental disagreement with Wilbur J. Cash, who a decade earlier had crafted an eloquent argument that "a unity of cultural values kept economic, social, and political conflict in check despite the disruption of Southern institutions." Where Woodward credited the Civil War with the overthrow of the planter class, in *The Mind of the South* Cash stressed continuity of leadership and values. For Cash, however, the planter ideology remained, as it had been from the beginning, essentially bourgeois.[2]

As the core of the continuity-change debate, the planter-industrialist dichotomy established by Cash and Woodward has itself become a first-rate specimen of continuity. So powerful is its spell that other historians whose findings fall between the two extremes have found themselves either forced to take sides or simply assigned by reviewers to the Woodward or the Cash camp. Those who wish to explore other facets of the social, political, and economic structure of the post-Reconstruction South must do so with great care lest they be trampled by the galloping ghostly cavalrymen used by Cash to symbolize planter-inspired continuity or crushed by the bourgeois-piloted bulldozers that for Woodward served as the vehicles of change.[3]

On the twentieth anniversary of the publication of *Origins of the New South*, Sheldon Hackney marveled that there had been so little fundamental challenge to the story sketched by Woodward. Hackney's article quickly became a period piece, for in the ensuing fifteen years Woodward's description of the wholesale demise of the planters at the hands of upstart businessmen and industrialists has been tested and found wanting by a number of scholars. Although they have left the overall credibility of *Origins* intact, their studies have reenergized the planter-industrialist debate, raising so many questions and stimulating so much new research that future textbook authors are likely to stop well short of I. A. Newby's 1978 assertion that the postbellum planter class "lost its preeminence to a business and professional elite centered in the towns and cities."[4]

As the premier student of irony in southern history, Woodward can surely appreciate the irony in the fact that some of his foremost critics are those who pursued his suggestion that the South's experience might be better understood if studied in a comparative global context. Though by no means all of the evidence marshaled against Woodward's transfer of leadership came from Marxist scholars operating in a comparative framework, those who drew the most attention employed this approach.[5]

The most notable of the new studies whose findings appeared to contradict Woodward were Jonathan M. Wiener's *Social Origins of the New South,* a study of Alabama, and Dwight B. Billings Jr.'s *Planters and the Making of a New South,* which focused on North Carolina. Wiener's primary contention was that Alabama planters continued to rule the roost in the postbellum decades, successfully turning back a political challenge from the state's expanding industrial classes and effectively impeding the economic modernization of Alabama. Billings, on the other hand, argued for planter persistence but found them at the forefront of the move to industrialize the Tarheel state. Both Wiener's planters and Billings's planter-entrepreneurs led their respective states down a path described by both authors (with allusion to the writings of Barrington Moore) as the "Prussian Road" to a modern society. In reality, neither Wiener's Alabama (where planters opposed industrialization) nor Billings's North Carolina (where planters orchestrated it) were truly comparable to the Prussian setting wherein the Junker elite retained social and political supremacy while allowing a shaky new middle class to promote the expansion of commerce and industry necessary to make Prussia a modern state. As used by Wiener and Billings, the Prussian Road model simply implied a planter elite, alive and well, bent on controlling or restricting growth, and determined to forestall the kind of social and political transformation that had accompanied the transition to modernity in England.[6]

Using a similar approach in his dissertation study of Mississippi, Lester M. Salamon found a corresponding pattern of "limited modernization" mandated from above by a dominant planter class. Although he offered no Prussian analogy, economist Jay R. Mandle traced "the roots of black poverty" to the enduring influence of the planter class. In Mandle's view, planters resisted agricultural mechanization, blocked large-scale industrial development, and managed, through coercion and the manipulation of racial prejudices, to consign blacks to the status of a permanent regional peasantry.[7]

Despite their vastly different approaches, these studies seemed to support the subjective but deeply considered observations of Cash. Yet what the Prussian Road, planter-persistence theorists offered, according to Michael Wayne, "is Cash's theme of continuity, but turned inside out. The continuity they describe is marked by anti-bourgeois, rather than bourgeois, tendencies." More recent works have indicated that the findings of both Woodward and his Marxist critics need to be qualified. Wayne's own study focused on Mississippi and Louisiana planters who succeeded in preserving their "material interests" but failed to "preserve their world." Wayne described the transformation, rather than the destruction, of a ruling class. Still, he saw a "profound break" between the old order and a new one that exhibited growing bourgeois sensibilities. In her more recent study of slavery and freedom on the "middle ground" of Maryland, Barbara Jeanne Fields described the revolutionary impact of emancipation on white and black society.[8]

In their analyses of late nineteenth-century South Carolina, both David L. Carlton and Lacy K. Ford documented the rise of a merchant, town, and mill-building class in the South Carolina upcountry. Canton described the townspeople, though "not 'modern' in any ideal-typical sense," as "a modernizing elite" whose "conservatism" and attachment to the past did not "make them in any way extensions of the planter class or analogues of the Prussian Junkers." Ford found that "the power of the large landowners, the so-called planter elite of the New South, had been circumscribed, though by no means destroyed, by the myriad of difficulties in using free labor in plantation agriculture and by the concomitant rise of a dynamic merchant class that turned Upcountry towns into pulsating nodules of economic activity."[9]

Efforts to shed light on the planter-industrialist question have provided at least tentative evidence that the identity and relative influence of the New South's movers and shakers varied with historical and geographical context. For the most part, planter-merchant conflict centered not on alteration of the means of production but on preeminence within the rapidly evolving system of agricultural tenancy, specifically on the question of who would get first crack at expropriating the surplus produced by the region's expanding ranks of landless farmers. Throughout the South merchants and townsmen fared better in their relationships with planters and emerged more readily as local leaders in areas most removed from the heart of a state's plantation belt.[10]

Despite geographic and contextual variations, these collective findings indicated a significant commercial and industrial presence, but they also challenged Woodward's notion of a thoroughly decimated planter class. In an important summary article, James Tice Moore implied that what Woodward saw as a bourgeois revolution was actually more like an incomplete agrarian restoration.[11]

Responding to Moore and other critics, Woodward reentered the fray in 1986, asserting that he still believed "something that can be called a revolution occurred and that in the process the planter class took a terrific tumble." Even for those planters who maintained their footing, Woodward pointed out that "land at depressed values, crops at depressed prices, and labor with 30 percent lower productivity were not the real sources of power, nor were celebrated genealogies." In a study that appeared shortly after Woodward's rejoinder, Gavin Wright offered some support for Woodward's sketch of a planter class transformed — in Wright's view from "laborlords" to "landlords" struggling "to deal with a nonslave labor market." Under such circumstances surviving as planters may have meant little, but Woodward conceded that resourceful landlords may have "moved to towns, opened stores, run gins, compresses, and banks, invested in railroads and mills, and played the speculative markets." In so doing, he explained, "they transformed themselves into members of the new class that was creating a commercial revolution and fostering an industrial revolution."[12]

Although it had the appearance of a strategic retreat, Woodward's explanation actually gave little ground on the question of the persistence of planters as a governing elite. "If after the Revolution," Wright asked, "the members of a class vigorously pursue goals they staunchly opposed before, in what economic sense has that class survived?" Had there been a consensus that post-Reconstruction governments were wholly dedicated to industrial and commercial development, the question of continuing planter involvement might, as Wright suggested, have ceased to be of interest to anyone except sociologists. Yet a number of scholars who doubted that late nineteenth-century southern policymakers were committed to economic growth attributed this perceived reluctance largely to the persistent influence of the planter class.[13]

In his analyses of the antebellum South, Eugene D. Genovese has led the way in creating a vision of southern planters as committed opponents of industrialization, but many recent studies dispute Genovese's contentions. The view of antebellum planters as enemies of industrialization rests largely on their chauvinistic oratory and limited participation in manufacturing. The antebellum South was a society in which planter was the career of choice and one where the prospect of industrial upheaval, however improbable, was troubling to some. As Fred Bateman and Thomas Weiss have pointed out, however, for all their self-serving rhetoric, politically powerful antebellum planters left little in the way of legal restraints on industrial growth in the South. Their investment behavior was more conservative than anti-industrial, reflecting an altogether rational preference for the somewhat less lucrative but more secure and socially esteemed career of a slaveholding planter over the uncertain and unfamiliar role of pathbreaking industrialist.[14]

For the postbellum era, Wiener produced the most convincing evidence of planter opposition to industrialization. Much of the rhetoric he quoted would not have seemed anachronistic in the antebellum era. Yet the growth of Birmingham, both in type and time context, was clearly exceptional. The city's relative proximity to the Black Belt combined with its rapid growth to make the prospect of full-scale industrial development far more real in the Black Belt of Alabama than it ever became in any other "deep plantation" region of the South. Wiener's Alabama planters were less leery of small-scale, agriculture-related industry that promised to expedite their own operations without creating competition for their labor. In this regard they were little different from their antebellum ancestors and not terribly unlike twentieth-century textile, garment, and other industrialists who assented to complementary low-wage industry but vetoed any that might threaten their domination of local labor markets.[15]

Meanwhile, according to Numan V. Bartley's study of the "in between" state of Georgia, planters neither vigorously opposed industrial development as they did in Wiener's Alabama nor spearheaded the crusade to industrialize as they did in Billings's North Carolina. Surveying the entire region, James Tice Moore challenged Woodward's probusiness interpretation of the Redeemers, observing that "a case can be made that the Democratic elite provided more consistent and reliable support for farmers than for businessmen." On the other hand, however, Moore failed to demonstrate that attentiveness to planter and agricultural interests amounted to hostility to commercial and industrial ones. He described the Redeemer program as "abounding in ambiguities" and offering at least "uncertain and tenuous encouragement for the entrepreneurial classes."[16]

If the antebellum legal framework lacked laws and procedures necessary to facilitate significant industrialization, manufacturers received mixed signals in the late nineteenth-century South. At one time or another five states offered tax concessions to new industry, several provided public aid for railroad construction, and some were generous in their sales or outright grants of land to corporations. On the other hand, however, as Bartley has observed, nine of the eleven new state constitutions adopted in the 1870s and 1880s denied state aid to "private endeavors" and "in other ways circumscribed expenditures for the internal improvements that would have been necessary to promote rapid industrial growth." Jonathan Wiener cited the failure of the "Whig-planter-businessmen" who dominated the 1865 Alabama constitutional convention to "institute the major legal requirements of modern corporate development, thereby indicating their intention to continue to hold back the industrialization of the state." In 1883 agricultural interests in the South Carolina upcountry supported repeal of a tax-exemption provision for new industry. Lacy Ford did not go as far as Wiener, however, concluding that "opposition to publicly financed railroads and to special tax privileges for industrialists does not suggest that Upcountry farmers opposed economic development but simply that they opposed the building of the New South at their own expense." Behind the failure of these farmers to invest in cotton mills David Carlton found both a "chronic lack of capital" and "ambivalence toward cotton mills and the concentrations of economic power they represented."[17]

As the works of Carlton and Ford demonstrated, the debate over state aid to industry involved not only planters but lesser farmers as well. The outcry against the heavy tax burdens of the Reconstruction era, analyzed in a recent essay by J. Mills Thornton III, almost certainly carried over to the legislative and constitutional debates about incentives for industry. More often than not, the more vocal opponents of these measures were self-proclaimed spokesmen for the common man who assailed tax exemptions and other concessions as examples of favoritism and special privilege. In Mississippi, for example, the Illinois Central Railroad, the lifeline of the Yazoo-Mississippi Delta, incurred the wrath of "redneck" hill country representatives who made little distinction between the special treatment accorded the railroad and the inordinate political clout wielded by the self-styled Delta aristocrats whose interests the railroad served. That this hostility grew out of a rejection of elitism and privilege rather than an aversion to industrial development is suggested by the fact that in 1896, as the state took to the courts to revoke the railroad's tax exemption and collect back revenues, the legislature granted any outside manufacturer locating in Mississippi an automatic ten-year tax deferral.[18]

Taken together the findings summarized here provide little basis for regionwide generalizations about the attitudes of planters toward industrial development. Except for the rhetoric supplied by Genovese and Wiener, the most we have on which to posit planter opposition is a failure to facilitate industrialization. This failure, no doubt, reflected some misgivings, but planter antipathy to industrial expansion hardly ranks as a central theme of the political and economic history of the late nineteenth-century South. On the other hand, had a dominant new class of leaders intent on mobilizing the region for industrial development been firmly in control, they surely could have rammed through more of the proindustry constitutional provisions. Had they done so, however, there is little reason to believe that the course of southern economic development would have been fundamentally altered. In the second quarter of the twentieth century, when the southern states turned to much more extensive programs of subsidies and assistance to industry, they succeeded only in confirming the pattern of dependence on labor-intensive and/or resource- or raw material–oriented industry that was already established in the late nineteenth century when such subsidies were unavailable.[19]

Jonathan Wiener emphasized the role of planters in steering the South onto the Prussian Road and away from "the classic capitalist path that had been blazed by England in the seventeenth and eighteenth centuries and followed by the Northern states." The validity of the Prussian Road model has been challenged by those who doubt that postbellum planters enjoyed the political and economic dominance attributed to the Junkers. "As Prussians, Alabamians cut a sorry figure," quipped Michael O'Brien. The concept of a "classic capitalist path" to a modern society is also a dubious one, resting only on a particular interpretation of the experiences of industrializing England and the northern United States. After all, as Barbara Fields observed, "The English agricultural revolution could happen only once, and the northern American version — occurring in a huge, sparsely populated continent — could repeat itself only in the rare instance (for example, Australia) in which this situation was replicated."[20]

As Fields's observation indicated, the South's journey toward economic modernization came in a different historical, cultural, technological, and resource context than did that of the North. The fortuitous combination of world demand, resources, technological innovation, and immigrant labor that fed the economic revolution in the North was by and large lacking in a South that found itself in decidedly uneven competition for investment capital with its more fortunate northern neighbor. David Carlton took note of this mismatch, explaining that "unfortunately for the southern economy, it had to coexist, within national boundaries, with a well-developed industrial region which could provide strong competition to any southern 'infant industry' requiring a skilled labor force and experienced entrepreneurs." Despite his emphasis on planter opposition to industrial development, Wiener also pointed to the initial refusal of northeastern investors to pour capital into the development of Birmingham. "These financiers," Wiener realized, "were engaged in the first stages of the consolidation of capitalist enterprises in their own rapidly developing region — a consolidation that absorbed a great deal of capital and paid an embarrassingly handsome return." So long as this remained the case, except for the petroleum-rich areas of Louisiana, Texas, and Oklahoma and, ultimately, the iron and coal region of Alabama, the South's hopes for expanding its industrial base centered on the creation of a highly attractive investment climate for competitive, labor-intensive industries that could no longer operate profitably in the North.[21]

The respective social and political routes to modernization taken by the North and by the South were hardly a simple matter of choice for the political and economic elite of either region. For the leaders of the economically vibrant North a measure of political democracy and social consciousness was but a grudgingly yielded hedge against instability and upheaval, one whose costs were bearable so long as rapid growth continued. Meanwhile, in the South a lingering dependence on labor-intensive agriculture and the courtship by default of industries highly sensitive to labor, tax, and material costs helped to shape a society whose leaders saw social control as a better, less expensive investment than social uplift. Regardless of who ruled the late nineteenth-century South, the prevailing core of reactionary, socially insensitive policies that characterized the era was far more likely to please than to put off the industrialists who were choosing southern locations. As for more dynamic enterprises, it was not the South's social and political structure but the distribution of labor, markets, capital, and resources within the national economy that kept them out of the region.

William N. Parker concluded that the post-Reconstruction South's economic experience "could hardly have occurred otherwise except as part of a national economic and social policy which would have redistributed labor and capital within the nation . . . without regard to race, locality, or previous social structure." According to Parker, bringing the South into the nation's economic, social, and political mainstream after the Civil War would have "required not only a national policy of the scope of the New Deal . . . but also the assistance of massive jolts from physical, technological and extraneous market and political events."[22]

If the South was not a region whose economic development was thwarted or compromised by its own leaders, be they planter or industrialist, it was a society in transition, one whose governing elites could not ignore the needs of a still powerful agricultural sector, but one where aggressive business and industrial interests, with momentum on their side, were beginning to make themselves felt. The complex relationship between economic, social, and political conditions went beyond the simple question of the relative influence wielded by planters and industrialists.

Reinhard Bendix noted that "the evidence concerning changes of social stratification in the course of industrialization does not present the simple picture of a declining aristocracy and a rising bourgeoisie. In most European countries there is evidence rather of the continued social and political preeminence of preindustrial ruling groups even when their economic fortunes declined, as well as of the continued, subordinate social and political role of the 'middle classes' even when their economic fortunes rose." In an industrializing society existing social and political arrangements may "lag" and thus fail to provide an accurate reflection of the transition that is under way. Tensions are inevitable in such societies, but in the case of the South, the transformation was gradual enough and the primary concerns and goals of planters and industrialists compatible enough to support a central set of policies that served the interests of both groups without necessarily reflecting the relative strength of either.[23]

For example, C. Vann Woodward has argued that "in order to accumulate the capital required for the industrial plant, or to attract it from outside," late nineteenth-century lawmakers "cut appropriations for public services to the bare bone" and "starved the public schools to the point of emaciation." Woodward also linked labor repression, disfranchisement, and legislative malapportionment to the industrial development effort.[24]

Summarizing literature that examined the same policies but found them "less oriented toward business and industrial development than had been generally assumed," Numan Bartley concluded that "the Bourbon preoccupation with social stability, low taxes, and limited government does not necessarily suggest a governing elite preoccupied with economic development." As Bartley's comment indicated, the same policies that Woodward saw favoring business and industry have been cited by others as evidence of persistent planter influence.[25]

These conflicting assessments of the goals and orientation of government in the New South point to a common core of policies acceptable both to planters and to industrialists. So long as industrial-development initiatives posed no threat to white supremacy, labor control, fiscal conservatism, and political stability, the interests of the region's planters were in no danger of compromise. Buttressed both by circumstances outside the region and by the unpleasant realities of race, class, and relative wealth within it, New South development policies translated, as Woodward wrote, into "juleps for the few and pellagra for the crew."[26]

The "crew" did not suffer their subjugation in silence. Unable to reorder the priorities of the central policy core or to resist a growing subordination to single-crop commercial agriculture, the South's small farmers joined the Farmers' Alliance and Populist crusades. These uprisings were a protest against the unresponsiveness of a political system dominated by large-scale agricultural, commercial, and industrial interests, but their long-term effect was to increase the cohesion of these elites.[27]

As the South entered the twentieth century the accelerating momentum of the business and industrial sector manifested itself in the many growth-oriented reforms of the Progressive Era. During the first three decades of the twentieth century the South actually adopted a strategy employed by other, less developed regions. Growth-minded southern leaders relaxed their grip on the public purse enough to invest more heavily in education, transportation, and public health as a means of accelerating economic expansion. Between 1900 and 1920 per capita per pupil expenditures increased by 416 percent in the South, while they grew in the nation at large by only 250 percent. Many of these Progressive Era reforms reflected a genuine humanitarian concern for lower-class whites, but they aimed primarily at stabilizing an industrializing society and vaulting it over some of the earlier stages of economic development by providing it with the modernized system of transportation and public services and the reliable, competent labor force thought necessary for more advanced industrial economies.[28]

Dewey W. Grantham has described southern Progressivism as an effort to reconcile "progress and tradition." From the perspective of political economy, southern Progressives achieved this reconciliation by improving the South's infrastructure, upgrading its industrial labor supply, and mobilizing its state and local governments for industrial development without provoking a political confrontation with southern planters or stripping them of their dominion over the lower tier of the South's low-wage economy. One key to the success of this effort was the fact that although the expanded commitment to transportation, education, and public health created new revenue demands, per capita tax collections remained well below national norms. Moreover, the primary benefits of the modernizing reforms of the Progressive Era fell squarely on the white side of the color line. The "for whites only" nature of educational reform was a prime example. As Gavin Wright argued recently, improvements in black schools were likely to undermine a planter's ability to hold on to his black tenants. Consequently, efforts to strengthen public education during this period often amounted to improving only the white schools and, not infrequently, to improving them at the expense of the black ones.[29]

Where education for whites was concerned Wright also concluded that, like their planter contemporaries, "southern entrepreneurs" operating as "low-wage employers in a high-wage country, . . . could not take vigorous steps to open communication and interaction with the outside world, without risking loss of labor." The proponents of Progressive Era educational reform took care to avoid such risks, however; their goal was not to unleash white labor but to "domesticate" it as a part of their overall effort to, in David Carlton's words, "organize a turbulent and diverse society through the training of its children." As described by James L. Leloudis II, North Carolina's Woman's Association for the Betterment of Public School Houses supported "a program of social control," one "intent upon training children 'to fill the positions defined by circumstances' without going 'so far as to make [them] discontented with their lot or [to] fill their minds with vain ambition.'" No matter how sincere the humanitarianism of these reform advocates, their goal was not socioeconomic uplift but moral and behavioral discipline through the inculcation of middle-class values in a group of people who had (and were given) little hope of becoming middle class.[30]

A contemporary observer quoted by George B. Tindall concluded that "'the business class political philosophy of the new South is broad enough to include programs of highway improvement, educational expansion, and health regulation. But it does not embrace any comprehensive challenge to laissez faire ideas in the sphere of relationship between capital and labor, and the section is lagging in social support of such matters as effective child labor regulation and compensation legislation.'" Actually, business progressives did challenge laissez-faire in the relationship between capital and labor as state and local governments cast their lot with capital, promising labor control and ultimately offering financial assistance for industrial expansion.[31]

The desire to insure social stability in the midst of economic change had even encouraged a limited retreat from laissez-faire in the social welfare sector. Still, southern governments continued to hang back in this area where, again quoting Tindall, it was assumed that race relations were a "settled problem" and that the remedy for "the larger economic problems" of tenants and industrial workers "would come, if at all, through economic expansion."[32]

Business progressivism made bedfellows of boosterism and reform, and the ensuing union was an enduring one, described by Tindall as the new "norm of Southern statecraft in the decades that followed." Tindall's conclusion actually understated the case. The all-out devotion to the cause of growth and the unexamined faith in growth as a panacea for all that ailed the South formed the basis of a consensus broad enough to span the region's ideological spectrum.[33]

An indelible belief in the ameliorating potential of economic growth led a number of the South's small cadre of moderates and liberals to accept low wages, discriminatory hiring, blatant anti-unionism, tax exemptions, and worker exploitation as unpleasant means to an ultimately redemptive end. Hodding Carter Jr. led the industrial recruitment charge in Greenville, Mississippi, and marshaled community support for a bond issue to finance a tax-free building for the Alexander Smith Company. Carter's *Delta Democrat-Times* emphasized "the truly splendid one-hundred-year human and industrial record" of the carpet manufacturing firm that was then in the process of fleeing Yonkers, New York, and abandoning its unionized work force of 2,500. The company soon occupied a new fifteen-acre plant in Greenville where none of its workers bore the taint of unionism. In an interview some years later Carter explained how he must have rationalized his support for this and similar industrialization efforts by noting that economic progress was the real key to racial progress in the South. "You know," Carter declared, "people who get decent jobs don't stay rednecks for very long. That's the hope of the South, of course."[34]

Because it promised economic rewards and posed no threat to their social and political dominance, the growth ethos appealed to conservatives as well as to liberals. In Mississippi, for example, it became the only subject on which Hodding Carter and Ross R. Barnett could agree. The optimism of Henry W. Grady and his New South disciples stood at one time in stark contrast to the standpattism of the planter, but as the realities of building an economy based on competitive, low-wage, labor-intensive industries sank in, the rhetoric of change began to sound increasingly like the rhetoric of more of the same. Racism, sectionalism, and economic and physical coercion became the stock-in-trade of many southern leaders committed to economic growth.

In the hands of its conservative proponents the desire for industrialization became a potent propaganda weapon because it melded that old standby, defense of tradition, with a more dynamic and captivating rationale — the pursuit of progress. Integration, unionization, progressive taxation, and government regulation could all be lumped together as a part of a massive Yankee plot to undermine the South's traditions and derail its progress. The Citizens Council propagandized nonstop for white supremacy, but it was hardly bashful about its affection for the right-to-work law either. When Mississippi voted to put such a law in its constitution, the council-dominated Delta counties turned in some of the most impressive majorities for the proposal. Labor organizers found direct ties between the Citizens Council and anti-union groups like the Arkansas Free Enterprise Association and the Louisiana Right To Work Councils.[35]

From the heart of the South Carolina textile belt the editor of the *Anderson Independent* wrote: "'In the 1850's there were the Abolitionists. In the 1950's there is the NAACP. In the 1850's the South's economy was becoming too strong to suit New England's interests. In the 1950's the migration of industry poses the same challenge to the North and East.'" Lieutenant Governor Ernest F. Hollings tapped similar racial and sectional prejudices when he vowed that "'we are not going to have labor unions, the NAACP and New England politicians blemish the Southern way of life.'" Hollings's assertion testified to the ease with which the proponents of industrialization were able to cast themselves both as the guardians of the past and as the architects of the future. Lacy Ford saw in his emergent South Carolina upcountry elite an essential faith described by Alexander Gerschenkron as the belief "'that the golden age lies not behind but ahead of mankind.'" As the twentieth century unfolded the descendants of these men were soon using the same tactics to pursue their golden age as the planters had once employed to protect their own golden age.[36]

At the center of the common core of planter-industrialist interests was the need for an adequate supply of low-cost labor. As Harold D. Woodman observed, "The desire for a dependent, easily controlled, docile, and cheap labor force burns as fiercely in the heart of a thoroughly bourgeois factory owner as it does in the heart of a plantation owner." On the farm and in the factory, Woodman concluded, southern employers stood apart from their northern brethren in their ability "to exercise a more complete control over their work force."[37]

Given the importance of labor both to planters and to industrialists, the greatest source of tension between them was the possibility of competition for workers in a particular geographical area. For the early postbellum era Wiener presented the clearest evidence of planter-industrialist tensions arising from labor concerns, but the rapid expansion of the railroads and the explosive growth of Birmingham created a market for black industrial labor that was uncharacteristic of the South or Alabama at large in subsequent decades.

Save for industries like timber, naval stores, and meat processing, jobs in southern manufacturing were reserved largely for whites with just a few of the most onerous and distasteful tasks open to blacks. The greatest threats to a Black Belt planter's labor supply came either from the out-migration of black labor or from other planters or lesser farmers who periodically needed extra help with chopping or picking. When a Mississippi planter charged with peonage explained that he was "damn tired of people trying to get my Negroes," he was talking not about industrialists but other planters.[38]

The Yazoo-Mississippi Delta was a bastion of large-scale, labor-intensive agriculture, but there is surprisingly little hard evidence of any sustained, effective opposition to industrialization on the part of that region's landed elite. Sawmills and other such intermittent, seasonal operations that passed for "industry" in much of the Delta could save planters considerable investment in tenant or wage-hand upkeep during slack labor periods. Such industries were more than willing to accommodate local wage scales. When local planters objected to wages paid to black laborers by a Natchez sawmill, the mill's owners cheerfully cut paychecks in half.[39]

The assumption that planters were the chief opponents of economic modernization in the South hardly squared with Gavin Wright's observation that while federal wage and hour laws affecting industry had to be "imposed on the South from outside," the federal farm policies that triggered mechanization and the demise of the sharecropping system "were virtually written by the planters." Because of this involvement, although their ranks had been thinned by the boll weevil invasion, the Depression, and the ensuing consolidation of landholding, at the end of the 1930s it was those planters who survived, rather than those who had passed on, who found themselves in "planter's heaven . . . , with generous government subsidies, protection against risk, ready financing for new machinery, and cheap harvest labor to make it all possible."[40]

As mechanization reduced the demand for farm labor, Mississippi Delta planters pledged their support for the recruitment of agriculture-related industries. While this position may have indicated some anxiety about the prospect of full-scale industrialization, there was actually little need for planters to fret. Except for river towns like Greenville and Natchez, interest in Delta area locations was confined primarily to small-scale agricultural support and processing industries.[41]

Historically, planters and farmers had been less than generous in their contributions to private industrial subsidy schemes, but the Delta legislators offered strong support for Mississippi's 1936 Balance Agriculture with Industry (BAWI) law. This plan allowed local governments to provide municipally financed and tax-exempt buildings for new industries. Similar programs soon cropped up across the South, incurring little opposition from planters and farmers because, unlike earlier efforts, they spread the costs of industrial subsidization across the entire population. Delta planters served regularly on the Agricultural and Industrial Board that oversaw the BAWI program, although relatively few industrialists expressed interest in Delta locations. Early BAWI plants that came into the area went to Natchez and Greenville and hired almost exclusively all-white workforces. Before Armstrong Tire arrived in Natchez, its officials announced they would employ "only a few colored for porters and mixing carbon black." Both towns were ardent in their courtship of these industries and generous in the terms they offered.[42]

By the time that equal employment legislation and the accelerated southward migration of industry had combined to create a greater demand for black industrial workers, mechanization had minimized the labor needs of southern planters. In areas affected by mechanization, such as Mississippi's infamous Tunica County, blacks charged that the entire white power structure had dragged its feet on industrial development in order to force out-migration by blacks who were unwanted as voters and no longer needed as laborers. This accusation may have been correct in a number of cases, but concerns about unionization, educational levels, and the prospect of political upheaval also encouraged relocating industrialists to spurn old plantation-belt areas with large black populations.[43]

Ironically, as the South became increasingly committed to industrial development, it was not planters and farmers but industrialists and industrial promoters who often spearheaded resistance to the recruitment of better paying and faster growing industries. Fearful of wage pressures and the contagion of unionism, the same local employers who loved to extol the virtues of competitive free-enterprise capitalism fought energetically and effectively to protect themselves from labor competition with high-wage, unionized firms. Industrial developers in Raleigh welcomed white-collar firms swarming with Ph.D.s to the Research Triangle but turned a cold shoulder to unionized blue-collar operations. Even at the height of the Sun Belt hysteria of the 1970s, from Greenville in the Piedmont to Greenville in the Delta, local economic growth agencies mustered their forces to turn back potentially unionized firms that might disrupt local wage scales and redistribute local workers. Most such firms eventually found homes in the South but usually not in communities where low-wage industries were still the dominant local employers.[44]

In addition to cheap labor, industrial development advocates remained concerned about low taxes and conservative government. Here again there was little reason for significant planter-industrialist conflict. An ongoing pattern of industrial expansion in rural areas and small towns not only retarded urbanization, but it left the region's urban businessmen heavily dependent on trade with the agricultural countryside and wedded them to the status quo in that countryside. Until the post–World War II era, malapportionment and notorious anti-urban political systems like Georgia's county unit plan simply mirrored the structural and spatial realities of the South's economy. Across the South, despite the expanded role of government as an agent of modernization, economic decentralization helped to preserve political decentralization and a conservative style of government that served the needs of the industrialist without damaging the interests of the planter. At the middle of the twentieth century Alabama retained its malapportioned legislature in which Black Belt planters remained the tail that wagged the dog only because, as one journalist put it, it was Birmingham's Big Mule economic elite "'who are the masters of that highly versatile tail.'"[45]

The conservative orientation of the southern growth ethos was rooted in a regional economy where labor-intensive industry and labor-intensive agriculture maintained a delicate coexistence. In the second quarter of the twentieth century when the relative importance of these two dominant components of the southern economy began to change dramatically, the old planter-industrialist policy core quickly reflected the shift in priorities induced by these changes. Triggered by the cumulative impact of the boll weevil, the Great Depression, and New Deal crop reduction subsidy programs, the mechanization of southern agriculture proceeded with even greater vigor under the influence of the economic tonic provided by World War II. These same factors combined to intensify the crusade for industrial development, which began to enjoy greater success in the wake of the war. This great lurch forward culminated in a major restructuring of the region's political economy as growth proceeded at an uneven pace and in an uneven distribution. Low-wage industries continued to seek rural locations, but the gains of the postwar years, the impact of federal minimum wage legislation, and the diminished relative importance of agriculture spurred ambitious urban leaders to seek a fuller integration of their communities into the national economy through the recruitment of larger, more dynamic firms. These aspirations led emergent metropolitan elites to challenge certain previously acceptable political traditions like legislative malapportionment and the year-round open season on blacks and city slickers.[46]

Finally, facing external pressure from the federal government and internal pressure from disruptive, image-scarring civil rights demonstrations, the leaders of cities like Atlanta, Charlotte, and Dallas took steps to avert the violence and school closings that they believed would be bad for business. On the other, trailing edge of the South's changing economy, however, sat many of the region's small towns and some cities like New Orleans and Birmingham, whose well-developed heavy industrial base helped to make its Big Mule leadership less interested in further growth than in the maintenance of segregation. In Jackson a fledgling business community proved reluctant to challenge the Citizens Council or a state legislature that still fixed an adoring gaze on South Africa. There was trouble at the trailing edge, trouble so disturbing and ugly that it made the pragmatic tokenism at the leading edge seem farsighted and progressive indeed. In reality, economically motivated moderates seldom went beyond what it took to forestall federal intervention or further protests. Moreover, their ties to business and industrial interests re-

inforced their fiscal conservatism and their skepticism about government's ability to provide meaningful assistance to the disadvantaged.[47]

A century after Henry Grady's New South speech the fundamental
elements of what manufacturers describe as the South's good business
climate are still policies that promise cheap labor, low taxes, and stable,
conservative government. The continuing appeal of these policies to industrialists (in an era when planters are as rare in the South as Republicans used to be) does not indicate that those who saw them in their late
nineteenth-century context as pro-planter were wrong. It does suggest,
however, that a static planter-industrialist model has limited value as a
means of explaining changing social, political, and economic linkages in
the post-Reconstruction South.[48]

Planter influence may have imposed some initial social and political restrictions on the New South development strategy, but for the
most part those restrictions were either acceptable or downright appealing to the types of industries that were most receptive to the South's
overtures. In response to these economic realities, the New South crusade moved quickly from a dualistic attempt to promote economic development while preserving social and political stability to one where
preserving social and political stability actually became part of the development effort.

The latter phase proved difficult to transcend. By the middle of the
twentieth century the need to upgrade the South's industrial base and
boost regional wage levels was well recognized, and, as a number of major American firms started to lose ground in an increasingly competitive
world manufacturing economy, they began to consider new locations in
areas of lower operating costs. In order to stem the tide of industrial
out-migration, however, old Manufacturing Belt states began to offer
financing, tax incentives, and a host of other southern-style induce-
ments as a means of hanging on to precious payrolls.

Meanwhile, the competition for American industrial investments expanded from an interregional contest to an international one. With its
low wages and good business climate growing steadily less meaningful
in comparison to its northern and midwestern competitors and already
meaningless relative to its "Third World" rivals, the South's political and
economic leaders confronted a dilemma. On the one hand, a continued
appeal to industry based on cheap labor and low taxes promised steadily
diminishing returns. On the other, abandonment of these policies was
likely to cost the South dearly in the short run so long as the worldwide

bidding war for industry continued. This second prospect became all the more apparent as the region suffered heavy job losses in its traditional mainstay industries like textiles and apparel, where executives often bowed to competitive pressures by transferring their operations to Third World labor markets. The need to hold on to these industries until they could be replaced by more stable, better-paying ones ran afoul of efforts to recruit these latter firms, not only because of potential wage competition but because of the increased tax revenues needed to fund the educational and other institutional improvements deemed necessary to attract more desirable industries. Beset by uneven growth rooted in the contradictory forces that pulled it in opposite directions, the South's economy hung suspended between the future and the past. For white-collar, metropolitan workers the interregional earnings gap effectively disappeared, but for unskilled, blue-collar workers outside the cities, South/non-South wage differentials showed little sign of shrinkage.[49]

As in the late nineteenth century, conditions throughout the world economy continued to shape efforts to direct and accelerate the South's industrial development. Through interaction with indigenous cultural and historical forces, these far-ranging economic influences set the stage not just for a regional drama but for a global one, as in settings as diverse as South Africa, South Korea, and South Carolina industrialization accommodated itself to what Woodward called "an astonishing variety of social systems, ethical doctrines and political purposes."[50]

In the case of the South this process of accommodation involved more than the competitive or cooperative efforts of planters and industrialists to shape the region's economic development to their own interests. It should also be examined within the larger context of an evolving national and international economy that helped to make certain elements of the social and political organization of a fading plantation society not just compatible with but almost integral to the establishment of a new industrial one. Seen in this perspective the story is one of continuity and change, not in conflict but in synthesis, their fortunes so interwoven that the effort to separate them — to isolate the hoofbeats of the cavalry from the roar of the bulldozer — promises to become the lost cause of southern historiography as the New South enters its second century.[51]

World
War II
and the
Mind
of the
Modern
South

As he brought his classic *Mind of the South* to a close, Wilbur J. Cash surveyed "the forces sweeping over the world in the fateful year of 1940" and warned that "in the coming days, and probably soon," the South was "likely to have to prove its capacity for adjustment far beyond what has been true in the past." As its "loyal son," Cash could only hope that in the coming confrontation the South's virtues would "tower over and conquer its faults." Yet, there was next to nothing in his decidedly pessimistic treatise to suggest that the South's "capacity for adjustment" would see it through or, for that matter, that it even possessed such a capacity. As the conflict with the Yankee escalated from words to war, a pervasive and enduring conformity had descended on the region, stifling creativity and intellectual curiosity by stigmatizing them, in Cash's words, as "anemic and despicable," not just alien and unsouthern but unmanly to boot. (The southern mind as Cash saw it was not only all white but — despite its showy and largely symbolic celebrations of white womanhood, which were closely related to its very real racial and sexual paranoia — all male as well.) Crippled by racism, an exaggerated sense of individualism, a tragic proclivity for violence, and the "savage ideal" of hostility to criticism or innovation, what Cash presented as a deeply flawed mind was actually more like a regional temperament, a remarkably consistent behavioral pattern forged in the crucible of Civil War and Reconstruction and still dominant and unyielding more than sixty years later.[1]

Unfortunately, the uncertain prospect of a second global conflict had driven an already neurotic Cash even closer to the edge. Hoping for the best, but expecting the worst, Cash knew that something big was about to happen to the South. He could hardly have dreamed, however, that had he not taken his own life in 1941, five months after his book was published and two months after his forty-first birthday, he might actually have lived to hear southern historians begin to attach a significance to World War II once reserved exclusively for the Civil War.[2]

Indeed, to paraphrase Gerald R. Ford, had Cash been alive, he would have been spinning in his grave when he learned that at the November 1982 meeting of the Southern Historical Association in Memphis, Morton Sosna, then of Stanford University, planned to read a paper whose title suggested that in its impact on the South, World War II had actually been "More Important than the Civil War." As a commentator on this session and a friend of Mort's, I felt obliged to warn him that while such radical notions might be tolerated or even encouraged at Stanford, it was quite another thing to stand at the northern terminus of the Mississippi Delta and dare to suggest that any event in human history, save perhaps for the birth and resurrection of Jesus Christ, was more important than the Civil War. To my dismay, Sosna ignored my warnings, and to my surprise, he not only delivered his paper but lived to see it published.[3]

In reality, Sosna's paper was not quite as audacious as his title implied. Several years earlier, for example, historian John R. Skates Jr. had insisted that "the Second World War was a watershed for Mississippi, a convenient and readily identifiable era, before which there was basic historical continuity for more than a century, but after which nothing ever again was quite the same."[4]

By the 1980s, after three decades of relatively unproductive historical wrangling about the genealogy and ideology of the post-Reconstruction South's political leadership, historians were beginning to realize that it was not the misdeeds of Redeemer Era politicians but fundamental economic and demographic factors that had been the primary influences in making the South of 1930 look so much like the South of 1877. Writing in 1980, economist William N. Parker implied that it was time to move on, arguing that the South's socioeconomic and political development between the end of Reconstruction and the beginning of the Great Depression could have been altered only by a national economic and social policy that would have "redistributed labor and capital within the nation . . . without regard to race, locality or previous social structure." The first attempt to enact such a policy came with the New Deal, and Parker believed that it was not until the New Deal/World War II era that "southern institutional peculiarity" began to break down and the region's "energies and resources" were freed "to be merged with the national society."[5]

In 1983 Numan V. Bartley observed that "while it would not be entirely appropriate to insist that nothing very important happened in the 1860s and the 1890s, those decades no longer seem . . . to be the great watersheds" that historians once assumed they were. Instead, Bartley believed, contemporary scholarship increasingly suggested that far more fundamental changes came out of the middle years of the twentieth century, with perhaps 1935 to 1945 best qualifying as the latest crucial decade of New South historiography."[6]

The changes that occurred during this decade were dramatic indeed. One of the most significant and relatively immediate ones was the transformation of southern agriculture. The New Deal's acreage-reduction incentives and the resultant consolidation and mechanization of agriculture were reinforced by the pull of military service and the opportunity for relatively lucrative employment in the defense industries. Between 1940 and 1945 alone, more than 20 percent of the South's farm population abandoned the land. The modernization of southern farming all but mandated a much more intensive emphasis on industrialization, forcing the region's commercial and professional classes who were once primarily dependent on agriculture to seek a broadened industrial base that would in turn expand both regional and local consuming potential. Efforts to recruit new industry had already accelerated significantly in response to the Depression, and the industrial stimulus of the war both intensified and institutionalized this trend. Launched in 1936, Mississippi's Balance Agriculture with Industry program of municipal subsidies to new industrial facilities had produced just twelve plants employing only 2,700 workers by 1940. As a result, disenchanted legislators allowed the BAWI law to lapse. Spurred by the wartime economy, however, the twelve plants were operating at full capacity by 1944, with the Ingalls Shipyard at Pascagoula providing more jobs than all the other subsidized plants combined. The Mississippi legislature speedily reinstated the BAWI program, and the other southern states quickly followed suit with subsidy plans of their own. By the early 1950s, a southern governor's obligation to recruit new industry was second only to his obligation to defend segregation.[7]

In time, economic development would even supersede the defense of Jim Crow as, however unevenly, in state after state, the post–World War II era saw the reins of power pass to more dynamic, metropolitan-oriented elites who sought fuller integration of both local and state economies into the national and global economy. "More young men came home from World War II with a sense of purpose than from any other American venture," former Mississippi congressman Frank Smith insisted. He was one of them, and so was Greenville's Hodding Carter. The war against Nazism inspired Carter's postwar crusading for improved race relations as did his service as editor of the Middle East edition of *Stars and Stripes,* which allowed him to see firsthand the resentment harbored by native peoples against British racial and colonial policies. In the wake of the war, Carter was soon clashing with Greenville whites who objected to an honor roll for World War II veterans that would include the names of both black and white servicemen.[8]

Another veteran who came home with a sense of purpose was Doyle Combs, who became an NAACP leader in Northeast Georgia and vowed to vote even if he "had to kill somebody" because "I went into combat and lost a portion of my body for this country." The growth of black dissatisfaction during the war was more than obvious to contemporary observers, and the widespread participation of black veterans in postwar civil rights activities is well documented. In Mississippi the list included Medgar Evers, Amzie Moore, and Aaron Henry, while veteran Harry Briggs was the plaintiff in the legal assault on segregation in Clarendon County, South Carolina, that paved the way for the 1954 Brown decision. Many black former GIs showed a surprising level of militance. In Monroe, North Carolina, Robert F. Williams armed himself and other black veterans, and his "Monroe Rifle Club" became the only organization ever identified with both the NAACP and the National Rifle Association.[9]

At the same time, some white veterans admitted, more of them privately than publicly, that their wartime experiences had changed their racial views. One of the most startling public statements to this effect came from Lieutenant Van T. Barfoot of Carthage, Mississippi, who was awarded multiple decorations for his heroism in combat. In June 1945, Mississippi senator James O. Eastland had insisted that "numerous high ranking generals" had told him that "nigra soldiers" had proven an "utter and abysmal failure" and had "disgraced the flag of their country." Not surprisingly, Eastland's remarks were seconded by the state's other senator, Theodore G. Bilbo. When Bilbo, Eastland, and the rest of the Mississippi congressional delegation sought a photo session and the opportunity to bask in the glow of the heroic Barfoot, Bilbo asked him eagerly, "Did you have much trouble with nigras over there?"[10]

Bilbo was soon red-faced and squirming as Lieutenant Barfoot announced, "I found out after I did some fighting in this war that the colored boys fight just as good as the white boys. . . . I've changed my ideas a lot about colored people since I got into this war and so have a lot of other boys from the South."[11]

Barfoot's case was by no means an isolated one, but it was hardly a representative one either. If it was true, as Frank Smith insisted, that many Americans returned from World War II with a sense of purpose, it did not follow that they all returned with the same sense of purpose. Smith discovered this himself when he encountered a young Mississippi farmer who told him, "Fight integration? Why, I've just begun to fight. When I was on a beach in the South Pacific I was fighting and I didn't know why. Now we know what we are fighting for, and nothing is going to hold us back."[12]

As a racial moderate, Smith often clashed with the Citizens Council founded at Indianola by World War II paratrooper Robert Patterson. Another thorn in Smith's side was a former Marine wounded in the Pacific, Byron De La Beckwith of Greenwood, who would eventually be convicted of the murder of fellow veteran Medgar Evers. Finally, Smith admitted that as many as half of his former student colleagues who had served in World War II and survived wound up as active members of the Citizens Council or "their political satellites."[13]

The Ku Klux Klan, the Columbians, and several other hate groups also drew a number of recruits from the ranks of former soldiers. Deploring veteran participation in the revival of the KKK, the editor of the *Montgomery Advertiser* found it difficult to understand "how a veteran who risked his life to stop the terror of Hitlerism can come home to play Hitler himself."[14]

During the war, racial tensions had exploded during six civilian riots, over twenty military riots and mutinies, and from forty to seventy-five lynchings. The resurgence of Ku Klux Klan activity paralleled a horrifying explosion of postwar violence, much of it directed against returning black veterans. Georgia and Alabama were the most homicidal states in the nation in 1946, with murder rates nearly seven times that of New

York. Walton County, Georgia, was the scene of one of the most shocking racial murders involving two black men, one of them a veteran, and two black women, one of them pregnant. Clinton Adams, a frightened white youngster, watched from hiding as a group of white men executed the four. In 1981 Adams finally confronted one of the killers, who explained that black veteran George Dorsey had been killed because "Up until George went into the army he was a good nigger. But when he came out, they thought they were as good as any white people."[15]

Violence also crept into postwar southern politics, especially the so-called GI Revolts that erupted at the state and local level in the first few elections after the war as militant former soldiers sought to overturn entrenched political machines. In Hot Springs, Arkansas, future governor Sid McMath spearheaded a victory over the McCloughlin machine that involved armed partisans on both sides, as well as the sabotage of phone lines by the veterans in order to frustrate opponents' efforts to steal the election with fraudulent ballots.[16]

Expanded economic opportunity was often a goal of politically active veterans, but as Jennifer Brooks has shown, they sometimes disagreed as to how this worthy goal might be best achieved. In the spring of 1947, veterans took over the picket lines when tobacco workers struck against the R. J. Reynolds Tobacco Company, carrying signs reading "From the Firing Line to the Picket Line" and vowing that "R. J. Reynolds can't beat us when the Nazis couldn't." Other veterans organizations, however, warned that labor unions were a serious threat to the economic aspirations of returning GIs. The Veterans Industrial Association recruited veterans as strike breakers, insisting, "We have as hard a war to win freeing ourselves from the so-called labor leaders here as we had with Germany, Japan, and Italy."[17]

For all the disparity and contradictory sense of purpose manifested in the activities of World War II veterans, it was nonetheless possible to discern among them a widespread inclination toward a more "modern" or "progressive" approach to government and politics, one that stressed economic development and favored moderation over demagoguery on the race issue. Georgia's demagogue for all seasons was Eugene Talmadge, whose red-suspendered rusticity and cagey manipulation of the state's outrageously antiurban county-unit electoral system had made him the dominant force in Georgia politics for the better part of two decades. In 1946, "Old Gene" faced a formidable challenge from James V. Carmichael, a former legislator who had managed the Bell Bomber plant in Marietta during the war. While not all of Georgia's veterans supported

Carmichael, a large number did, many of them echoing the sentiments of a Navy veteran who noted that "Hitler, Mussolini, and Tojo are gone" and expressed his hope that "Eugene Talmadge is joining them." Veteran after veteran linked Carmichael with "good government," and organizations such as the "B-29ers-for-Carmichael Club" appeared all over the state.[18]

Although Carmichael won the popular vote, the county-unit system gave the election to Talmadge, who proceeded to die of cirrhosis of the liver before he could take office. Foreseeing this possibility, Talmadge supporters had engineered a general election write-in effort for Talmadge's son Herman, who was in fact a veteran himself. In the end, the younger Talmadge's flimsy claim to the governorship rested on the last-minute discovery of additional write-in ballots from voters in Talmadge's home county who, in a remarkable display of loyalty, had risen from the grave to mark their sheets for Herman and, in an equally inspiring display of unity, had marked them all in the same handwriting. During the ensuing controversy, Georgia had not one but three governors, but when a special election finally put Herman in office, he surprised a great many Georgians. Though he went on to author a pamphlet that insisted that "God Advocates Segregation," Talmadge also pursued an impressive agenda of educational reform and industrial recruitment, explaining, "When I came along it was after World War II, and I think the people of Georgia had made up their mind that they wanted to see more progress in state government."[19]

Though no admirer of Talmadge, another Georgian, Katharine Dupre Lumpkin, expressed similar sentiments. As she surveyed the South in 1946, Lumpkin noted that the cumulative impact of depression, war, agricultural mechanization, and industrial development was weakening the region's resistance to change: "I know the old life continues, but not serenely, not without a struggle to maintain its existence. . . . The Southern people are pressing against the enclosing walls." In the same year that Lumpkin offered this observation, Helen Douglas Mankin drew heavily on the support of newly enfranchised blacks to become the first woman elected to congress from Georgia.[20]

While it was difficult at the end of the 1940s to look back much beyond the war itself, the perspective of the 1990s both affords us the luxury of the longer view and requires that we take it. When we do, we can see that, to some extent, the changes in southern agriculture, the outmigration of blacks, and the move to industrialize were actually rooted in conditions and trends visible as early as or even before World War I.

In fact, the years from the boll weevil invasion of the early twentieth century through the beginnings of the Great Migration of blacks to the North and the descent into the Great Depression might be seen as the harbingers of a great turning period, a protracted drama for which the New Deal and World War II constituted the final acts.[21]

Most scholars have argued that of the two acts, World War II clearly deserves top billing, but it is virtually impossible to assess the impact of the New Deal and World War II separately. Both the New Deal and the war contributed heavily to the modernization of southern agriculture and the South's subsequent efforts to industrialize. While the New Deal's acreage-reduction programs rendered much of the old farm labor force marginal, if not superfluous, however, the war offered alternative employment opportunities and threatened to create a labor scarcity sufficient to boost farm wages above levels that southern landlords were willing to pay. Meanwhile, although the war seemed ultimately to undermine southern liberalism and strengthen anti–New Deal conservatism, the conflict did not cancel the Roosevelt administration's stated commitment to improving economic conditions in the South and arguably even facilitated it by removing the restrictions on spending that had hampered New Deal recovery efforts.[22]

The $52 billion paid out on just the ten largest government defense contracts between 1940 and 1944 was roughly equivalent to total government expenditures between 1932 and 1939. Not surprisingly, southern manufacturing employment grew by 50 percent during the war, and annual wages climbed by 40 percent between 1939 and 1942 alone as war-induced competition for labor quickly rendered the New Deal's Fair Labor Standards minimums obsolete in some southern industries. For all the undue influence still wielded by reactionary southern politicians, the Roosevelt administration also seized numerous wartime opportunities to exempt the South from its official "hold the line" policy on wages while affording significant support to organized labor as well. Although the South remained a decidedly low-wage region, it emerged from the conflict with an expanded industrial labor force and a markedly more affluent consumer pool, which became a crucial part of the region's postwar attraction for market-oriented industries. If it is correct to credit the war with finishing what the New Deal started, it seems reasonable as well to think of World War II functioning, at least in part, as a sort of unarticulated Third New Deal, one freed from some of the most severe economic constraints that hampered the first two.[23]

Wartime spending created many new job opportunities for southerners, although not all enjoyed equal access to them. On any construction site, as one black southerner who spoke from experience explained, "If a white man and a black man both walk up for an opening and it ain't no shovel in that job, they'd give the job to a white man." This generalization applied to black veterans as well. Promiseland, South Carolina, veteran Isaac Moragne angrily rejected a Veterans Administration staffer's recommendation that he apply for a common laborer's position, explaining later, "I was a staff sergeant in the Army, . . . traveled all over England . . . sat fourteen days in the English Channel . . . I wasn't going to push a wheel barrow." A Southern Regional Council field agent reported that "Hattiesburg, Mississippi, is the most progressive city in Mississippi, yet the Negro veteran who struggles away from the battlefields of the world can expect to move back to the same old pattern of living, if he moves back to the 'progressive' city of Hattiesburg."[24]

During the war, men and women left the South's farms for its factories in almost equal numbers, and in many cases employers preferred to hire the women. This was especially true when the choice lay between a white woman and a black man. In some instances, defense employers simply drew on the existing textile labor pool where white women were heavily represented and blacks hardly at all. Although many of these white women withdrew or were pushed out of the industrial workforce when the war ended, postwar economic expansion soon afforded them new opportunities to return to the factories while the concomitant shrinkage of the South's agricultural sector often made such a move a matter of absolute necessity. In Mississippi, the number of women employed in manufacturing increased by nearly 60 percent between 1940 and 1950, a rate nearly twice as high as that for their male counterparts. At the same time, continuing discrimination forced blacks of both sexes to pursue wartime opportunities in the North.[25]

In both the short and long terms, the war's impact on worker mobility was crucial in a number of ways. At the national level, while 12 million Americans were being shipped overseas, another 15 million moved to cities elsewhere in the nation, with half of these moving to different states. Meanwhile, between 1940 and 1945, three times as many people left the South each year as had departed during the preceding decade. A total of 1.6 million civilians moved out of the South during the war, and almost as important, three times that many moved elsewhere within the region. Prior to the war, southern workers had been far less mobile, sticking close to home either because they could not afford to move, had no incentive to move, or simply could not bring themselves to move.

This labor market inflexibility was far less pronounced in the postwar South as out-migration, in-migration, and intraregional migration continually responded to and shaped economic, racial, political, and cultural trends.[26]

Among the cultural trends most affected by this newfound mobility and other war-induced changes was the evolution of southern music. As Bill C. Malone wrote, "while promoting major transformations in the habits, employment, and residence of rural southerners, the war effectively nationalized their music." Country music went both national and international thanks not only to the proliferation of country radio programming in response to the out-migration of southern whites but to the Armed Forces Radio Network, which carried what had once been seen as strictly regional "hillbilly" music all over the world. The major beneficiary of this was Grand Ole Opry star Roy Acuff, whose distinctive voice became so well known in the steamy jungles of the South Pacific that some Japanese troops reportedly spurned "banzai" in favor of "To Hell with Roy Acuff." Although this hateful rallying cry proved ineffectual in the short run, the Japanese finally won a measure of revenge in the 1990s as their karaoke machines subjected thousands of southerners to the drunken wailings of would-be country boys trying to sing "The Wabash Cannonball." A second beneficiary of wartime developments was the Texas Troubadour Ernest Tubb, who pioneered in a musical style known as "honky-tonk" which drew its name from establishments known for drinking and dancing and not infrequently fighting and shooting as well. The repeal of prohibition, the sense of rootlessness and transiency, and the loosening of morals and family constraints occasioned by economic expansion and population redistribution shaped both the thematic and stylistic contours of honky-tonk. The loud, twangy pedal steel guitar was a perfect accompaniment for tunes such as "What Made Milwaukee Famous Has Made a Loser Out of Me," and it also allowed the song to be heard over the clamor of the laughing, cursing, and fighting that filled the bars and beer joints where it was most often played.[27]

It was symbolically prophetic that the Japanese attack on Pearl Harbor bumped country music's pioneering Carter Family from the cover of *Life* magazine in December 1941 because the wartime changes in country music seemed to spell nothing but trouble for many traditional artists. Bill and Earl Bolick, the Blue Sky Boys, had been phenomenally popular performers on Atlanta's WGST before the war but soon fell by the wayside when they refused to add amplified instruments to back up their close and plaintive mountain harmonies. Fittingly enough, when the Blue Sky Boys broke up, Bill Bolick returned to his native North Carolina, but Earl remained in Atlanta and went to work for Lockheed in the postwar South's largest industrial plant. Elsewhere, however, Bill Monroe, another successful prewar traditional musician, began his ascent to legendary status in 1945 when he incorporated the new three-finger banjo-picking style of Earl Scruggs into his music to create blue-grass, a musical style now viewed by self-appointed purists as "traditional" but described correctly by Alan Lomax as a sort of modernized "folk music with overdrive." Meanwhile, the commingling of country and black styles helped to insure the postwar appeal of Hank Williams, underscoring Charles Gillett's observation that during the 1940s "country music probably absorbed more elements of black music than were accepted into the mainstream pop of the time." This coming together or at least coming closer together of country music and black music was another striking development of the early postwar years. Southern black musicians who remained economically successful after the war did so primarily by electrifying their music, following the lead of Muddy Waters, who abandoned his tractor on the Stovall plantation near Clarksdale and headed north to Chicago in 1943, finally making good on his threat that "If I feel tomorrow, the way I feel today, I'm gonna. . . . pack my bags and make my getaway."[28]

During the war and after, younger and more urbane black audiences readily demonstrated their preference for the amplified dance-oriented stylings that became known as "rhythm and blues." Researchers who studied black life during the war had discovered a marked trend toward secularization as rural blacks acquired radios, automobiles, and telephones, and generally transcended the barriers that had once insulated them from mass-society influences. Disgusted by the changes she observed, lifelong Mississippi Delta churchgoer Matilda Mae Jones complained, "Songs they sing in church now feel like fire burning. . . . all fast and jumpy and leapy like. . . . that's just the way these swing church songs are now." Jones's complaint foreshadowed a trend that would see performers like Clarksdale-born gospel singer Sam Cooke, who began his career singing songs such as "Jesus Gave Me Water," go on to fame as a rhythm and blues superstar with hits like "Chain Gang" and "Everybody Loves to Cha Cha Cha." Cooke's career paralleled those of countless others, such as James Brown, Otis Redding, and Ray Charles, who, in succeeding years, not so much left gospel music as took it with them when they entered the secular, sensual world of rhythm and blues.[29]

For many black as well as white performers, their musical odyssey led to Memphis, where a war-inspired economic boom had played the key role in bringing both Firestone Tire and International Harvester plants to the city. Opportunities were by no means equal for both races, but the city offered the proverbial "day jobs" that would allow aspiring artists to play their music at night. It was here at Memphis's Sun Studios that rhythm and blues met country-derived rockabilly to produce the revolutionary musical hybrid known as rock and roll. As Pete Daniel observed, "The leisurely pace of rural life collided with urban haste, and the city allowed all genres of contemporary music to mix. The rhythm of the land collided with the beat of the city, and the energy generated by this chain reaction redefined American music." [30]

Writing in 1935, Greenville writer David L. Cohn described the Mississippi Delta as a land of "complete detachment," explaining that "change shatters itself on the breast of this society as Pacific breakers upon a South Sea reef." "Disturbing ideas" might "crawl like flies around the screen of the Delta," wrote Cohn, but "they rarely penetrate." In the wake of World War II, Cohn painted a decidedly different portrait, however, noting that "many changes have occurred in the life of the Mississippi Delta as elsewhere. We had scarcely emerged from a shattering economic depression before we were plunged into man's most catastrophic war. The foundations of our faith are severely shaken. We no longer believe, as we once did, in the inevitability of progress. Our compass is aberrant, our course erratic. We are more than a little fearful that we shall not make our landfall." [31]

Cohn's observation seemed to bear out George Orwell's contention that "if the war didn't kill you, it was bound to start you thinking," but in reality, southerners were already thinking, particularly about the South, well before World War II. The region once dubbed "The Sahara of the Bozart" by H. L. Mencken could by 1941 boast of having the nation's most dynamic literary community. The pivotal member of that community, William Faulkner, sought vainly to enlist in the military during World War II but wound up sitting out the war as a screenwriter in Hollywood, working on "Battle Cry," "God Is My Co-Pilot," and a number of other patriotic films. Still, Faulkner revealed his emotional involvement in the conflict in a letter to his stepson, who was then serving in the military: "A change will come out of this war. If it doesn't, if the politicians and people who run this country are not forced to make good the shibboleth they glibly talk about freedom, liberty, human rights, then you young men who have lived through it will have wasted your precious time, and those who don't live through it will have died in vain." Looking beyond the war, Faulkner could only hope that there "will be a part for me, who can't do anything but use words, in the rearranging of the house so that all mankind can live in it." [32]

Ironically, some literary scholars now quote these eloquent lines as they mark World War II as the beginning of the end for Faulkner as a great writer, arguing, with *Intruder in the Dust* as a case in point, that his subsequent fiction became more didactic and mechanical and less open-ended and artistically valid. Whether Faulkner was a less gifted writer is of less significance for our purposes than the fact that after the war he was far more widely read and appreciated. The contradictions raised by World War II and subsequently magnified by the tensions of the Cold War focused national and international attention on the South's deficiencies. World War II brought more than twice as many Yankee soldiers to the South as the Civil War, and their wartime experiences often yielded specific and personal testimony to the South's backwardness. By 1948, then, Faulkner's Charles Mallison could perceive among nonsoutherners "a volitionless, almost helpless capacity to believe almost anything about the South not even provided it be derogatory but merely bizarre enough and strange enough." In a larger sense, the war had not only highlighted the South's abnormalities but helped to transform the nation into one where these abnormalities could no longer be tolerated. The result was the creation of what Sosna called "a bull market . . . for regional exposure, explanation, and analysis." [33]

Certainly, the war years inspired and nurtured a host of writers of both fiction and nonfiction who wrote with the clear purpose of focusing attention on the South's problems and stressing the urgency of finding solutions. Serving as a naval officer in India, young historian C. Vann Woodward was struck by his visit with the leader of India's untouchables who "plied me with questions about the black 'untouchables' of America and how their plight compared with that of his own people." Already the author of a revisionist biography of Populist Tom Watson, Woodward returned from the war to write a sweeping reinterpretation of the Redeemer Era South and then to pen *The Strange Career of Jim Crow*, an enormously influential volume that struck at both the legal and emotional underpinnings of segregation. [34]

Meanwhile, Woodward contemporary John Hope Franklin, who had just received his Ph.D. from Harvard, offered his services as a historian to the War Department. Because he was black, he was rebuffed without receiving serious consideration. Then, responding to naval recruiters' appeals for clerical personnel, Franklin was again rejected solely on the basis of his race. Finally, ordered to report for a draft physical, Franklin was subjected to further indignities, leading him to conclude that "the United States did not need me and did not deserve me." Consequently, he spent the rest of the war outwitting the draft board and "feeling nothing but shame for my country — not merely for what it did to me, but for what it did to the millions of black men and women who served in the armed forces under conditions of segregation and discrimination." Franklin went on to revise the traditional historical view of Reconstruction and of the role of blacks in southern history and to serve (as did Woodward, in a lesser capacity) as an adviser to the NAACP Legal Defense Team representing the plaintiffs in the *Brown v. Board of Education* case.[35]

Franklin's wartime experience reflected the ambivalence and frustration with which many black intellectuals approached the conflict. Determined to link the fighting abroad to the struggle for racial justice at home, poet Langston Hughes exulted in "Jim Crow's Last Stand" that "Pearl Harbor put Jim Crow on the run / That Crow can't fight for Democracy / And be the same old Crow he used to be." Hughes also urged black soldiers to get those "so bad, Evil and most mad, GO AND GET THE ENEMY BLUES." As segregation continued to flourish throughout the war effort, however, a disappointed Hughes also mocked, "Jim Crow Army and Navy, Too / Is Jim Crow freedom the *best* I can expect from you?"[36]

By the time the war began, Richard Wright's angry fiction had already established him as the nation's preeminent black writer. As an increasingly disenchanted member of the Communist Party, however, Wright found himself zigging and zagging in response to a party line that was zigging and zagging as well. In the wake of the Nazi-Soviet Pact, he insisted that the conflict was "Not My People's War," pointing out that "the Negro's experience with past wars, his attitude towards the present one, his attitude of chronic distrust, constitute the most incisive and graphic refutation of every idealistic statement made by the war leaders as to the alleged democratic goal and aim of this war." After Hitler's invasion of Russia, however, the party suddenly had no more use for Comrade Wright's pacifism, and slightly more than a week after Pearl Harbor, a frustrated Wright pledged his "loyalty and allegiance" to the American cause, promising that "I shall through my writing seek to rally the Negro people to stand shoulder to shoulder with the administration in a solid national front to wage war until victory is won."[37]

Meanwhile, irreverent novelist and folklorist Zora Neale Hurston had drawn consistent criticism from Richard Wright and other black intellectuals for her failure to use her writings as a weapon in the struggle against racism and Jim Crow. Yet for all her apparent reluctance to devote her energies to solving the race problem, in the original manuscript for her autobiographical *Dust Tracks on a Road,* she pointed out that "President Roosevelt could extend his four freedoms to some people right here in America. . . . I am not bitter, but I see what I see. . . . I will fight for my country, but I will not lie for her." Like several others, this passage was subsequently excised after Hurston's white editor deemed it "irrelevant." After the war, however, writing in *Negro Digest,* Hurston cited Roosevelt's reference to the United States as "the arsenal of democracy" and wondered if she had heard him correctly. Perhaps he meant "arse-and-all" of democracy, she thought, since the United States was supporting the French in their effort to resubjugate the Indo-Chinese, suggesting that "the ass-and-all of democracy has shouldered the load of subjugating the dark world completely." Hurston also announced that she was "crazy for this democracy" and would "pitch headlong into the thing" if it were not for the numerous Jim Crow laws that confronted her at every turn.[38]

World War II also stiffened white crusader Lillian Smith's resolve to fight against segregation. She insisted in 1943 that fighting for freedom while acquiescing to Jim Crow amounted to "trying to buy a new world with Confederate bills." Condemned by Georgia governor Eugene Talmadge as "a literary corn cob," Smith's 1944 novel *Strange Fruit* was a searing story of miscegenation and murder that concluded with the lynching of an innocent young black man. It lay bare the pain and suffering caused by white racism and the hypocrisy and sexual repression that festered just beneath the surface of the southern way of life.[39]

The uncompromising Smith was hardly more contemptuous of those who defended Jim Crow than those who urged moderation in the fight against it. Yet, with external pressures mounting as the Supreme Court struck down the white primary in 1944, many white southerners who had once seemed most dedicated to racial justice found themselves urging the proponents of desegregation to slow down. Ardent and courageous spokesmen like Hodding Carter and Ralph McGill insisted that ending segregation would take time, and when they bristled at northern critics — members of the "hit-and-run school of southern writing," as Carter called them — they sounded a great deal like Faulkner's Gavin Stevens in *Intruder in the Dust* and Faulkner himself a few years thereafter. As Numan V. Bartley observed, in the wake of the war "the very word 'liberal' gradually disappeared from the southern political lexicon, except as a term of defamation." Meanwhile, although the contradictions raised by Jim Crow were inconsistent with the United States' rise to free-world leadership, the anti-Communist hysteria of the early Cold War years made even northern liberals initially reluctant to encourage anti-segregation litigation and protests.[40]

Alabaman Virginia Durr claimed that when she introduced Senator James Eastland to a group of Mississippi Methodist women lobbying for repeal of the poll tax, he had spluttered that they apparently wanted "black men laying on you." The anti-poll-tax movement weathered such opposition from Eastland and other southern politicians but fell apart after losing crucial support when the National Committee to Abolish the Poll Tax refused to purge itself of members belonging to groups targeted by the attorney general's list of "subversive" organizations."[41]

Even before World War II, some southern intellectuals were beginning to behave according to a pattern that now seems fairly typical of emerging or developing nations around the world, agonizing about their region's backwardness but also expressing their fears about the loss of cultural identity and virtue that might accompany the accelerating effort to modernize their society. No writer struggled more painfully or brilliantly with the persistence of the South's deficiencies or the decay of its virtues than William Faulkner. In the wake of World War II, Faulkner's fictional Jefferson was already experiencing what Walker Percy later called "Los Angelization," its "old big decaying wooden houses" giving way to antiseptic one-story models crammed into subdivisions "with their neat plots of clipped grass and tedious flowerbeds" and its housewives "in sandals and pants and painted toe nails," puffing "lipstick-stained cigarettes over shopping bags in the chain groceries and drugstores." Meanwhile, mechanization of agriculture brought a dramatic change in the rhythm of southern rural life as machines came between men and women and the land and further separated them from the product of their labors. "I'd druther have a mule fartin' in my face all day long walkin' de turnrow than dem durned tractors," a Delta farmhand told David Cohn. "There ain't nothing about a tractor that makes a man want to sing," complained another worker. "The thing keeps so much noise and you so far away from the other folks."[42]

In "The Displaced Person," Flannery O'Connor told the story of a Polish immigrant, Mr. Guizac, who finds work as a hired hand on a run-down farm in early postwar Georgia and revitalizes it through his energy and mechanical expertise. Yet, for all the economic benefits he brings,

Guizac is also infected with alien values. His employer, Mrs. McIntyre, is impressed by Guizac's accomplishments and happy with the potential profits his efforts might reap for her, but she also worries that Guizac is a stranger to the society and culture in which he lives. Her fears are confirmed when she learns that he plans to get a female cousin into the United States by betrothing her to a local black man, and in the story's startling conclusion, she looks on silently, offering no warning, as the unsuspecting Guizac is flattened by a runaway tractor.[43]

In his semi-autobiographical novel *The Year the Lights Came On,* Terry Kay described the postwar scene in Royston, Georgia: "The cotton mill placed an advertisement in *The (Royston, Ga.) Record,* seeking employees. A sewing plant was officially opened by His Honor the Mayor. Farmers began to listen to what county agents had to say about subsoiling, land testing, seed treating, or about planting kudzu and lespedeza to stop top-soil from washing away in the ugly scars of erosion. The sound of John Deere tractors stuttered even at night." In Royston, no less than else-where, Kay believed "everyone seemed aware of being embraced by a new history of the world, and everyone knew it would be a history never forgotten."[44]

Like Kay and O'Connor, Walker Percy was also witness to the desta-bilizing effects of urbanization, industrialization, and agricultural mech-anization in the postwar South. Even as O'Connor worried that the changes sweeping across her region might purge the South "not only of our many sins but our few virtues," Percy was noting the "growing de-personalization" of southern social relations and suggesting that north-ernization of southern life would mean a society "in which there is no sense of the past, or of real community, or even of one's own identity." Percy would ultimately emerge as one of the dominant literary figures in the post–World War II South, and a new generation of writers such as Richard Ford and Josephine Humphreys now explore in their own work the validity of Percy's insistence that modern life subjects southerners, like all other Americans, to "deep dislocation in their lives that has noth-ing to do with poverty, ignorance, and discrimination."[45]

Expressing similar concerns, John Egerton worried in 1974 that the "Americanization of Dixie" simply meant that the South and the nation were "not exchanging strengths as much as they are exchanging sins." In his 1995 study of the pre–Civil Rights generation in the South, how-ever, Egerton was more upbeat, crediting World War II with bringing the South into "the modern age" by turning "hard times into hopeful times," moving "people up and out," and changing "our ways of thinking and working and living. Practically everything about this war," Egerton believed, "from the way we got into it to the way we got out of it, suggested transformation."[46]

Confirming Egerton's assessment of the war as a watershed, Bertram Wyatt-Brown insisted in 1991 that "the South Cash knew has largely disappeared. In matters of economic prosperity, racial demography, urbanization, and politics, the fact is that the region has altered much more since the early 1940s than it did between 1865 and 1941."[47]

Few contemporary observers seem inclined to dispute Egerton or Wyatt-Brown, but if we are to understand the full impact of World War II on our region, we must take into account not only the magnitude but the limitations of the changes induced by the war. Upon close examination, we can also see that although the war is responsible for many of the differences between the South that Cash saw in 1940 and the South we see today, it also contributed to some of the similarities as well. For example, if the war made the South more attractive to industrial investors, its failure to destroy the region's heavy concentration in low-wage industries helped to explain why the postwar South retained a cheap-labor appeal that those investors still find significant. In addition, the war's stimulus to industrial mobility and to southern efforts to attract new and better industries meant that the South ultimately went from offering thousands of dollars in subsidies to underwear plants to offering hundreds of millions of dollars in subsidies to automobile plants.[48]

On another front, the war's acceleration of black migration from states where blacks could not vote to states where they could played a key role in spurring the Democratic Party's advocacy of civil rights, but in doing so, it also fed the nationwide white backlash that all but derailed the Civil Rights movement. Similarly, if the war-inspired Civil Rights revolution allowed southern blacks to claim the political rights and influence so long denied them, it also triggered the massive exodus of racially conservative southern whites from the Democratic Party, the cumulative result being a South that quickly amassed the nation's largest concentration of black officeholders while becoming its most predictably Republican region in presidential elections and a growing number of lesser contests as well.

While Cash would have found officeholding by Republicans or blacks almost equally startling, he would probably have been even more amazed to see that the changes set in motion or intensified by the war had rendered his version of the southern mind essentially obsolete, replacing it with a more heterogeneous and less exclusionary model, one open to anyone who saw themselves as southerners regardless of race or gender or even regional or national origin. Not only were blacks just as likely as whites to identify themselves as southerners by the 1990s, but in many cases, they actually seemed more confident of what that meant. Enduring taunts and threats and all manner of abuse from those who sought to preserve Cash's South, Charlayne Hunter-Gault had broken the color barrier at the University of Georgia in 1961. In 1988 she returned to Athens to deliver the commencement address, embracing the South as "my place" and paying tribute to southerners of both races whose "tumultuous" but shared history had melded them into the nation's only "definable people." Numerous such examples along with contemporary polls identifying Robert E. Lee and Martin Luther King as the South's most revered historical figures seem to point to a southern mind dramatically different though hardly less paradoxical or contradictory than the one that tormented Cash.[49]

Confirming the anxiety Cash had felt in 1940, Morton Sosna concluded that the South had emerged from World War II as "an arena where the forces of good and evil, progress and reaction, rapid change and seemingly timeless continuity were about to engage in a battle of near mythological proportions." As Sosna indicated, for the South, the end of the war meant not peace but another quarter century of struggle. More than any single preceding event, World War II helped to shape not only the contours of this struggle but its outcome, an outcome that finally allowed us to contemplate a South whose virtues, if they did not tower over its faults, were at least no longer totally obscured by them. All of this seems to have come out far better than Cash dared to hope. Yet, before we credit World War II with unloosing forces that destroyed Cash's South, we should first take note of the racism, violence, anti-intellectualism, and social indifference that now permeate American society at large and ask how the postwar historical context so clearly conducive to mitigating these characteristic vices of the southern mind in 1940 could have also set the stage for their ominous emergence as defining features of the national mind in 1996.[50]

Does "Mind" Still Matter?

The South, the Nation, and

The Mind of the South,

1941–1991

Two major symposia and a number of sessions at scholarly conferences marked 1991 as the fiftieth anniversary of the publication of Wilbur J. Cash's *The Mind of the South*. In this monumental work, Cash contended that a unified and continuous set of distinctly southern values and attitudes had not only defied but actually fed upon the upheaval of Civil War and Reconstruction and then persisted through four decades of the twentieth century despite the economic and demographic transformations accompanying urbanization and industrial expansion. Cash's brilliantly descriptive terminology, such as the "Proto-Dorian convention" (which bound all whites, regardless of class, in a common, overriding commitment to white supremacy) or the "savage ideal" (a peculiarly southern strain of conformity and aversion to criticism or innovation forged during Reconstruction and dominant throughout the ensuing decades), soon served as conceptual coin of the realm for historians of the South. Meanwhile, Cash's name itself became synonymous with the seemingly indelible image of an intellectually stunted, emotionally dysfunctional South too obsessed with the past to cope with the present, much less comprehend the future.[1]

Although it was once the symbolic centerpiece of numerous inconclusive symposia dedicated to examining the

South's distinctiveness or determining its precise whereabouts on an imprecise continuum linking continuity and change, *The Mind of the South*'s reputation as the last word on Dixie began to crumble at the end of the 1960s. Discussions of Cash's book circa 1991 are likely to focus not on its relevance but on its quaintness. Once a ready source of insight into the psyche of southern whites, Cash's classic work now seems more like an artifact, better suited for the display case than the seminar room.

The Mind of the South appeared in 1941 to almost unanimous critical acclaim. It drew praise from journalists and literary figures as well as from historians such as Clement Eaton and C. Vann Woodward, who despite some reservations praised Cash's "literary and imaginative rather than . . . scholarly approach" and cited the "brilliant analysis" and "penetrating observation" that characterized the final quarter of the book. Although *The Mind of the South* was warmly received, even the most enthusiastic reviewers could hardly have foreseen its remarkable durability. Yet after twenty-five years in print, *The Mind of the South* still collected accolades. Dewey W. Grantham Jr. praised Cash's "brilliant essay on the southern character," and other contributors to the 1965 historiographical compendium *Writing Southern History* used terms such as "magisterial," "provocative," and "imaginative" to describe Cash's book. Such was high praise indeed for any book, let alone one with nearly a quarter century of exposure to a profession known neither for coddling its young nor deferring to its elders. *The Mind of the South* had made a spectacular debut, but its twenty-five-year run as the undisputed first title on almost everybody's list of books about the South was even more impressive.[2]

The second quarter century of *The Mind of the South*'s existence was to prove quite different. Two years after its almost unprecedented staying power had been documented in *Writing Southern History,* Cash's book was under full assault by Woodward, who had become the most influential figure in the field. By the end of the 1970s, intellectual historian Michael O'Brien had concluded that *The Mind of the South* no longer deserved "a paramount, perhaps not even a prominent, place in our approach to southern history." In an essay that appeared a few years later, Bertram Wyatt-Brown reluctantly agreed that "Cash was once a thinker to be reckoned with. Such is no longer the case." Wyatt-Brown added that "condescension is the prevailing mood whenever Cash's name does appear."[3]

In sharp contrast to the attention accorded Cash's book in *Writing Southern History* in 1965, the 1987 historiographical volume *Interpreting Southern History* mentions Cash in the text only three times, and in only one of those cases is he discussed in relation to a major historiographical concern, this despite the book's pages being filled with references to scholarship that relates in some measure or another to his treatment of southern society. By 1988 O'Brien found it difficult to resist the temptation simply to put out of its misery a once-heralded book he now described as a "corpse" so "riddled" by critics that "it would require a necromancer to piece together the shattered bones, torn sinews, and spilled blood."[4]

O'Brien found it ironic that Cash had committed suicide because he believed that Nazi agents were hounding him, "whereas, in fact, after a respectful silence, it has been historians who have preyed upon him." The lengthy ascendancy that preceded the cruelly abrupt demise of *The Mind of the South* does indeed suggest that historians, perhaps especially those who study the South, should never assume that they will somehow escape their fate as grist for the slow but exceedingly fine-grinding mills of the critical gods. More important, however, the startling contrasts between the two quarter centuries that constitute the literary life of Cash's book demonstrate as well the particularly crucial role of contemporary societal concerns in influencing both the ideological goals and the critical perspectives of those who write southern history.[5]

No historian's career better illustrates the interaction of the perceptions of the present with those of the past than that of C. Vann Woodward. At the end of the 1930s the young Woodward, excited mightily by what he saw going on at "the peak . . . of the Southern Literary Renaissance," was sorely disappointed when he began graduate study in southern history at the University of North Carolina and discovered that there was "no renaissance here, no surge of innovation and creativity, no rebirth of energy, no compelling new vision." Instead of joining in the celebration of creativity and innovation that was rocking the southern literary world, the masters of Woodward's chosen field were "united not so much in their view of the past as in their dedication to the present order, the system founded on the ruins of Reconstruction called the New South." Beyond that, as far as Woodward could see, the study of southern history amounted to little more than "summing up, confirming, illustrating, and consolidating the received wisdom" of a prevailing consensus proclaiming "the enduring and fundamentally unbroken unity, solidarity, and continuity of Southern history. Only with the support of such a consensus," Woodward argued, "could a writer like Wilbur J. Cash have undertaken a book about 'the mind' of the whole region from past to present and gained wide acclaim and credence for his efforts."

Joel Williamson also has suggested that the sense of unity and continuity that characterized the South in the 1930s enabled Cash "to write such a book as *The Mind of the South*."[6]

Cash may well have been influenced by the solid South mentality, but his work offered little comfort to southern historians or anyone else who was intent, in Woodward's words, on "vindicating, justifying, rationalizing, and often celebrating the present order." On the contrary, Bruce Clayton concluded that Cash "clearly intended to throw a stick of dynamite into the southerner's stream of consciousness." Elsewhere, Daniel Joseph Singal described Cash's book as "a complete reversal of the vision of the region's history once offered by New South writers — it read like a compendium of those aspects of the South they had deliberately screened out." As what Richard H. King called "a quintessential expression of the regional self-scrutiny which marked the Southern Renaissance," *The Mind of the South* brought to the study of the South's past the curiosity and the spirit of critical inquiry that Woodward had found so sorely lacking among other southern historians at the end of the 1930s.[7]

In his willingness to challenge the received wisdom of the traditional view of southern history, Cash was, in fact, comparable to Woodward. Certainly Cash was an advocate of the same "tough minded realism" Woodward found so praiseworthy in the subject of his 1938 biography of Thomas E. (Tom) Watson and so laudable in Howard W. Odum and his regionalist colleagues in Chapel Hill. Like Odum and his cohorts, albeit with considerably less optimism, Cash hoped that the South might transcend its burdensome past and become a more "'rationally' coherent" region. Cash also clearly shared Woodward's disdain for the existing order in the South, and by emphasizing how the region had been failed or sold out by its leaders, both Woodward and Cash interpreted the past in a manner that was wholly unsupportive of what they saw in the present. At any rate, the immediate and widespread acceptance accorded *The Mind of the South* below the Mason-Dixon line had considerably less to do with its emphasis on continuity than Woodward suggested. The success of Cash's book actually reflected — despite the apparent penchant for hagiography among southern historians at large — the new sense of urgency about the South's problems and the search for solutions that had been gaining intellectual momentum among social scientists, journalists, and major literary figures in the South throughout the 1930s.[8]

This unprecedented spirit of critical analysis quickly put the lie to the New South myth of progress. With its depression-era suffering captured beneath the microscope of Roosevelt's New Deal, the South's enormous problems in areas ranging from public health to education to deeply entrenched poverty became all too obvious. Studies by Odum, Rupert B. Vance, and Arthur F. Raper showed a South blighted by staggering deficiencies in its institutional and human resources. The works of John Dollard and Hortense Powdermaker documented the relationship between the South's racial inequities and its economic disparities. The photographs of Dorothea Lange and Margaret Bourke-White provided dramatic visual documentation for the scholarly observations and statistics offered by concerned academics. In *You Have Seen Their Faces,* Bourke-White's photographs and Erskine Caldwell's captions offered a portrait of a South, as one reviewer described it, "so sick from its old infections of prejudice and poverty that it is a menace to the nation." Such was the suggestion as well of the National Emergency Council's report that included Franklin Roosevelt's designation of the South as "the Nation's Number One Economic Problem," and such was the alternately pathetic and menacing South that leapt from the pages of *The Mind of the South,* establishing Cash's book, in the words of William J. Cooper Jr. and Thomas E. Terrill, as "a primer for southerners who were determined to shake the ghosts of the past and build a modern South."[9]

World War II encouraged expressions of national solidarity and unanimity of purpose, but the racial and ideological contradictions raised by the war, as well as the economic and demographic upheaval that it induced or accelerated, soon contributed to renewed pressure to bring the South into the American mainstream. This pressure intensified with the postwar emergence of the United States as the leader of the free world. In Woodward's view, Cold War America "presented herself to the world as a model for how democracy, power, opulence, and virtue could be combined under one flag." The major visible defects in this model seemed to be concentrated in the nation's southeastern quadrant, but these defects were too pronounced to ignore if the nation was to be effective in its role as global policeman and shining example of Western-style democratic capitalism. Hence, among the burdens shouldered by the United States in the early Cold War years was that of dealing with an economically and culturally deprived, socially and politically embarrassing South. As Immanuel Wallerstein somewhat laboriously explained, its status as a "world hegemonic power" was incompatible with the existence of a "'backward' geographical zone" within its borders, and therefore "the homogenization of America" emerged as "an urgent political (and diplomatic) need of the U.S. federal state" in the years after World War II.[10]

Such was the global and ideological setting in which a venerable literary and intellectual tradition that Fred Hobson called the southern "school of shame and guilt" not only persisted but flourished for a quarter of a century. Works like Lillian Smith's *Killers of the Dream* followed Cash's lead by presenting southern life as, in one reviewer's words, "a schizophrenic invention without parallel, an insane dichotomy from the cradle to the grave." Stetson Kennedy's *Southern Exposure* described the South as "the nation's pathological problem No. I" and warned that the insanity of the South "infected the entire nation."[11]

As the Cold War intensified and the Civil Rights movement cranked up as well, the academic community also attacked the credibility of southern mores and institutions. In 1949 political scientist V. O. Key Jr. presented a state-by-state analysis that emphasized the irrationality of southern political culture and pointed, as Paul M. Gaston observed, to the "cold hard fact that the South as a whole has developed no system or practice of political organization and leadership adequate to cope with its problems." Two years later Woodward provided a stunning revisionist history of the post-Reconstruction South. The works of Woodward and Key laid the foundation for an interpretive synthesis that established the parameters of inquiry for a generation of scholars writing about the political history of the post-Reconstruction South. Essentially, Key's study documented the "debilitating" legacy of the Populist failure and the policies of disfranchisement, segregation, and one-party politics that Woodward saw accompanying the Redeemer to Progressive transition in the New South.[12]

The Woodward-Key synthesis fused the work of two southern liberals who believed that the destruction of what Hugh Davis Graham called "the South's unique political legacy of the turn of the century — *i.e.,* disfranchisement, malapportionment, the one-party system, and Jim Crow" — would pave the way for the rational, class- (rather than color-) based political system that Cash had found so sorely lacking in the region. Pursuant to that end, Woodward's *The Strange Career of Jim Crow* appeared in the immediate aftermath of the 1954 Brown decision to, as Richard King wrote, "demythologize the existing social and legal institutions that regulated race relations," and suggest that the racial attitudes of white southerners might be more susceptible to modification than some Americans believed. (King noted that as of the mid-1950s Woodward's work "was a fitting tribute to the critical consciousness that Cash saw emerging during the Depression decade.") Shortly after Woodward's book appeared, Kenneth Stampp offered an impressive refutation of Ulrich B. Phillips's slavery as a "school for civilization" thesis in a book that emphasized the cruelty of slavery and suggested the destructiveness of its legacy. Published in 1961, John Hope Franklin's *Reconstruction: After the Civil War* was soon joined by Stampp's *The Era of Reconstruction* in overturning the old William A. Dunning view of Reconstruction as a tragically mistaken attempt to use federal authority to promote social reform in the South.[13]

Unlike Cash's book, many of these and other similar works stressed conflict and discontinuity, and almost all of them differed significantly with *The Mind of the South* on one or more points of emphasis, interpretation, or analysis. As Wyatt-Brown explained, however, "the common way of handling Cash's ideas was to praise them, then to ignore their ramifications." The time for debate about historical complexities of the South's problems would come later. For the new, post–New Deal generation of scholars, writers, and activists, a more immediate concern seemed to be the creation of a broad-based, historically informed consensus on the necessity of devoting the nation's energies and resources to righting what was wrong with the South. Carrying the stamp of historical legitimacy and benefiting greatly from its timely reissue in paperback in 1960, Cash's book reigned as the acknowledged, handy one-volume troubleshooter's guide to the problem South.[14]

As Bob Smith recalled, "In the fall of 1960 Cash's book blossomed on the reading lists in Harvard's Yard like some lush tropical growth. Everywhere the young in mind wanted to know about the South, and, of course, only Cash could tell it like it was. The book was instant revelation to a generation of yearlings who had never been south of the Jersey Turnpike; they picked about it for cryptic wisdom . . . or they swallowed it at an indigestible gulp like one of those dreadful purgatives of eighteenth-century medicine, sustained only by faith."[15]

Writing in 1967, Woodward observed that *The Mind of the South* had "long been the first and often the only book of a historical nature that visiting journalists, pundits, and other authorities on the contemporary South read to fill them in on background. It is cited, quoted, paraphrased, and plagiarized so regularly as to have practically entered the public domain." This was particularly ironic because the book was clearly subversive of the regional dogma that prevailed when it appeared, yet it quickly and painlessly became, as Woodward saw it, "part of the received wisdom" about the South. Actually, the same might also be said of the early works of the revisionist Woodward himself, who like Cash, in Wyatt-Brown's words, "simply became part of a Southern scholar's world."[16]

Southern scholars began to reexamine their world in the late 1960s. With even the most militant defenders of Jim Crow in full retreat and the South's long-anticipated political and economic transformation well under way, ideological pressures to focus public attention on the seriousness and tenacity of the South's problems — rather than to explore the complexity of their origins — became noticeably less urgent. As a result, historians began to evaluate the assumptions and expectations that lay behind some of the major contributions to the liberal reformist scholarship of the post–New Deal era. Although his own work (along with that of Key, Stampp, and others) was soon under intensive reexamination, Woodward set his critical sights on *The Mind of the South*. As "the preeminent interpreter of the region in print," Cash had for some time actually shared star billing with Woodward, "the premier academic historian of the region," although their ostensibly peaceful coexistence had been shaky from the start. Even in his essentially positive 1941 review of Cash's book, Woodward had suggested that Cash had neglected both conflict and change as significant themes in southern history. Cash's dismissive treatment of the Populists was clearly contrary to the much more positive interpretation advanced in the Watson biography by Woodward, who in both *Origins of the New South* and *The Strange Career of Jim Crow* also emphasized class conflict and institutional upheaval not seen in Cash's South. In an essay first published in 1958, Woodward clearly rejected Cashian notions of continuity as he described a South beset by a "Bulldozer Revolution" that threatened to level "many of the old monuments of regional distinctiveness."[17]

Both Cash and Woodward hoped to see fundamental changes wrought in southern society, but as Bruce Clayton explained, Cash saw change in terms of the triumph of an externally derived "modern mind" over an indigenous southern "folk mind" historically averse to change in any form. By giving little attention to internal dissent, Cash discouraged those inclined to entertain the persistent entreaties of contemporary southern moderates who argued that, given time, the white South could play a meaningful role in saving itself. Cash clearly hoped the South would change and had even detected a few hopeful signs in the 1920s and 1930s that it might be changing, but he found little evidence of a capacity for self-redemption when he examined the South's past.[18]

Although he also championed liberal reform, Woodward took a

different view of southern history. In an oft-quoted and unmistakably apt passage, Michael O'Brien explained, "Woodward has consistently stressed change in the Southern past, because he has wanted change. If Southern history is a remorseless unity, unbroken in its social conservatism and unchallenged by a significant radicalism, the task of the Southern reformer is futile." For this reason, O'Brien observed, "Woodward has always sought the indigenous solution, obliged to find his glimmers within the Southern tradition." [19]

Given Woodward's determination to glean what he deemed usable from the South's past and Cash's contrasting view of a southern past that was anything but user-friendly, it was hardly surprising that Woodward would at some point choose to distance himself from Cash. His first significant effort to do this came in 1967. In his *New Republic* review of Joseph L. Morrison's biography of Cash, Woodward noted the "virtually unchallenged popularity" of *The Mind of the South* but declared that a "reassessment" of Cash's book was "long overdue." He proceeded to recount but a few of the "limitations" of *The Mind of the South,* noting that adequate space was not available to do justice to the task. Still, Woodward managed to point out that "Cash knew nothing firsthand of the Tidewater, the Delta, the Gulf, the Blue Grass, or the Trans-Mississippi South." Rather, his was "an unbiased history of the South from the hillbilly point of view." Woodward also noted the "historical blind spots" in a book that was "really about the period from the 1830's to the 1930's" and devoted nearly half of its space to the 1920s and 1930s. Assailing the exaggerated emphasis on continuity that characterized the book, Woodward noted that "on the smooth rhetoric of 'proto-Dorian' consensus, the Southern mind slides over Secession, Civil War, Emancipation, Reconstruction, and industrial revolution without altering its course, unchanged and unchangeable." Woodward concluded that "it would take a lot of printers' ink to straighten out the resulting distortions." [20]

Woodward titled his essay "White Man, White Mind," no doubt to protest the fact that in Cash's book "Negroes are left virtually mindless." Noting the short shrift Cash gave to slavery, Woodward concluded that "the tragic theme was simply not Jack Cash's dish" and surmised that this was why Cash had so little apparent appreciation for Faulkner, "all of whose important novels appeared before Cash's death." (This comment was particularly puzzling since just three years before Cash's death in 1941, Woodward had hardly seemed a Faulkner admirer himself when he observed that Faulkner "seemed to draw most of his subjects out of abandoned wells.") [21]

Woodward's review of Morrison's biography of Cash, in which he devoted only one unflattering paragraph to the biography itself — "It tells us all we need to know (and perhaps a little more) about the obscure struggles of this modest, neurotic, but rather appealing and courageous writer" — suggested that he would have more to say, and this he did in a paper presented at the Southern Historical Association annual meeting in Washington, D.C., in 1969 and in an essay published the same year in the *New York Review of Books* and then expanded upon in 1971 in Woodward's *American Counterpoint*. In this latter essay, Woodward both broadened and intensified his attack, questioning Cash's selection of a title (to Woodward, "The Mindlessness of the South" might have been a better choice) and objecting to Cash's inattention to such heavy-duty thinkers as Jefferson, Madison, and Calhoun, to name only three. Woodward rebuked Cash for his neglect of significant examples of dissent, ranging from antislavery activists to unionists to native Republicans, and expanded his criticism of Cash's inadequate discussion of blacks as individuals and unsatisfactory treatment of slavery as well. Woodward again complained about the geographical limitations of Cash's book, referring to the famous Manhattan-centric *New Yorker's Map of the United States* and suggesting that in Cash's world, "North Carolina would easily qualify as the New York of the great South." Finally, again and again, Woodward returned to his fundamental and overriding objection to *The Mind of the South*—that Cash had seriously overestimated the degree of continuity in the distinctive history of a people who, "unlike other Americans, repeatedly felt the solid ground of continuity give way under their feet."[22]

The racial, political, and economic changes that had rocked the South in the last half of the 1960s only reinforced Woodward's caustic dismissals of Cash's obsession with continuity. His scholarly preeminence already well established, Woodward's criticisms signaled the onset of an interpretative tug of war in which he and Cash anchored opposing schools of thought regarding the relative significance of change and continuity in the southern experience. In the short run, momentum clearly belonged to the Woodward squad. In 1970 Paul Gaston echoed Woodward's sentiments, charging that "Cash's popular theory of historical continuity . . . was constructed by misjudging the significance of key elements in the Southern experience; and the Old South — New South dichotomy which he minimizes is in fact a crucial one with which every search for the 'central theme' of Southern history must come to terms at one point or another." Shortly thereafter, Woodward protégé Sheldon Hackney dismissed Cash as "the South's foremost mythmaker" and assailed him for promulgating "the New South propaganda's image of the planter's son becoming first a captain of cavalry and then after the war a captain of industry as the civilization of the Old South blended into the New South with scarcely a ripple in the social structure."[23]

Not all the criticisms launched at Cash concerned his insistence on continuity. Eugene D. Genovese attacked Cash for promulgating an inaccurate view of a southern white society burdened by guilt over slavery — "guiltomania" Genovese called it. Genovese also assailed Cash for his overzealous dismissal of the aristocratic claims of the planter class. Genovese argued that Cash, who was so intent on deromanticizing their prevailing popular perception of the planter class, was himself the captive of "a pathetic fascination with the romance of aristocracy." Hence to Cash "the planters could not have been an aristocracy because too many of them were not really genteel but acquisitive, vulgar, mean, foulmouthed, and perhaps even unwashed." Genovese dismissed this "petty-bourgeois" view by asking "what aristocracy ever arose from any other kind of men?"[24]

The specific criticisms introduced by Woodward and Genovese went largely unrebutted during the 1970s. Michael O'Brien noted the "declining prestige" of *The Mind of the South* in 1978, and when tempted a decade later to "assist" in the "repudiation" of the book, he asserted that "the ammunition for such a repudiation is ready to hand more than sufficient." He then offered what amounts to a reasonably up-to-date summary of the major criticisms that have been leveled at *The Mind of the South*:

It is said that *The Mind of the South* ignores the colonial history of the South, scants the Old South, and misunderstands the New South. It barely mentions slavery and is more or less racist in its characterization of blacks. It neglects women, except as totemic objects of Southern mythology. It diminishes the existence of class conflict in the Old South and insists upon its relative impotence after the War. It misunderstands the nature of aristocracy. It overstresses both the unity and the continuity of Southern history. It has very little grasp of political history and has no coherent explanation for the Civil War. It is provincial in its emphasis both upon white males and upon the Piedmont of North Carolina as the archetypal South. It exaggerates the guilt of southerners over slavery. It shows little understanding of the formal ideas of generations of southern intellectuals. Its view of Reconstruction is primitive. It overestimates the static quality of agricultural society.[25]

Devastating as it seemed, the lengthy list of indictments presented by O'Brien merely recycled the criticisms of Woodward (in some cases, reaffirmed and expanded upon by Joel Williamson) and Genovese and added only a few of O'Brien's own complaints for good measure. These criticisms are no less valid because they come from a relatively small, though unquestionably influential, group of scholars. Indeed, one might argue that Cash's detractors did their job so well that in recent years a number of historians have apparently seen little need to refer to Cash directly, even if their own research appeared to relate directly to one or another of Cash's arguments or assumptions.

For example, whereas Cash had maintained that during the antebellum period the plantation system and the planter interests it embodied were "wholly dominant, possessing, for practical purposes, absolute control of government and every societal engine," in their respective studies of secessionist politics in Alabama and Georgia, J. Mills Thornton III and Michael P. Johnson found little evidence of planter hegemony. Moreover, despite Cash's contention that the common white in the South had not challenged "the right of his captains to prescribe the public course" because prior to "the nineties at least" the "prescriptions" of the planter class had "never . . . crossed his ego," Steven Hahn has traced the roots of southern populism to the distinct class interests and values of small-scale yeomen, "petty producers" in upcountry Georgia during the 1850s.[26]

Elsewhere, James Oakes, while emphasizing "substantial mobility" into the slaveholding class prior to 1830, conceded that the declining percentage of slave owners thereafter meant that "slaveholders approached the secession crisis fearful of an uncertain consensus among free Southerners." Finally, Lacy K. Ford's study of antebellum South Carolina emphasizes white unity in 1860, although it stresses the political independence of the upcountry yeomen, the neighbors of Cash's "stout young Irishman," whose reluctance to secede in 1850 had played a crucial role in keeping the state within the union for another decade. Interestingly enough, none of these scholars suggested that their findings differed or coincided with those of Cash. Viewed in conjunction with the scant attention given Cash's book in *Interpreting Southern History* in 1987, such evidence seems to affirm O'Brien's description of *The Mind of the South* as a corpse — so shredded and picked over that even the normally ravenous historiographical vultures no longer bother to circle about it.[27]

O'Brien described Cash as "preyed on" by historians, and Wyatt-Brown noted that although Cash had feared a savage response from his fellow southern whites, "his sternest reviewers came out of the faculty common room, not the county courthouse." Before we reach any conclusions about the cause(s) of the alleged death of Cash's version of Dixie, however, it might be wise to make one last check of the vital signs and ask not only whether *The Mind of the South*'s demise may not be somewhat exaggerated but whether that demise is wholly ascribable to the scholarly criticism it has received.[28]

The Mind of the South did not come under sustained scholarly analysis until it was nearly thirty years old, and, not surprisingly, many of the shortcomings that O'Brien listed could be chalked up to the age of Cash's book or to the limitations in understanding and sensitivity that characterized even liberal-minded white southerners of his era. O'Brien has pointed out that making allowances for *The Mind of the South* because of its age merely concedes the "diminishing exactitude" of Cash's work, but how significant is such a concession? So long as historians continue to evaluate the work of others and defend or revise their own work in response to the criticisms they receive, the passage of time all but guarantees that the relevance or persuasiveness of the initial version of any historical argument will diminish. For works of history, questions of diminishing exactitude are less matters of "whether" than "how much?" In his 1991 biography of Cash, Bruce Clayton rightly asks, "How many other historians, fifty years after their deaths, provoke any comment at all?" Moreover, by taking his own life shortly after his book appeared, Cash removed himself from the process of intellectual exchange by which historical exactitude is evaluated, effectively leaving assessments of his credibility solely to the perceptions of his critics. When, after an extraordinarily lengthy honeymoon, significant criticisms finally did appear, *The Mind of the South* became, as O'Brien described it, a book that had to stand or fall on the basis of the "coherence and integrity" of an astonishingly ambitious "cumulative argument" that had been painstakingly constructed but then quickly abandoned, left unrevised and unprotected for more than a quarter of a century.[29]

Wyatt-Brown has suggested that had Cash "lived into the era of sweeping Supreme Court interventions, Martin Luther King, and the Voting Rights Act" and witnessed the "Bulldozer Revolution" as well as the other changes that reshaped the post–World War II South, "he would have been tempted to tinker with the text." Contrast Cash's plight with that of Woodward, who, since his 1967–1971 assault on *The Mind of the South,* has occupied the position of the great anti-Cash, his monumental scholarly status serving, symbolically at least, as an inverse barometer of Cash's overall credibility. Happily for us all, Woodward has had the opportunity to reply to his own critics and to qualify and clarify his arguments and conclusions on a number of occasions. Having opened the gates for the flood of criticism that seemed to sweep Cash from the mainstream to the periphery of southern historical thought, Woodward opted in 1986 to recapitulate his own remarkable career in *Thinking Back: The Perils of Writing History.* Woodward dedicated the volume to his critics, and he adroitly and graciously responded to those who sought to refute or amend his findings on a variety of topics. Owing to the length of Woodward's career and the breadth of his inquiry, *Thinking Back* served as a first-rate brief history of the study of southern history itself.[30]

The value of *Thinking Back* only causes us to wish that Cash had had a similar opportunity to respond to his critics and to clarify and qualify his arguments. Cash has shown no inclination to return to a world every bit as troubled as the one he so tragically abandoned a half century ago, however. Hence, we are fortunate to have the insights of intellectual historians Bruce Clayton, Fred Hobson, Richard H. King, and Bertram Wyatt-Brown, each of whom, without becoming apologists for Cash, has nonetheless provided some much-needed perspective on Cash's work and suggested that a number of his ideas continue to be relevant and viable.

In response to criticisms of the "limited geographical range" of Cash's book, Fred Hobson suggested that a comparison of William Faulkner's Thomas Sutpen with Cash's "new raw planter" indicated that Cash did indeed understand "the mind of the upland cotton country of the Far South." Like Cash's "generic southerner," Sutpen "was an upland planter, a shrewd, strong, courageous, and ambitious man who started with nothing, worked hard, acquired wealth and position, built a big house, aped Tidewater manners when he chose, wanted education, culture, and good marriages for his son and daughters — and wanted to found a dynasty." Certainly Sutpen exhibited both the "innocence" and the fierce individualism of Cash's prototypical southerner. Sutpen's rise to "aristocracy" is much accelerated over that of Cash's southerner on the climb, but as Hobson points out, Cash in fact concluded that "in many parts of the South, as in Mississippi," such success stories un-folded, "because of the almost unparalleled productivity of the soil, in accelerated tempo."[31]

Hobson conceded that to Cash "the Mississippi Delta and Catholic Louisiana were as foreign . . . as California." When *The Mind of the South* appeared, the reigning expert on the Mississippi Delta was David L. Cohn, whose *God Shakes Creation* (published in 1935 and reissued in an expanded version in 1947 as *Where I Was Born and Raised*) had introduced the world to a distinctive southern subregion far removed geographi-cally from Cash's Piedmont. Yet in his review of Cash's book and in his own descriptions of the Delta, Cohn gave no evidence that he found Cash's work inapplicable to his native Delta. In fact, Cash's South, with its startling juxtapositions of hedonism and Puritanism and hospitality and homicide, seemed very much like the Delta that Cohn described as "a church-going and whisky-drinking society" that despite its facade of placidity was little less than an "armed camp." At its best, Cohn's Delta, like Cash's South, was known for its courtesy, generosity, and pride. At its worst, the blindly destructive individualism and social indifference, the excessive "attachment to racial values" and the "tendency to justify cruelty and injustice in the name of those values" that marked the South at large marked the Delta in particular.[32]

Criticisms relating to the geographical limitations of Cash's book — in Jack Temple Kirby's words, complaints that Cash's "'mind' is really the guts of the Carolina Piedmonters and Appalachian hillbillies" — amounted to saying that Cash generalized about some parts of the South that he did not know. In fact, however, Cash's regionwide generaliza-tions were wholly in keeping with his thesis about the cultural unity of the white South. Varieties in physical terrain made little — granted, per-haps too little — difference; Cash was concerned about commonalties of cultural terrain. It may be legitimate to raise questions about the geo-graphically narrow realm of experience on which Cash drew (although impressive recent studies of the upland South by Steven Hahn, David L. Carlton, and Lacy Ford have encountered few suggestions that their significance is limited), but to raise such questions is by no means to show that Cash had no insight into the South beyond the Piedmont.[33]

Joel Williamson charged that Cash "took his understanding of what had been the nature of the black presence from the Southern white world in which he came to maturity." Because it was "uniquely out of touch with the realities of black history in America and with the history of race relations," Williamson wrote, Cash's world was one "in which blacks had become, to use Ralph Ellison's perfect phrase, 'Invisible Man,' and he probably never really knew any of them, and neither did the great mass of his contemporaries." Richard King conceded that "Cash edged toward a vague, hazy sort of racism" when he discussed the sensuality of black women and the "grandiloquent imagination" and "facile emotion" of blacks in general, although he was quick to add in Cash's behalf that "whatever critical remarks he offered about blacks he attributed the same or worse to whites." King also noted that although he devoted only five pages to the effects of slavery on blacks, Cash pulled no punches in outlining the "corrupting and brutalizing effects" of slavery on all of southern culture. Unlike many of his white contemporaries, Cash harbored no "sentimentality" about slavery nor did he buy into Phillips's then widely accepted contention that slavery had exerted a civilizing influence on blacks.[34]

Others have contended that Cash may well have understood better than Williamson suggests what Richard Wright meant when he wrote that "the white South," which said it "knew 'niggers,'" had never "known" him. Hobson argued that Cash probably realized that it would be presumptuous of him to attempt any analysis of the black mind. Cash indicated as much when he wrote that "the white South delighted to say and believe that it knew the black man through and through. And yet even the most unreflecting must sometimes feel in dealing with him that they were looking at a blank wall, that behind the grinning face a veil was drawn which no white man might certainly know he had penetrated." Citing this passage, Clayton contended that "Cash was forever free from embracing the white southerners' cherished notion, expressed by racist and well-meaning liberal alike, that they 'understood' the Negro and knew what was best for both races."[35]

Clayton went further, asserting that after four decades of "reading, thinking, brooding, worrying, talking, and writing, Cash had shaken free of his region's racial prejudices and illusions." Michael O'Brien probably provided a more accurate summary of Cash's racial attitudes when he wrote that "Cash himself was a liberal in racial matters by the standards of his time, that is, he had adjusted his views to deprecate the enemies of blacks, but not yet altered his own opinions to sympathize with black culture and personality."[36]

By way of comparison, "black culture and personality" are hardly dominant themes in Woodward's early monographs either, even when the subject was, as King put it, "those policies and practices that affected black life." Howard N. Rabinowitz has suggested that "by largely ignoring black attitudes and behavior" in the pre-1974 editions of *The Strange Career of Jim Crow*, "Woodward missed an opportunity to provide a more compelling treatment of the origins and development of segregation." Rabinowitz noted as well that in the book's earlier editions, Woodward described blacks as "not aggressive in pressing their rights" and "confused and politically apathetic." None of this is to imply that Woodward's racial egalitarianism was ever open to question, although Cash's clearly was and should have been. It does suggest, however, the value of fully two generations of scholarship, much of it with an Afro American focus, to Woodward as he revised and reshaped his work. Lacking access to such scholarship and unexposed to civil rights-era consciousness raising, Cash meanwhile is regrettably but justifiably condemned to eternal identification with a practice still widespread among historians of referring to southern whites as "southerners" and southern blacks as "blacks."[37]

If, for whatever reason, Cash did not treat blacks as southerners, he nonetheless understood the formative influence of blacks on the white mind. As Hobson has pointed out, "the Negro is at the center of his book." Cash's Proto-Dorian bond largely anticipated George M. Fredrickson's explication of the idea of Herrenvolk democracy (for whites only), and for all the evidence presented in recent years of complexity and tension within the social structure of southern white society, there is no denying that in developing the concept of the Proto-Dorian bond, Cash identified a remarkably potent and durable vehicle for social control.[38]

O'Brien's charge that Cash's book "neglects women, except as totemic objects of southern mythology" is essentially correct, although the three citations pertaining to women that appeared in *Writing Southern History* in 1965 suggest that, writing in 1941, Cash was hardly more guilty than his academic contemporaries of neglecting the role of women in southern history. More than most of these scholars, at least, Cash clearly understood the powerful social and political symbolism attached to the pedestalized white female and was willing to explore the interplay of racial and sexual anxieties subsequently analyzed so skillfully by Winthrop D. Jordan. By emphasizing what Richard King called the "close identification of the South with the white woman," Cash demonstrated that defense of one was essentially tantamount to defense of the other. As King explained, "Racial purity was absolutely central to the legitimacy of white southern society." Hence to Cash (and to Jordan as well), wrote Wyatt-Brown, "fear of the contamination of blood lineage was not purely a sexual fear, but was a dread loss of race command, the nightmare of impotence, both physical and social." Coming to a similar conclusion after studying the caste system of the Mississippi Delta, John Dollard observed that "the race-conscious white man has a proprietary interest in every white woman" and explained that "behind the actual or posited desires of Negro men for white women is seen also the status motive, the wish to advance in social rank, to be as good as anyone else, and to have available what everyone else has." Hence when a Mississippi white man attacked a black voter registration activist, yelling "you sonofabitch, you sonofabitch, you'll never marry my daughter," his words would have neither puzzled nor surprised Cash. Indeed, his response reaffirmed not only Cash's description of the southern white mind but his analysis and understanding of it as well.[39]

Cash's view of Reconstruction was strikingly similar to prevailing popular and historical attitudes of his day — and, in that regard, strikingly dissimilar from most of the rest of his book. Yet Cash's now-discredited treatment of Reconstruction notwithstanding, his analysis of its impact on the mind of the white South, that is, in Richard King's words, the creation of "a collective psycho-cultural entity — the South," was surely on or near the mark. Wyatt-Brown concurred, noting that Cash's bitterness and his uncharacteristic face-value acceptance of the mythology of black rule and a carpetbagger-inspired reign of terror "had a beneficial side" in that "it enabled him to perceive that, like Ireland, Poland, Finland, Bohemia, and other exploited lands, the South found a new unity in the fury of war and the resentment of defeat." Wyatt-Brown added that "like the Celtic Fringe of Great Britain, the former slave states were compelled to assume the peripheral, subordinate role assigned agrarian outlands in relation to rich metropolitan centers." Here was essentially the same theory of "internal colonialism" that, as Wyatt-Brown pointed out, "received brilliant illustration in Woodward's *Origins of the New South*."[40]

Wyatt-Brown also argued that the distance between Cash and Genovese might not be as great as it seemed. In 1969 Genovese charged that Cash "identifies as aristocracies only those classes exhibiting the grace and *noblesse-oblige* of fourth- or fifth-generation gentlemen." To illustrate the error of Cash's ways, Genovese used William Styron's fictionalized account of the Turner family of Virginia (who should have met Cash's requirements as members of the South's tiny but true aristocracy), wherein the gentlemanly Samuel Turner was contrasted with his loutish brother Benjamin. The latter threw a visiting minister into "a desperate fidget" by continuing his conversation with the man of the cloth as he (Benjamin) was engaged in "taking a piss, which Benjamin did without a flicker of thought and in the most public way whenever he drank in the company of men." Genovese made his point — and suggested by inference, at least, that had he been born 150 years earlier, Billy Carter would have made a first-class aristocrat. In the long run, however, as Wyatt-Brown has argued, Genovese and Cash may not have been so far apart as Genovese first indicated. Both agreed that the behavior of the so-called "southern gentleman" was "not very gentlemanly." Moreover, Cash's emphasis on the "common commonness" and "class unawareness" that permeated southern white society resurfaced, without mention of Cash, in Genovese's 1975 essay concerning "Yeomen Farmers in a Slaveholders' Democracy."[41]

Wyatt-Brown also believed that "on this point, Cash and Faulkner shared the same vision of historical reality." Wyatt-Brown cited the violent decapitation of Faulkner's Thomas Sutpen by poor white Wash Jones (whose granddaughter Sutpen had seduced and cruelly rejected when she bore him a female child) as evidence that both Faulkner and Cash saw of southern white society as one where "those who hold power must meet their obligations according to subtle rules of gentility that Sutpen failed to learn."[42]

Not all of the reaffirmations of Cash's insights came from intellectual historians. Woodward's series of attacks on *The Mind of the South* established the importance of his differences with Cash on the question of continuity in southern history, and these differences framed the research agendas of a host of scholars in the 1970s and 1980s. In 1971 Woodward reiterated his belief that "abrupt and drastic breaks" had characterized the South's entire history as a region. The ensuing decades, however, yielded a number of studies by political, economic, and cultural historians whose discoveries of continuity pointed to a South that, to paraphrase Hugh Graham, reflected "more Cash than Woodward." By the end of the 1980s, there was also a growing body of literature that seemed to suggest both Cash and Woodward.[43]

Woodward's insistence on the postbellum demise of the planter class met with a stiff rebuttal from a number of state-based studies that found considerable evidence of ongoing planter dominance at the state and local level and generally reaffirmed Cash's contention, as James Tice Moore put it, that "all things had not changed with Appomattox, much less with the Compromise of 1877." In his study of North Carolina, for example,

Dwight B. Billings Jr. found Cash's thesis of the continuity of planter influence "right on target" and "wholly consistent" with Billings's depiction of "a revolution from above in North Carolina resting on agriculture and aimed at sustaining the position of a traditional landed upper class."[44]

Studies of the South Carolina Piedmont by David Carlton and Lacy Ford revealed that after the war momentum and influence were captured by a dynamic merchant- and town-building class, but their findings also indicate that the genealogy and antebellum pursuits of the South's postbellum white leadership were less crucial than the values and attitudes that they brought to their tasks. Such was also the argument of Michael S. Wayne, who found the late nineteenth-century planter leadership in the Natchez District profoundly changed in outlook and sensibilities. In his *Old South, New South,* Gavin Wright explained that emancipation automatically transformed the South's economic elite from antebellum "laborlords" (who pursued wealth in labor) into postbellum "landlords" (who pursued wealth in land). Wright actually placed former slaveholders alongside businessmen and industrialists in his emergent landlord class because, as one reviewer saw it, "regardless of whether the landlords were 'new' *men,* their sudden commitment to enhanced land values constituted a 'new' *mission* and . . . made them a 'new' class."[45]

Other recent studies have bypassed questions of the class identity or values of southern leaders, focusing instead on the relationship between the structure of the regional, national, and global economy and the persistence of certain conditions formerly attributed to the survival of planter influence in the South. Observing that "discussions of the New South in recent years have tended to view its social characteristics, from 'paternalism' to low wages to worker powerlessness, as internally generated, the creations of a persistent ruling class," David Carlton concluded that the "revolution from above" that Billings described in North Carolina was not "sponsored by southern Junkers so much as imposed upon them." Elsewhere, James C. Cobb pointed to "an evolving national and international economy that helped to make certain elements of the social and political organization of a fading plantation society not just compatible with but almost integral to the establishment of a new industrial one." Along these lines, for example, the growing mobility and competitiveness of post–World War II industry clearly played a major role in sustaining opposition to union expansion in Dixie. As Wright observed, "Whether the South ever becomes highly unionized . . . is an open question. But if it does not, it will be a sign of the late twentieth-century American times, not the persistence of the Old South."[46]

As some scholars pursued the themes of continuity and change within the context of the South's economic development, others examined the emergence of two-party politics and the cultural implications of the South's post–World War II economic transformation. In their broad-based attempt to test V. O. Key's prophesy that black enfranchisement would give the South a rational two-party system, Numan V. Bartley and Hugh Graham conceded that "the South of the 1970s is not the same South that the tortured Wilbur Cash knew." Bartley and Graham none-theless concluded that southern white voters, still seemingly hexed by history in the mid-1970s, adhered to a decidedly Cashian pattern of po-litical behavior that "confounds our more rational and optimistic predic-tions and masks deeply rooted continuity behind the symptoms of ba-sic change." The wholesale desertion of the national Democratic party by southern whites of all classes after 1964 attested to the continuing vi-ability of Cash's Proto-Dorian convention and led Bartley and Graham to suspect that the ascendance of the Republican party in presidential politics in Dixie "may well have reflected a quite traditional southern tri-umph, under a new partisan label, of her more dominant social conser-vatism over her game but historically outweighed populism." More than a decade after Bartley and Graham's book appeared, Earl Black and Merle Black predicted that despite the massive economic and demo-graphic changes that had swept across the region, southern politics would remain conservative and therefore "perpetuate much of the past even as a different future beckons."[47]

In 1977 Carl N. Degler also took issue with Woodward and others who emphasized discontinuity in the southern experience. Melding Cash's themes of continuity and distinctiveness, Degler introduced and concluded his argument with Cash's comparison of the South to "a tree with many age rings, with its limbs and trunk bent and twisted by all the winds of the years, but with its tap root in the Old South." For Degler "the reality of the continuity of southern history" lay "in the persistence for more than 150 years of those characteristics that have made the South distinctive."[48]

In support of his argument, Degler cited the findings of sociologist John Shelton Reed, who consistently discovered distinctively southern values and attitudes lurking amid the skyscrapers and shopping malls of the Sunbelt South. By 1983, however, Reed believed that identification with the South was actually strongest among those white southerners most affected by the same Bulldozer Revolution that Woodward had seen "erasing the very consciousness of a distinctive tradition along with the will to sustain it." Reed found that those largely bypassed by the Bulldozer Revolution, the poorly educated and less affluent whites who clung to the outdated values and prejudices decried by Cash, were actually less concerned with their identity as southerners than were their better-schooled, upwardly mobile brethren. Though less likely to embrace the racism and traditionalism that were the distinguishing features of Cash's South, these relatively prosperous and sophisticated southern whites were much more inclined not just to acknowledge but to express pride in their southernness. Reed concluded, therefore, that it was no longer those "most isolated from the American mainstream . . . who will find their regional identity most salient. Rather it is those who are most modern in background and experience." Reed attributed the determination of upscale whites to assert their southernness to their desire to avoid the loss of identity that would accompany total immersion in the American mainstream, and he noted that in their determination to remain "different" these southerners were, paradoxically enough, becoming "no different — no different from the other cultural minorities that make up late twentieth-century American society."[49]

Reed's discovery of the unexpected relationship between socioeconomic change and the persistence of a distinctively southern, but no longer quite so distinctively Cashian, regional identity demonstrated how hopelessly blurred and relatively unproductive the Cash-Woodward continuity-discontinuity debate had become by the 1980s. Bruce Clayton argued in 1991 that the "jury is still out" on the matter, but if so, there is little reason to expect a verdict any time soon. That the case of Woodward v. Cash would ultimately end in a hung jury should hardly surprise Richard King, who pointed out in 1980 that while Woodward focused primarily on "observable forces, movements, and institutions," Cash was more concerned with the "cultural psychology in which Southern institutions were grounded." In that sense, King noted, "Cash and Woodward simply talked past one another; they were interested in different things." Although there were those who sought to impose order on the Woodward-Cash confusion by insisting that one side or the other had gotten the better of it, the reality was that by the end of the 1980s, the dialogue on continuity and change in the southern experience had moved so far beyond the original premises on which either Cash or Woodward had operated that their names were far more likely to be invoked to symbolize a point of view than to substantiate it.[50]

The foregoing review of the criticisms, scholarly analyses, and "tests" of *The Mind of the South* points to a book that has been both questioned and corrected on a number of points. In the interest of perspective, however, it is worth noting that Woodward's *Origins of the New South,* published a decade after *The Mind of the South* and considerably narrower in its chronological focus, has also drawn its share of critical comment on a number of significant issues without losing its overall credibility. Moreover, as with Woodward's work, criticism of Cash's book should be discounted against the reaffirmations and clarifications that have been offered in its behalf. If one also acknowledges that *The Mind of the South* was a work of extraordinarily ambitious scope published fifty years ago for a nonscholarly audience but nonetheless left orphaned and defenseless on the doorstep of the academy, the book appears to have emerged from its belated trial by historiographical cross fire in surprisingly good condition.[51]

If this assessment is correct, our effort to understand why so many historians now dismiss *The Mind of the South* as a "period piece" or a hopelessly dated "artifact" must move beyond Cash's academic detractors to consider the changing regional and national context in which their criticisms were raised. After all, the lengthy tenure of *The Mind of the South* as the most influential book on Dixie had little to do with its ability to withstand scholarly scrutiny. In reality, as we have seen, once the initial reviews were out of the way, the book seemed to enjoy a virtual twenty-five-year exemption from such scrutiny. One of the few historians to suggest during this period that *The Mind of the South* might actually have some shortcomings was Dewey Grantham, who pointed out in 1961 that Cash had offered his readers little insight into "the historical rubric or conceptual framework out of which he wrote." Grantham's observation helps to explain why, during the charmed first half of its existence, historians smothered Cash's book with almost perfunctory accolades, but, as Wyatt-Brown explained, few of them seemed to see "*The Mind of the South* as a point of departure" for their research. Instead, they and the students under their direction simply acknowledged Cash as an imposing and apparently immutable fixture of the historical landscape, cited or quoted him if it was advantageous to do so, and then, in Williamson's words, "moved confidently and comfortably on." The first historian to provide a full-blown assessment of the historiographical significance of *The Mind of the South* was Woodward, who simultaneously became the book's harshest and most influential critic. Until Woodward forced his fellow historians to confront the broader interpretative ramifications of *The Mind of the South,* the apparent accuracy of Cash's compelling description of the character and mind-set of southern white society had simply overshadowed the question of the historical perspective from which Cash's portrait derived.[52]

Instead of attracting scores of would-be revisionists or reaffirmers, *The Mind of the South* rested comfortably for twenty-five years on a cushion provided by the widespread perception of the enormity and gravity of the South's problems. This perception was reinforced not only by mountains of statistical data and volume after volume of scholarly research but, more important for Cash's thesis, by the consistently outrageous, irrational, socially and politically primitive behavior that continued to be associated with white southerners as a group.

Jack Kirby described Cash's book as "the magnum opus to the visceral, mindless South." David Hackett Fischer observed that by taking "the plantation legend" and "turning it upside down," Cash effectively "stood Scarlett O'Hara on her head." As a result, Fischer complained, "there wasn't much to be seen of Scarlett's upper parts, but there was considerable display of her lower ones," and he concluded that it was "a little disconcerting to find, in a book called *The Mind of the South,* so little brain and so much bottom."[53]

Like his mentor H. L. Mencken, Cash's writings clearly encouraged reasonably well-read northerners (and outsiders in general) to, as Faulkner's Chick Mallison complained, "believe anything about the South not even provided it be derogatory but merely bizarre enough and strange enough." In fairness to Cash, however, he was hardly without literary and journalistic contemporaries and successors who made considerably more lucrative careers out of demonstrating that, in Fischer's words, "Scarlett's lower parts" made such "a splendid spectacle." As Daniel Singal pointed out, "From Erskine Caldwell to Tennessee Williams, from C. Vann Woodward to Marshall Frady, southern authors carried the critical spirit to its logical extreme, until Americans living outside the region formed a picture of southern society as one immense *Tobacco Road.*" Moreover, it was hardly Cash's fault that the behavior of his subject population so often suggested an insufficiency of brain and an excess of bottom, although it was to this widely held stereotype and its consistent reaffirmation by the southern whites of whom he wrote so despairingly that Cash largely owed his quarter-century reign as the martyred guru of southernology.[54]

Observers indicated on a number of occasions that the outrageous behavior of southern whites during the 1940s, 1950s, and 1960s had reinforced the credibility of *The Mind of the South*. That Cash's book rang true to readers throughout the 1940s was hardly surprising. Eugene Talmadge and Theodore G. Bilbo did not meet their demise until the end of the decade, and when they did, the insurgent Dixiecrats soon rushed in to reaffirm the region's commitment to political depravity. As Kirby observed, "To a generation witnessing the Dixiecrat movement of 1948, the *Brown* school desegregation decision's aftermath, the Montgomery bus boycott, and the ensuing 'Negro revolt' in the South, Cash's South was more than adequate as an explanatory model. It was brilliant." Although he endeavored to show in 1954 that *The Mind of the South* had "serious defects," Louis D. Rubin Jr. conceded that despite the book's unevenness, "a second world war, a police action, a Republican administration, and a vast increase in Southern industrialization have not managed to outdate very much of it."[55]

Forged in the crucible of the first Reconstruction, the "savage ideal" continued to flourish as the long-feared second one finally became a reality. The bloody reception accorded the Freedom Riders in 1961 and the mini-war that erupted as James Meredith entered Ole Miss in 1962 insured that *The Mind of the South* would remain unchallenged yet a while. Citizens Council propaganda presented in 1964 in James W. Silver's *Mississippi: The Closed Society* gave striking testimony to the persistence of a distinctively Cashian southern mind, alive and still not well:

> One of the main lessons in the Old Testament of our Bible is that your race should be kept pure. . . . A friend had 100 white chickens and 100 reds. All the white chickens got to one side of the house, and all the red chickens got on the other side of the house. You probably feel the same way these chickens did whenever you are with people of a different race. God meant it to be that way.[56]

Likewise, the "I love Mississippi! I love her people! I love her customs!" speech of Ross Barnett that elicited a "reasonless, incoherent, delirious response" at the Ole Miss-Kentucky football game on the eve of the Oxford riot might have sent chills down the spine of a Cash who so clearly saw fearful southern parallels to the totalitarian demagoguery that held Italy and Germany in its grip at the end of the 1930s. Affirming the impression conveyed by Silver, Walker Percy wrote in chilling terms in 1965 of a Mississippi that presented an "extraordinary apposition . . . of kindliness and unspeakable violence" and boasted of its piety when in fact it lay in the grip of a religion "which tends to canonize the existing social and political structure and to brand as atheistic any threat of change." Such evidence from Mississippi and elsewhere across Dixie suggested that, as Cash had predicted, the white South's "capacity for adjustment" was indeed being tested and, as he had feared, it was failing the test.[57]

In his 1965 retrospective on Cash's book, Edwin M. Yoder concluded that "the essential behavior of the South as Cash described it" had not "changed radically in the last quarter-century. . . . [N]otwithstanding obvious economic and social modifications that are often heralded today, as in the 1890s, as constituting a 'New' South," Yoder wrote, the South continued to "defy the impersonal forces" and to project "a mental pattern familiar to Cash."[58]

The ongoing propensity of southern whites to project "a mental pattern" straight out of The Mind of the South helped to account for the fact that, as Wyatt-Brown observed, "Cash became an excuse for not probing, except for the most superficial renderings, such themes as lynching, sexual violations of the race bar, and personal violence." In essence, instead of serving as a stimulus to further inquiry into such behavior, The Mind of the South became an impediment to it. So long as Cash's South was the one they also read about in the morning papers or watched in horror on the evening news, scholars largely accepted his pronouncements as an explanatory end in themselves rather than challenge them or search for contextual or other influences that might seem to make the behavior of white southerners seem a bit less peculiar.[59]

Wyatt-Brown identified The Mind of the South as a pioneering contribution to American studies, a genre that relied on "typological schemes for explaining American characteristics," and he linked the declining prestige of Cash's work to the general loss of credibility on the part of the entire field of American studies during the mid-1960s. In Cash's case, however, the problem was less one of his typological approach than his reliance on a particular typology that seemed increasingly inappropriate once popular perceptions of southern whites no longer suggested the uniquely southern mind-set that Cash had emphasized.[60]

Woodward noted in 1952 that southerners owed much of their distinctive identity to the fact that they were the only Americans for whom history was not simply "something unpleasant that happens to other people." Hence it was probably not wholly coincidental that at the end of the 1960s when, as Woodward observed, "history" at last began to "catch up" with other Americans, questions about Cash's insistence on southern peculiarity finally caught up with *The Mind of the South* as well. Certainly Cash's argument for the distinctiveness of the southern white mind lost much of its persuasive power after long-awaited civil rights advances in the South combined with the concomitant revelation of the seriousness of the race problem in the rest of the nation to suggest that racism and irrationality were hardly as unique to southern whites as Cash had seemed to believe.[61]

In 1965 Yoder attributed George C. Wallace's political strength in Alabama to "a canny insight into the 'proto-Dorian' standing of the Southern poor white." Yoder was surely correct, but in the "white back-lash" atmosphere of the late 1960s, Wallace's unexpected appeal among whites outside the South left Cash's insistence on the peculiarity of southern white racial attitudes clearly open to question. Wallace's sur-prisingly strong showing in presidential primaries outside the South and his standing in the polls during the 1968 presidential campaign led re-porter Douglas Kiker, himself a southerner, to observe: "It is as if some-where, sometime a while back, George Wallace had been awakened by a white, blinding vision: they all hate black people, all of them. They're all afraid, all of them. Great God! That's it! They're all Southern! The whole United States is *Southern!* Anybody who travels with Wallace these days on his presidential campaign finds it hard to resist arriving at the same conclusion."[62]

The racially polarized atmosphere of the 1968 campaign, as well as the ugly scenes of Martin Luther King's visit to Cicero, Illinois, were part of a growing body of evidence that white racial paranoia was too potent an element of the national mind to be dismissed as a peculiarly southern trait. As Kirby observed, "Television recorded it all. Suddenly the devil-ish white South, for years evoked on live TV by plump mothers verbally abusing frightened little black children at schoolyards, dissolved in the vision of plump Yankees behaving the same way."[63]

Coming on the heels of the national retreat from the Second Re-construction were the bitter signs of polarization and intolerance that marked the Vietnam protest era and further suggested a savage ideal gone national. The same was true of the heavily coded "law and order" rhetoric of Richard M. Nixon's presidency. The box-office success of the *Walking Tall* movies suggested broad popular receptivity to the vio-lent expediency of Buford Pusser, who wielded a mean club and kept his search warrant in the boots that he used to kick in the doors of illegal booze and gambling joints. In the character of Pusser, as Kirby observed, "Southern violence was redefined, and Cash's savage ideal, thriving still, was no longer quite so solidly based upon Proto-Dorian bond of white supremacy." (Pusser, after all, had appointed a black deputy.) [64]

A decidedly less violent embodiment of a new, embraceable South appeared as well in the successful television series *The Waltons,* whose characters seemed to personify the best of the South's rural, down-home values of love, loyalty, and localism. By the early 1970s, a nation staggering from the disillusionments of Vietnam and Watergate seemed willing to look to such a South for leadership and guidance.[65]

The southerner who stepped forward bore scant resemblance to Cash's volatile, irrational, hell-of-a fellow. Simultaneously confident and humble, energetic and low key, deeply religious but freed from the racial and ideological constraints that traditionally bound his fellow white southern Baptists, save for his drawl, Jimmy Carter seemed less a southerner than, in William L. Miller's words, a "Yankee from Georgia." As president, this decidedly different southerner behaved in wholly un-Cashian fashion by quietly counseling reason and restraint. Unfortunately, Carter's words fell on the deaf ears of an electorate whose majority proved unprepared to accept anything less than instant gratification and a high-profile presence in the world. Unfortunately as well, Carter demonstrated how truly colorless Cash's generic southerner became when his Puritanism lacked even a redeeming smidgen of hedonistic counterbalance.[66]

By 1980 Carter's uninspiring persona and his inability to neutralize forces beyond his control proved to be major political liabilities as he confronted a Californian who urged an end to all this talk about reason and restraint. If one relied only on Cash's adaptation of Henry Adams's words about his Harvard classmate, the Virginian William Henry Fitzhugh ("Rooney") Lee — "simple beyond analysis. . . . No one knew . . . how ignorant he was. . . . He could not analyze an idea, and he could not even conceive of admitting two" — while observing the 1980 presidential campaign, it would have been difficult indeed to identify Carter as the southerner in the race. Political scientists Earl Black and Merle Black even described Ronald Reagan as "much more conventionally 'southern' in his style and practice of politics than either Lyndon Johnson or Jimmy Carter."[67]

Reagan's attitude toward civil rights was clear enough when he opened his 1980 campaign in Neshoba County, Mississippi, site of the 1964 slayings of three civil rights workers, and neither mentioned the tragedy nor hailed the improvement in race relations in the years since it occurred. Instead, in language Mississippians had not heard since the massive resistance era, Reagan defiantly proclaimed his belief in "states' rights" and promised to "restore to state and local governments the powers that properly belong to them." As president, he encouraged Americans to embrace a highly romanticized sense of nationalism, while his indifference to the nation's widening economic disparities and insensitivity to its pressing social problems evoked images of a Redeemer South governed by a philosophy described by Woodward as "juleps for the few and pellagra for the crew." Statistics on poverty, education, and public health indicated that the South remained the nation's most backward region, but with such concerns no longer a political priority and with job losses and homelessness suddenly plaguing all of the nation's major cities and many of its formerly prosperous industrial areas, the South's fifty-year claim on the nation's conscience was clearly a thing of the past by the end of the 1980s.[68]

Noting how effectively Jesse A. Helms had manipulated the "minority quota" issue in his 1990 North Carolina senatorial victory over black challenger Harvey Gantt, Edwin Yoder concluded that "the invidious use of race consciousness to undermine interest politics is alive and well." While it appeared at first glance that Helms had simply trotted out Cash's old Proto-Dorian convention in order to save his political neck, Yoder realized that this tactic — once the subterfuge of choice among southern Democrats — had now "gone national" and in fact "taken on a certain shoddy respectability" among national Republican party leaders.[69]

Even more chilling was the case of former neo-Nazi and Klansman David Duke whose flaying of affirmative action and welfare programs won him a seat in the Louisiana legislature and contributed to his strong showing in his 1990 campaign for the United States Senate. Though clearly intended to play on white racial antagonisms and economic anxieties, the Duke campaign was seldom interpreted solely in "southern" terms. Indeed, Duke won praise from the *New Republic* (which had condemned George Wallace in 1968) and conservative columnist Patrick J. Buchanan, who urged national GOP leaders to quit "pandering" to blacks and to take "a hard look at Duke's portfolio of winning issues." George Bush's manipulation of the Willie Horton episode in his 1988 presidential campaign, his veto of the Civil Rights Act of 1990, and his injection of the minority quota controversy into the 1990 congressional election implied that Buchanan's advice had been taken seriously.[70]

Observing the tendency of southern liberals like V. O. Key to see the salvation of the South's blacks and lower-income whites in a biracial alliance of have-nots, Richard King noted that, given the South's "depressed, underdeveloped economy" and its persistent labor surplus, "it is far from clear that the economically rational course for marginal, struggling white farmers or white industrial workers was to support equal competition for their jobs by blacks." The same was true of a southernized national economy plagued by job losses and declining wages throughout the 1980s. Having played a crucial role in shaping the South's past, race-based politics seemed to have become a fixture in the national political arena as the 1990s began. This reality indicated that the consistent effectiveness of the Proto-Dorian appeal may have had as much to do with the South's distinctive economic context as the peculiar cultural one emphasized by Cash.[71]

In 1964 Howard Zinn had argued that "far from being utterly different," the South represented "the *essence* of the nation." Zinn's premise was hard to swallow in the wake of Oxford, Birmingham, and Selma, but the events of the ensuing quarter century seemed to confirm Zinn's contention that the differences cited by Cash between the South and the nation at large "have been matters of degree, based on time and circumstance." Zinn conceded the South was "racist, violent, hypocritically pious, xenophobic, false in its elevation of women, nationalistic, conservative, and it harbors extreme poverty in the midst of ostentatious wealth." "The only point I have to add," wrote Zinn, "is that the United States as a civilization, embodies all of those same qualities."[72]

Writing at perhaps the peak of the United States' strength and influence around the globe, Zinn argued that it was "particularly appropriate in this time, when the power of the United States gives it enormous responsibility, to focus our critical faculties on those qualities which mark — or disfigure — our nation." For a nation willing to undertake such painful self-scrutiny, the South became "marvelously useful, as a mirror in which the nation can see its blemishes magnified, so that it will hurry to correct them."[73]

At the time Zinn wrote, however, it seemed both more urgent and more expedient to deal with the South's blemishes than to inspect the national complexion too closely, and by the time Zinn's words rang true, the nation was no longer in a blemish-correcting mood. Still, the mere acknowledgment of the Americanness of the South's imperfections spelled a loss of credibility for *The Mind of the South,* a realization that the distinctions Cash had drawn between the South and the nation as a whole were now, and perhaps always had been, largely differences of degree rather than kind. In an otherwise positive review, David Cohn had responded in 1941 to Cash's book with the question of whether it was "possible to isolate so-called Southern characteristics or failings from national characteristics or failings." F. Garvin Davenport Jr. observed in 1970 that the pride, bravery, courtesy, generosity, and other virtues Cash ascribed to the South at its best were nothing more than "the myth of American democracy with its individualized, spontaneous, simple way of life." Meanwhile the South's "vices," which Cash identified as "an incapacity for analysis, an inclination to act from feeling . . . sentimentality and a lack of realism," simply struck Davenport as "for the most part images of national scope."[74]

As a "loyal son," Cash had closed his book with the hope that the South's "virtues will tower over and conquer its faults," but once Dixie's worst flaws were finally either ameliorated or exposed as national rather than regional in scope, the spell of *The Mind of the South* was broken. To be sure, anecdotal evidence of the survival of Cash's South remains abundant. The message of *The Mind of the South* permeates the lyrics and repertoires of country musicians such as Willie Nelson, who typically opens his performances with "Whiskey River" and closes them with "Amazing Grace." Surely, once he overcame his embarrassment, Cash would have had a field day with the Delta matron who told Tony Dunbar in 1989 that her adolescent memories were a mixture of Sunday school ("I went to the Methodist Church every Sunday. Church was very important in our family, and I went to Sunday school every week until I got out of college") and sex ("I was deflowered on a John Deere tractor. That doesn't sound very romantic, does it, but I assure you it was. We have such beautiful moonlight here"). Finally, V. S. Naipaul sounded much like Cash himself when he announced in *A Turn in the South,* published in 1989, that he had found below the Mason-Dixon line "a whole distinctive culture, something I had never imagined existing in the United States."[75]

If such evidence might be counted on to elicit "I told you so's" from die-hard Cashites, it was equally likely to meet with the "ho-hums" and "so what's" of a growing number of Americans for whom the debate over southern distinctiveness seemed increasingly tiresome and uncompelling. When Edwin Yoder hailed the continuing relevance of *The Mind of the South* in 1965, he gave thanks for "the tacit alliance that reaches down from the rarefied meditations of professors, authors, and journalists to the inchoate consciousness of the leather-jacketed hot-rodder who sports a Confederate battle flag on the rear bumper." Yoder believed that without "working mythologists to go on holding up a mirror to *The Mind of the South*' this mind would vanish as a distinctive study in self-consciousness." Eighteen years later, Yoder waxed nostalgic about the civil rights era, "when so much of national importance was happening in and to the South." He associated the late 1950s and early 1960s with "a cresting of interest in what it was like to be southern. We southerners were studied hard, everywhere, like savages brought in from a newly discovered continent in the Elizabethan Age." As Yoder sized up the situation in the early 1980s, however, the once intense national fascination with the South had given way to what he called a general "mood of boredom and impatience," and he confessed that even he felt a "certain burden and exertion" in trying to make a case for the persistence of a meaningfully distinct South.[76]

As Yoder wrote, however, there were still quite a few southerners who stood ready to shoulder the responsibility of keeping a fading South alive. The phenomenon of southern self-assertion that John Shelton Reed had documented in the early 1980s was even more pronounced by the end of the decade. *Southern Living,* described by Reed as a "sort of how-to-do-it manual, in living the Southern good life," boasted over two million subscribers by 1990, and even the short-lived *Southern,* whose motto was "the South, the whole South, and nothing but the South," had a circulation of approximately three hundred thousand when it folded in 1989. Meanwhile, the University of North Carolina Press published the *Encyclopedia of Southern Culture,* a massive volume dedicated, according to Alex Haley, "to distilling and presenting our southern distinctiveness." The encyclopedia appeared in 1989 to great national and international fanfare, but its decidedly regional sales pattern indicated that it might serve primarily as a bible for the converted, an ideal coffee-table tome for those desiring to reaffirm their faith and be born again — perhaps, in good Baptist fashion, again and again — in their own southernness.[77]

It is surely worth noting that while Cash was largely relegated to the footnotes of *Interpreting Southern History* in 1987, his name and his words are spread throughout the *Encyclopedia of Southern Culture.* The placement of Cash's biographical entry in the section of the *Encyclopedia* titled "Mythic South" was especially appropriate. Described by Yoder as the individual most responsible for keeping "Southern self-consciousness" alive "beyond its natural span," Cash has become, however unwittingly, the patron saint of Yoder's "working mythologists" who are determined to keep southern distinctiveness alive. Whereas Yoder had given thanks for such activity in 1965, however, he worried in 1983 that what he called "the southernizing enterprise" or "The Dixiefication of Dixie" actually amounted to little more than "obscurantism and self-caricature." Yoder's changing attitude toward those who sought to keep the candle of southerness burning reflected the dramatically altered national context that had undermined the credibility of *The Mind of the South*.[78]

John Egerton complained in 1974 that "the Americanization of Dixie" and its concomitant, "the southernization of America" (which might have been more accurately described as simply the *discovery* of the southernness of America) actually meant that the South and the nation were "not exchanging strengths as much as they are exchanging sins" and were thus "sharing and spreading the worst in each other, while the best languishes and withers." Certainly once the South's most negative traits were either neutralized or nationalized, determined advocates of southern distinctiveness found themselves scrambling not so much to document the South's continuing uniqueness as to demonstrate that this uniqueness had any particular meaning for those who lived beyond the always indistinct and now increasingly uncontested boundaries of Dixie itself. Whereas Cash had hoped to see the South's virtues triumph over its faults, he could hardly have imagined that as the latter began to fade the former would prove so difficult to keep in focus. Cash would also be stunned to find that a South once so contemptuous of its own intellectuals and even more resentful of the critical national attention accorded its problems and peculiarities had not only become the most dissected and analyzed area of the United States but a region whose ongoing propensity for self-scrutiny was becoming increasingly difficult to justify to the rest of the nation.[79]

If, in the long run, the credibility of *The Mind of the South* seems to have been more affected by events in the real world than in the scholarly one, the rapid rise, long reign, and unceremonious demise of Cash's book presents a prime example of how closely interrelated these two worlds are. This interrelationship surfaced in the example of the Columbia, South Carolina, military historian who observed in January 1991 that 40 percent of the military reservists mobilized for Operation Desert Shield came from the Southeast and brandished a copy of *The Mind of the South* as he explained, "It's part of our heritage to fight." Overwhelming national popular support for the United States's military action in the Persian Gulf indicated that the speaker might have profited from rereading *The Mind of the South* without regard to the geographic limits imposed by Cash. Indeed, much of the foregoing discussion also suggests that Cash's book should be reconsidered for its national rather than its regional implications. It would be the ultimate in both irony and improbability if the most insightful book ever written about the South one day assumed a new role as a valuable window on the mind-set of the nation at large, but given the striking contrasts between the first quarter century of *The Mind of the South*'s existence and the second, we should follow the example of its remarkable author and "venture no definite prophecies" about the third.[80]

From
Muskogee
to
Luckenbach

Country Music and the "Southernization"
of America

In 1969 Merle Haggard's "Okie from Muskogee" paid tribute to militant "hippie-haters" and generally reconfirmed the
traditionalism and authoritarianism long associated with the
South and country music. Eight years later Waylon Jennings's
"Luckenbach, Texas" described another small town in the
South not as a citadel of intolerance but as a live-and-let-
live haven where jeans-clad residents had rediscovered the
"basics of love." Whereas Haggard's "Okie" had enjoyed its
greatest appeal among conservative, country music–loving
southerners, Jennings's "Luckenbach" was on the lips not
only of traditional country fans but of shaggy teenagers and
young, middle-class adults across the nation. The dramatic
expansion of country music's appeal in the 1970s was particularly significant because for most of its existence the music
had encountered all the hostility and condescension traditionally reserved for things southern. The nation that embraced country music in the 1970s had been deeply affected
by the twin shocks of defeat and disillusionment, traumas
previously associated only with the experience and heritage
of the southern states. Thus the factors underlying country music's increased respectability in the 1970s also provide
important insights into the nation's belated acceptance of

the South, a phenomenon that some called the "Americanization of Dixie" but others more accurately identified as the "Southernization of America."[1]

The image of a "benighted" South emerged in mature form in the 1920s. World War I had unleashed a number of forces that spotlighted the region's deficiencies and even worse inspired many of its leaders to defend these shortcomings. The war had tossed southerners, black and white, into a whirlpool of new experiences — travel, interaction with nonsoutherners, even non-Americans. Concerns over the potential aggressiveness of returning black veterans resulted in intensified repression and occasional antiblack riots. Caught up in militant patriotism southern leaders made their defense of the region's social and political hierarchy synonymous with their devotion to traditional "100 percent Americanism." Thus the Scopes Trial, other examples of entrenched religious fundamentalism, and even the resurgence of the Ku Klux Klan were not embarrassing examples of regional backwardness but badges of honor proudly worn. With the rest of the nation hurtling down the road to modernism, relativism, and almost certain ruin, the South led an uncompromising defense of the absolute and the familiar.[2]

Not surprisingly, its reactionary position as defender of the faith subjected the South to a torrent of derision. H. L. Mencken, the region's superdetractor and arch nemesis, led the way, reviling Dixie as the "bunghole of the United States." To Mencken, even Virginia, the best of the southern states, had "no art, no literature, no philosophy, no mind or aspiration of her own." On the other hand, Georgia, the region's most primitive state, was "crass, gross, vulgar and obnoxious." Between these two lay "a vast plain of mediocrity, stupidity, lethargy, almost of dead silence."[3]

It was significant that country music began to have its first commercial impact as Mencken was deriding the South for its cultural barrenness and particularly for its spirited defense of traditionalism. Essentially the music of low-income, rural whites, early recorded country music was an amalgam of British and American folk and fiddle tunes, hymns, and old popular songs that had been preserved within the self-perpetuating, conservative matrix of values and tastes in the region. Recording companies began to realize the market potential for southern rural music after Georgian Fiddlin' John Carson's recording of "The Old Hen Cackled and the Rooster's Going to Crow" sold several thousand copies on the "Okeh" label. Talent scout Ralph Peer had described Carson's singing as "pluperfect awful," but conservative rural customers nonetheless seemed anxious to own recordings of songs that they had been hearing for years at minstrel shows, dances, and fiddling contests.[4]

Much of the original material performed by Carson and his contemporaries consisted of folk tunes and hymns, but as recording opportunities increased, the need for new material spawned the first generation of country songwriters. Like the early recorded folk and gospel music, the first commercial compositions expressed the values and prejudices of the rural South. Fiddlin' John Carson was a regular at Ku Klux Klan rallies, and his "Ballad of Little Mary Phagan" helped to exacerbate the anti-Semitism that was a major factor in the lynching of Mary's alleged murderer, Leo Frank. Fiddlin' John made light of the evolution controversy in "There Ain't No Bugs on Me" when he asserted "there may be monkey in some of you guys, but there ain't no monkey in me," but his contemporary Vernon Dalhart took a more serious view in "The John T. Scopes Trial," concluding that "the old religion's better after all." In addition to religious fundamentalism and ethnic bigotry, early country music stressed the sadness of life on this earth, particularly the pain of unrequited love and the inevitable sorrow brought on by man's sins. As it became increasingly commercialized, "hillbilly music" (named for a band known as Al Hopkins and the Hillbillies) proved acceptable neither to educated northerners who maintained a romanticized vision of the sturdy, noble Anglo-Saxon "folk" nor to progressive, upper-class southerners who saw the music undermining their efforts to build a "New South" while resurrecting the "culture" and "refinement" that they, and others, believed had been a prominent characteristic of the antebellum South.[5]

Although most Americans rejected country music as the primitive mode of expression of the southern "po' white," Jimmie Rodgers broadened the music's audience in the 1930s by employing a number of vocal and instrumental innovations. "Singing cowboys" like Gene Autry and Roy Rogers also lent appeal to country music by encouraging the use of "country-western" to describe what had once been "hillbilly" entertainment. Taking a cue from this development, country performers abandoned the garb of the rural poor in favor of the lavishly decorated cowboy outfit.[6]

Sequined shirts, ten-gallon hats, and fancy boots made country performers more glamorous, but World War II gave the music its greatest boost toward respectability. As the war scattered white southerners and their music all over the world, Armed Forces Radio broadcasts provided reassuring melodies for homesick GIs and won country music many new fans.[7]

The wartime experience convinced Nashville recording and publishing executives that the potential market for this music was more extensive than they had dreamed. Eddy Arnold typified a move to make country music less "country" by exchanging his checkered work shirt for a tuxedo, de-emphasizing his "Tennessee Playboy" nickname and crooning the tender ballads that quickly made him RCA's most popular recording artist. Meanwhile, star-crossed Hank Williams was repeatedly demolishing the barriers between country and popular music as his simple but emotionally appealing songs propelled him to stardom and his instability and alcoholism drove him to an early grave.[8]

Despite the beachheads established by Williams and Arnold, traditional country music was forced underground in the mid-1950s as rebellious youth made their ambiguous statement through rock and roll. Country music had fallen on hard times, but at the end of the 1950s a few performers were able to capitalize on the "urban folk revival," an academically inspired resurgence of interest in the "true" American folk music. Traditional artists like Maybelle Carter and Bill Monroe (whose "bluegrass" style was far more modern and innovative than most folk revivalists realized) became feature attractions at campus "hootenannies." Meanwhile, others like Johnny Cash were flexible enough to present themselves as folk singers. The urban folk revival had no time, however, for most country performers, whose music at this point was far too commercialized for an idealistic movement intent on celebrating a genuine, undiluted, and therefore, of course, nonexistent culture of "the folk."[9]

Most country performers were as unwelcome on college campuses during the 1960s as Fiddlin' John Carson would have been at H. L. Mencken's table during the 1920s. Country music remained very much the music of the southern redneck and thus elicited images of pickups with shotguns stacked in the back of the cabs, shotguns waiting to be used to terrorize or kill civil rights marchers or those who sympathized with them. Amidst the liberal fervor of "The New Frontier" and "The Great Society," the ugly scenes of New Orleans, Oxford, Birmingham, and Selma made the South seem every bit as primitive and savage as it had in the 1920s.

For years, observers had searched vainly for a genuine spokesman of the proletariat among country music stars, someone who might demonstrate significant commercial appeal as a "poet of the people." Hank

Williams, who seemed to some a likely candidate to become the "hill-billy" Woody Guthrie, had proven to be a simple, uneducated country boy who read comic books and shunned politics and social commentary. Johnny Cash's victory over drugs and empathy for the down-and-outer made him country music's first great hope of the counterculture in the 1960s. Unfortunately, however, Cash's decision to make commercials for the American Oil Company and, ironically, the fact that his success had made him so respectable cooled the ardor of many of his youthful fans.

Cash's most likely successor as country music's Bob Dylan was Merle Haggard, an ex-convict whose songs of poverty and alienation were welcomed as authentic vignettes of life on the other side of the tracks. Haggard seemed the perfect symbol for a campaign to convince blue-collar whites they were being exploited and take them out into the streets to join the student protests of the late 1960s. Like Cash, however, Haggard proved a disappointment. In 1969 a road sign pointing to Muskogee, Oklahoma, and a comment about the smoking preferences of its residents inspired "Okie from Muskogee," a song intended as a lighthearted commentary on the generation gap. Regrettably (except in the commercial sense), both hard hats and liberals insisted on interpreting the song literally, and when Haggard, a former Okie himself, recorded "Fightin' Side of Me," a musical version of the "America — Love It or Leave It" bumper sticker, his ties to the New Left were temporarily severed. Thus, as the 1970s opened and the bitter polarization of American society exploded in the tragedy at Kent State University, country music was there, apparently defending authoritarianism, repression, and excessive use of force.[10]

By the end of the 1960s many Americans outside the South were angry and bewildered by the tumult in their midst. Martin Luther King's attempts to take the Civil Rights movement north of the Mason-Dixon line had shown that nonsouthern whites were far more distressed about racism and discrimination in Dixie than in their own backyards. Alabama governor George Wallace had found a following among blue-collar voters (and not a few secretive white-collar contributors) in the industrial North. As attention focused on embarrassing racial problems in northern cities, C. Vann Woodward observed that "self-righteousness withered along the Massachusetts-Michigan axis." When the Nixon administration moved to cultivate the South and co-opt Wallace, it accelerated a snowballing tendency to forgive, forget, and even applaud the South's peculiarities.[11]

Both the Vietnam and Watergate experiences encouraged a revised and more favorable assessment of the South. The Vietnam conflict gave the nation its first taste of defeat and left it without so much as the satisfaction of having fought for a noble cause. Agonizing postmortems produced no comforting explanations for the Indochina failure. Southern leaders had shown the staunchest support for the war, even to the point of defending accused mass murderer William Calley. These same spokesmen, however, generally refused to join in the self-flagellation that became almost a national pastime as the United States backed out of Southeast Asia. The South had been saddled with the humiliation of defeat for over a century. Hence it was not surprising that of all Americans, southerners appeared to cope best with the Vietnam failure.[12]

The South's response to Watergate and other Nixonian excesses was similarly stoic. Despite the blind, last-ditch defense of Nixon offered by a great many conservative southern political representatives, Americans at large were more keenly aware of the ostensibly objective, level-headed performances of Senators Herman Talmadge, Howard Baker, and Sam J. Ervin. The last named's record of opposition to civil rights measures was forgotten as he quoted the Bible and the Constitution with equal aplomb and punched holes in the nervous testimony of once-powerful White House advisers. Despite the fact that many of them had supported Nixon to the last, after his resignation, southern political leaders refused to apologize or express disillusionment. To them, like supporting the Vietnam War, backing an embattled (and sympathetic) president had been a simple act of patriotism and was certainly no cause for remorse.[13]

As the nation lay locked in post-Vietnam, post-Watergate paralysis, expressions of confidence and purposefulness were rare except in the South, where the confrontation politics of George Wallace and Lester Maddox had yielded to the moderate progressivism of Reubin Askew and Jimmy Carter. Even as a fledgling presidential aspirant who seemed to have little chance of winning his party's nomination, Carter exuded quiet confidence. His staunch Baptist faith and studied humility, two of the most commendable "southern" traits, blended with his Yankee-like energy and commitment to efficiency to make him an attractive symbol of a reunified nation.[14]

Carter moved toward the White House to the accompaniment of an unfamiliar but welcome chorus of favorable media treatment of the South. *Saturday Review* hailed "The South as the New America." Even the formerly neo-abolitionist *New York Times* joined in celebrating the

South's reentry into the Union by noting that every southern city sported "transplanted Yankees who have adopted open collars, drawling speech and bourbon mixed with Coca-Cola" while the natives had reciprocated by sipping Scotch and "experimenting with skis." The implication of the media "bliss blitz" was clear to southerner Larry L. King, who exulted in the November 1976 *Esquire:* "We Ain't Trash No More!" [15]

Admiration for things southern was not completely without precedent in American history. Historically, however, the region's rare moments of approval had come when a mythical antebellum South of magnolias, belles, and cavaliers was praised by writers for its rejection of the crass acquisitiveness they saw in contemporary American society. Romantic unions between gentle, refined southern belles and energetic but crude Yankees were a popular theme during the Gilded Age as investors scrambled to stake their claims in an economically underdeveloped South. In a sense, this mythical "southern way of life" provided an attractive alternative to the tyranny of technology, bureaucracy, and the profit-motive fostered by the nation's relentless pursuit of "progress." [16]

Although not unprecedented, the rediscovery of the admirable, even adorable South in the 1970s was nonetheless striking because the nation appeared ready to look beyond the belles and beaux, put the Tobacco Road stereotype aside, and at last embrace that formerly repulsive rustic, the redneck. Movie performances by Burt Reynolds suggested that at heart working-class southern whites were too fun loving and well intentioned to get much of a kick out of night riding and lynching. *Time*'s portrayal of the "Good Ole Boy" revived the Jeffersonian ideal of the agrarian-as-salt-of-the-earth: "Behind his devil-may-care lightheartedness . . . runs a strain of innate wisdom, an instinct about people and an unwavering loyalty that makes him the one friend you would turn to." In a more serious vein, *The Waltons* reminded troubled television viewers that lower-class southern whites had always cherished strong family ties. The several movie versions of *Walking Tall* embellished the exploits of Buford Pusser, an impulsive but courageous southern sheriff with special appeal in a law-and-order decade. The redneck, who had once been scorned for his crudity and lack of sophistication, now emerged as a hero who had resisted the corrupting influences of mainstream society. [17]

The nation's new appreciation for the South had a strong economic component. Spurred by the population and aerospace boom in Florida, the region's economy "took off" in the late 1930s, registering dramatic improvements in almost every statistical category. The South became the cornerstone of the lower tier of fast-growing, easy-living states known as the Sunbelt. Although poverty remained a serious problem, by the mid-1970s the southward shift of population and investments suggested that the wheel of fortune had at least stopped on the South's number. Like the symbolic, if often superficial, cleansing afforded by the Civil Rights movement and the remarkable equanimity with which the region endured the successive traumas of Vietnam and Watergate, Dixie's newfound affluence greatly enhanced its respectability. Urban-industrial growth posed a serious threat to the South's reputation as an uncluttered land of relaxed, gracious living, but the region's leadership, intoxicated by impressive growth statistics and basking in the warmth of national approval, could see no evil in the Sunbelt boom.[18]

As economic prosperity put southern lifestyles and values in a new and more favorable light, country music moved rapidly toward mainstream acceptance. No longer did middle-class whites in the South or southern migrants to the North have to switch their radios to "pop" stations at stoplights or refrain from playing Loretta Lynn's newest hit on the jukebox. Country radio stations cropped up all over the dial. In 1961 there had been but eighty "all-country" stations in the nation, but by the mid-1970s there were more than a thousand, the most striking newcomer being New York City's WHN, which adopted a country format and doubled its audience in little more than a year. The boom had proven too big for a single town; while Nashville remained the capital of country music, Austin and Bakersfield could now rightfully claim "sounds" distinctively their own.[19]

Since its inception, commercial country music had sought a larger audience. Jimmie Rodgers had enhanced his music's appeal to urbanites by blending in blues, ragtime, and even Hawaiian touches. Hank Williams's songs had regularly appeared on the pop charts when recorded by artists like Tony Bennett and Frankie Laine, while crooners like Eddy Arnold and Jim Reeves had attracted a large number of fans who shunned more traditional performers. In the 1960s master guitarist Chet Atkins presided over the creation of a smoothed-out, jazzed up, electrified "Nashville Sound," and "country pop" singers like Roger Miller and Jimmy Dean demonstrated considerable appeal. It was not until the 1970s, however, that country music would enjoy repeated and widespread success among pop fans. Former Rhodes scholar Kris Kristofferson's bearded appearance and independent behavior set him apart from other country artists, and his popularity sent a clear message to fellow performers that, "properly packaged," country music could at last stake a claim on the lucrative youth market.[20]

Kristofferson's success paved the way for a number of veteran country performers to strip off their sequined suits and dive belatedly into the counterculture. Willie Nelson, long recognized in country circles as an excellent songwriter and singer, shattered the conservative image he had projected on the Ernest Tubb television series by sporting a beard and long hair and affecting the garb of a 1960s dropout. Nelson relocated to Texas in 1972 and became the pivotal figure in "the Austin Sound." Another Texan, Waylon Jennings, who once played with rock star Buddy Holly's Crickets, forsook his "ducktail" haircut for the "dry look" and a beard. Jennings's arrest on a drug charge actually seemed to boost his career, a fact of which he was well aware. With Nelson, Jennings symbolized the "outlaw" movement in country music, a curious phenomenon seemingly out of phase with prevailing trends toward conservatism and respect for "law and order." In fact, however, the appeal of the outlaw movement may well have been that it offered a brief nostalgia trip into the uninhibited lifestyles and flaunted traditions of the late 1960s without requiring any sort of ideological commitment. Nelson and Jennings seemed to have changed their philosophies relatively little, but their new appearance and demeanor helped to win the hearts of many of their newfound fans. As the seventies unfolded, other performers with roots in traditional country music adopted the Jennings-Nelson style with significant, although less spectacular, success.[21]

By the end of the 1970s female performers like Anne Murray, Crystal Gayle (the sister of Loretta Lynn), Emmylou Harris, and Linda Rondstadt enjoyed equally high standings in both the country and pop markets. Even the once "down-home" sound of Dolly Parton had been adapted to a more rock-oriented audience. The 1970s witnessed the emergence of "southern rock," a music more "rock" than "southern" whose performers — like Charlie Daniels and the Marshall Tucker Band — flaunted their "Deep South" heritages but dressed like cowboys. Meanwhile, the country market became so lucrative that traditional performers found themselves in competition with artists seeking to make a "reverse crossover" appeal to the country audience. Purists bristled as "outsiders" like Olivia Newton-John and John Denver received the industry's highest awards, but even old-timers like Roy Acuff and Maybelle Carter joined the Nitty Gritty Dirt Band on "Will the Circle Be Unbroken," an impressive album tribute to the roots of country music.[22]

Much of the expanded popularity of country music was the result of shameless image-making by performers and promoters. Still, there had been some changes in the music as well. The heavy bass beat of a Waylon Jennings tune called to mind much of early rock music, a form that appeared to stagnate in the 1970s. Thus former rock fans could hear in country music the pleasing rhythms they could no longer find in rock. Country music continued to act as a preservative for popular music, keeping alive old rock favorites like "That'll Be the Day" (Linda Rondstadt) or "Save the Last Dance for Me" (Emmylou Harris). The traditionally conservative lyrics now expressed a more explicit sexuality, as in Kris Kristofferson's "Help Me Make It Through the Night." More significant, female performers like Tanya Tucker ("Would You Lay With Me in a Field of Stone?") were expressing, even flaunting, their sexual liberation.[23]

Despite the changes, country music of the 1970s was still more traditionally "country" and "southern" than anything else. Country songs continued to emphasize the darker side of life, the unavoidable pain and punishment that a weak and sinful humanity forced a loving but stern God to inflict upon it. Country music's prescription for coping with life was a large dose of lowered expectations. With humans able to recognize their sinfulness but unable to control their sinning, life on earth could only be a sad experience, and even the brief pleasure of rebellious hell-raising only raised the price of atonement even higher. Like Kenny Rogers's "Lucille," the biggest country hits of the 1970s continued to center around lost love and other deep personal tragedy. In early 1977, 36 of the top 100 country songs dealt with marital infidelity. Country music in the 1970s, as it had been in the 1920s, was as blunt a reminder of human imperfections as could be found.[24]

Country music's unattractive description of human nature inferentially damned human society and institutions as well, but the music had produced almost no social commentary. For many Americans such causelessness was a welcome release from the crusading and protesting of the 1960s. Merle Haggard's odes to the "hard-hat backlash" were a bit crude for some, but country music produced other less primitive expressions of frustration at the rapidity of the changes taking place in American values and lifestyles. Tammy Wynette's "Don't Liberate Me, Love Me" was a commercially motivated appeal to record buyers who belonged to the "barefoot-in-the-kitchen" school of thought concerning the female's role in society. On the other hand, Loretta Lynn's "Don't Come Home A-Drinkin' (With Lovin' on Your Mind)" and "Your Squaw

Is on the Warpath" found an eager audience of women clearly tired of second-class citizenship at home and in the world at large but uncertain they wanted total "liberation."[25]

Many Americans probably shared the ambivalence about "progress" reflected in country songs, but to liberal observers the music was a reminder of the unfinished business of the sixties, a reminder that grated not only on their eardrums but on their psyches as well. The hard-core country music fan had long been the enemy of crusaders for social change. Those who threatened blacks and voted for Wallace also idolized Ernest Tubb. Writing in 1973, New Yorker Richard Goldstein admitted that country music represented "a culture against which I have very ancient and tenacious biases." Goldstein was even more candid as he explained further, "I can never encounter a white southerner without feeling a murderousness pass between us."[26]

Although the racist influence of the southern redneck had been undermined by the Civil Rights movement, northern liberals came away from the experience unsatisfied and confused. By the mid-1970s the traditional villains in the American morality play, the longtime opponents of social progress, were not only no longer pariahs, they were actually being venerated on jukeboxes throughout the land. Johnny Russell's 1974 recording of "Rednecks, White Socks, and Blue Ribbon Beer" was a thoroughgoing celebration of redneckery:

No we don't fit in with that white-collar crowd,
We're a little too rowdy and a little too loud
But there's no place that I'd rather be than right here
With my red neck, white socks, and Blue Ribbon beer.

One resentful writer called Russell's song "a truculent hymn to the twice-turned jockstrap that could someday become America's Horst Wessel," but despite such warnings, the odes to the blue-collar white continued, culminating in 1979 in Moe Bandy and Joe Stampley's popular album "Just Good Old Boys."[27]

A number of country songs of the 1970s went beyond a celebration of the common white folk of the South to pay tribute to the region and its deliverance from itself. Treatments like Jesse Winchester's "Mississippi, You're on My Mind" expressed confidence in the future but spent little time apologizing for the past. Tanya Tucker recorded the best-known version of Bobby Braddock's "I Believe the South Is Gonna Rise Again (And Not the Way We Thought It Would Back Then)," a song that rejoiced at the visions of "sons and daughters of sharecroppers drinking Scotch and making business deals." Braddock's tribute to Dixie emphasized a future of "brotherhood" and dismissed the past with "forget the bad and keep the good."[28]

Country music's failure to apologize for the southern past was mitigated to some extent by a fusion of the southeastern "Deep South" with the "Cowboy South" of the Southwest. Any knowledgeable listener knew better than to expect an apology from Willie Nelson or Waylon Jennings. Moreover, "redneck chic" blended with "Texas chic" in a manner not unlike the marriage of "country" and "western" music in the 1930s. The frantic, booming Southwest offered a paradoxical but appealing vision of "laid-back" cowboys sipping Lone Star beer and living life one day at a time. Waylon Jennings's "Luckenbach, Texas" glorified a wide spot in the road near Austin by depicting it as a place to escape the burdens of "keeping up with the Joneses," and Jennings and Nelson offered their own tribute to good ole boys in "Mamas, Don't Let Your Babies Grow Up to Be Cowboys," whose message might actually be translated: "They could do a whole lot worse."

Obviously much of the glorification of the South and its music was the result of commercial ballyhoo and popular whim. Behind the myth-making, however, was the reality that a traumatized post–Civil Rights, Vietnam, and Watergate nation had at last acknowledged its regional stepchild. Was this a positive step, a move toward final sectional reconciliation, or was it, as some feared, a "cop-out," a demonstration that many Americans would rather rationalize than remedy the deficiencies exposed in the late sixties and early seventies? Had the worst elements of the national character been allowed to triumph over the best? Were the values celebrated in country music values of which Americans might truly be proud?

The notion that the "southernization of America" marked a turn for the worse not only ignored the social, political, and economic advances in Dixie, it reflected the misconception that crusading liberalism and hunger for social justice had persistently characterized nonsouthern society. Writing in 1964, Howard Zinn had cautioned critics against dismissing the South as "un-American" and argued that southerners were correct in insisting that they were the most "American" of all the citizens of the United States. Zinn depicted the South as the regional embodiment of many basic American traits in their most extreme version. The South's flaws were merely the nation's flaws in concentrated and clearly focused form. Thus, the uncouth, racist, traditionalist South was actually an unflattering mirror image of the nation as a whole.[29]

Such an assessment was understandably upsetting to a generation of Americans who grew up thinking the South represented the antithesis of everything in which they were supposed to believe. Even in the rare moments when the region had been held up for admiration, it had been depicted as an alternative to American society's obsession with "progress." Still the white-backlash/George Wallace phenomenon, the widespread pessimism bred by Vietnam and Watergate, and the resurgent conservatism of the 1970s did a great deal to narrow the chasm between Dixie and the nation at large. Ironically, some of the best evidence that Zinn's "mirror image" thesis had gained implicit acceptance in the 1970s was the use of southern themes and settings to indict all of American society. Robert Altman's *Nashville* employed the country music capital as a cinematic setting for his argument that American society was rotten, not just at the top, as Watergate had shown, but at the grass roots, where the music of the masses was made. In conquering the nation, the country music industry had been ambushed by national values. Moved to philosophizing by several scotches, veteran country singer Faron Young ruefully admitted: "You got that dollar, you got America." In a similar vein the highly successful television series *Dallas* confronted viewers with J. R. Ewing, a good ole boy every bit as greedy and power-mad as a Jay Gould, Jim Fisk, or any contemporary northern robber baron. The South had at last arrived. It was no longer more sinful than society at large, but it had also become just as corrupt and cynical.[30]

As the nation embraced southern music, detractors could not resist pointing out that country songs remained "monotonous, sentimental, obvious, musically inferior, and lyrically sub-standard." What did such a lowbrow art form so emphatic in its emphasis on human limitations and deficiencies have to offer a nation so steeped in its self-congratulatory traditions of progress and success? Was not a more inspiring music in order?[31]

Actually, at the end of the 1970s the resonance of country music for a nation reeling from the disappointments of Vietnam and Watergate and the shocking discovery of the racial divisions and economic woes confronting communities outside the South should have been obvious enough. By the end of the 1990s however, country's traditional emphasis on humility and human limitations seemed largely inappropriate and outdated — ironically enough, nowhere more so than among white southerners who were settling into self-satisfied nonchalance about their region's economic, political, and cultural ascendance. Country music has seen white southerners through several generations of deprivation to ultimate acceptance and even emulation. Yet, as Tony Scherman observed wistfully in 1994, "Millions of country people are settled now in suburbia; they no longer need their struggle cathartically mirrored." Twenty years ago sensitive liberal commentators were warning that they could detect the ominous overtones of the South's conquest of the national mind-set — "the Southernization of America" — in the defiant and gritty lyrics of Merle Haggard. Paradoxically enough, they now seem equally distressed that they can hear in the bouncy and slickly produced stylings of Garth Brooks the loss of regional character and identity that has come with "the Southernization of America." [32]

The
Blues
Is a
Lowdown
Shakin'
Chill

Although they appeared in the Mississippi Delta at the end of the nineteenth century, not until the twentieth century was drawing to a close did the blues gain widespread acceptance as a legitimate American musical form. According to legend, the remarkable odyssey of the blues actually began in 1903 at the railroad station in Tutwiler, Mississippi, where W. C. Handy first heard "a lean, loose-jointed Negro" playing what Handy described as "the weirdest music I ever heard." Another of Handy's early encounters with the blues came when his band was performing for a dance at Cleveland and someone asked if he would mind if "a local colored band played a few dances." Clearly Handy was not impressed by the appearance of the hometown aggregation: "They were led by a long-legged chocolate boy, and their band consisted of just three pieces, a battered guitar, a mandolin and worn-out bass." Handy found the band's music "pretty well in keeping with their looks." It was characterized by an "over and over" strumming that quickly "attained a disturbing monotony, the kind of foot-thumping, eye-rolling music associated with cane rows and levee camps." Handy admitted that he found the music more "haunting" than annoying, but, although he would gain fame as the discoverer and popularizer of the blues, he doubted at the time that "anybody besides small town rounders and their running mates would go for it."[1]

Handy was not the last observer who would underestimate and oversimplify the blues. Although they were rooted in the system of labor and social relations that emerged in the Delta in the last quarter of the nineteenth century, their influence eventually reached far beyond the levee camps and cotton fields of the region. Not only did they offer valuable insights into the lives of Delta blacks, but their powerful and enduring legacies shaped the musical culture of several generations of white youths who knew little of the roots of the blues but nonetheless related to the sense of alienation and rebellion that permeated the music of those who occupied the bottom strata of Delta society.[2]

Individual blues performances typically focused on male-female relationships and other intensely personal experiences with both pleasure and pain. Yet, as an emotionally charged, deeply expressive, and unfailingly candid new music, the blues also offered an insider's perspective on the communal search for self-determination and stability that dominated the postemancipation experience of black southerners as a group.

The blues made their appearance almost simultaneously on the plantations and in the logging and levee camps throughout the Deep South. Although the blues flourished in a variety of locales, each of the music's several spawning grounds was a place where blacks came in search of a better life only to find themselves trapped in an endless cycle of hard work and meager reward amid almost intolerable living and working conditions. Given this realty, it is hardly surprising that the blues tradition developed so fully and rapidly in the Mississippi Delta, which was clearly the principal source of blues performers during the music's formative years. While the historical context of the Delta is by no means adequate to explain the entire content of the blues, the relationship between the two is important to an understanding of both.[3]

In 1909 a visitor to the Delta overheard a black woman singing as she plowed a cotton field. He compared what he heard to the "lamentation of a creature in great distress and isolation" and concluded that her song "made me feel as if I were traveling through an African region and had just been to visit a colony of prisoners in confinement." A number of scholars, including Lawrence Levine, have identified certain central elements of the African "traditional communal musical style" in the blues, but this new musical form actually evolved as part of a process whereby former slaves drew on both their African and American heritages to formulate a cultural response to the much-anticipated but generally disappointing experience of emancipation.[4]

Structurally and stylistically, the blues drew on the same traditions and material that had provided the basis for the slave spirituals and work songs. The blues derived most directly, however, from the field hollers that could be heard throughout the nineteenth-century South, not only on the plantations but anywhere blacks were engaged in hard manual labor. Linking the blues to the work environment of rural blacks in the Delta, blues performer Bukka White insisted, "That's where the blues start from, back across them fields. . . . It started right behind one of them mules or one of them log houses, one of them log camps or the levee camp. That's where the blues sprung from. I know what I'm talking about."[5]

Describing the field hollers, bluesman Son House recalled, "They'd sing about their girl friend or about almost anything — mule — anything. They'd make a song of it just to be hollering." Lawrence Levine cited the Coahoma County plowman who provided this example of a field holler suggestive of the blues-in-the-making, singing first to his mule:

O-O-O, This donkey won't drink water.
I'll knock him in the collar till he go stone blind . . .

And then to himself:

The gal I'm lovin' she can't be found.

David Evans concluded that somewhere near the end of the nineteenth century the "free, almost formless vocal expressions" of the field hollers "were set to instrumental accompaniment and given a musical structure, an expanded range of subject matter and a new social context" in a remarkable creative process that gave birth to the blues.[6]

As the music matured, blues lyrics typically appeared in a configuration marked by twelve-bar, three-line stanzas with the first statement repeated in the second line and supplemented or extended in the third. Levine used Charley Patton's "Green River Blues" as a classic example:

Some people say the Green River blues ain't bad.
Some people say the Green River blues ain't bad.
Then it must not have been the Green River blues I had.[7]

Across the South the blues emerged as blacks reached the final and unavoidable realization that the great promise of freedom was to be, if not denied, at least indefinitely deferred. Hence the Delta's misleading image as an attractive promised land for black farmers was no doubt crucial to its role as a breeding place for the blues. With its rich soil and intense demand for farm labor, the postbellum Delta had promised blacks the best opportunity available anywhere in the South to rise to independent landowning status. Lured by the chance to make a good crop under relatively good living conditions and to receive relatively good treatment from whites in the bargain, blacks had flooded into the Yazoo Basin, making it the premier testing ground for emancipation in the rural South of the late nineteenth century.

Among the black migrants who came to the Delta in the 1890s were Bill and Annie Patton and their twelve children. The Pattons had moved north from near Bolton and Edwards, anticipating that their large family workforce would bring them an advantageous sharecropping contract with a labor-hungry Delta planter. Believing they had found such a planter in Will Dockery, they settled on his plantation on the banks of the Sunflower River east of Cleveland. Although the Pattons were but one of thousands of black families who moved to the Delta in search of a better life, their decision to locate at Dockery's proved to be a pivotal event in both the history and mythology of American music.[8]

By the time the Pattons arrived, their son Charley was already playing the guitar, much to the consternation of his God-fearing, quick-to-punish father. Charley had learned music from the Chatmon family at Bolton, but the Chatmons' repertoire consisted of popular, ragtime, and white-oriented country dance tunes that bore little relationship to the music that would emerge as the Delta blues. At Dockery's Patton fell under the influence of Henry Sloan, a guitarist whose primitive rhythms captivated the young newcomer. The Patton family got along reasonably well at Dockery's, but young Charley, despite frequent and severe whippings from his father, fell into the hedonistic lifestyle of the musician. He drank heavily, worked infrequently, and managed somehow to stay on good terms with several women who worked for local whites and therefore could keep him well supplied with food. In the process of drinking, fighting, abusing and exploiting women, and avoiding insofar as possible having to work for whites himself, Patton also earned a lasting place in the history of American popular music through his influence on a host of bluesmen whose work in turn left a major imprint on several distinct musical forms.[9]

By 1918, when his mentor, Henry Sloan, left the Delta for Chicago, Patton already had a reputation as the finest musician in the area. One artist who fell under his spell and that of his companion, Willie Brown, was Tommy Johnson. He finally settled in Boyle, a village near Cleveland that was connected to Dockery's by the Pea Vine railroad. After two years in the Delta, Johnson returned to south Mississippi and began sharing what he had learned from Patton and Brown. Blues legend Robert Johnson first encountered Willie Brown in the mid-1920s, and it was through Brown that he met Charley Patton. Howlin' Wolf also moved to Dockery's in 1926 and soon became one of Patton's favorite protégés.[10]

The Delta's attraction for most blacks was the prospect of working rich land on favorable terms. For a small but gifted coterie of musicians, however, it also offered the chance to learn a new and increasingly popular music from those who had pioneered in it. Son House, who came to Robinsonville in Tunica County in 1930, soon fell under Charley Patton's influence. As a young man, Bukka White's ambition was to "come to be a great man like Charley Patton." Both House and White spent a great deal of time listening to Patton's recordings. White remembered being unable to squeeze into an overcrowded room in Clarksdale where a new Patton record was being played. The popularity of blues records among Delta blacks was reflected in their love of the phonograph. For most of them, the Victrola was their most expensive and prized possession. As Pete Daniel pointed out, during the 1927 flood fleeing blacks were more likely to try to save their Victrolas than anything else they owned.[11]

Blues records were precious commodities, but after a long, hard week in the fields, a Saturday night spent listening to live music at a blues juke joint or house party was a blessing indeed. W. C. Handy's doubts about the popular appeal of blues performers were soon dispelled by a shower of silver dollars that fell around the ragtag aggregation he encountered at Cleveland. At that point, Handy confessed, he suddenly saw "the beauty of the primitive music. . . . It touched the spot. Their music wanted polishing, but it contained the essence." More important, Handy realized that "folks would pay good money for it," and overnight he became a composer: "Those country black boys at Cleveland had taught me something. . . . My idea of what constitutes music was changed by the sight of that silver money cascading around the splay feet of a Mississippi string band."[12]

Charley Patton protégé Roebuck Staples, who lived on Dockery's plantation from age eight to twenty, recalled that on a typical Saturday afternoon "everybody would go into town and those fellows like Charley Patton, Robert Johnson, and Howlin' Wolf would be playin' on the streets, standin' by the railroad tracks, people pitchin' 'em nickels and dimes, white and black people both. The train come through town maybe once that afternoon and when it was time, everybody would gather around there, before and after the train came, and announce where they'd be that night. And that's where the crowd would go." When the crowd arrived, the scene was one of noise, excitement, and bright lights: "They'd have a plank nailed across the door to the kitchen and be sellin' fish and chitlins, with dancin' in the front room, gamblin' in the side room, and maybe two or three gas or coal-oil lamps on the mantel piece in front of the mirror — powerful light." [13]

Such gatherings were raucous and, as often as not, violent. "Them country balls were rough!" Son House recalled. "They were critical, man! They'd start off good, you know. Everybody happy, dancing, and then they'd start to getting louder and louder. The women would be dipping that snuff and swallowing that snuff spit along with that corn whiskey, and they'd start to mixing fast, and oh, brother! They'd start something then!" [14]

As the blues evolved, performers from different localities developed distinctive vocal and instrumental styles. Robert Palmer has stressed this diversity of the blues, noting that any sense of a cohesive identity for the music would require intensive examination of the repertoires of dozens of musicians. Still, these early Delta blues had some definite identifying characteristics: "The Mississippi Delta's blues musicians sang with unmatched intensity in a gritty, melodically circumscribed, highly ornamented style that was closer to field hollers than it was to other blues. Guitar and piano accompaniments were percussive and hypnotic, and many Delta guitarists mastered the art of fretting the instrument with a slider or bottleneck; they made the instrument 'talk' in strikingly speech-like inflections." [15]

Both the structure and the lyric content of the new music suggested that the key to the emergence of the blues was the development of "new forms of self-conception" among blacks. "The blues," Levine wrote, "was the most highly personalized, indeed, the first almost completely personalized music that Afro-Americans developed." Bluesmen performed solo — or at least blues performances featured a single performer — singing in the first person of his own experiences, suffering, and dreams and receiving a collective acknowledgment from an audience who had shared many of these feelings and experiences. The blues emerged in an era when prevailing mass culture values stressed rugged individualism as the key to upward mobility, but the values they exalted were hardly those of Horatio Alger or, more appropriately, Booker T. Washington. Instead of "Up from Slavery," the message of the blues was "Up from Slavery, but Not Far."[16]

David Evans explained that emancipation replaced the well-defined anonymity of slavery with the "responsibility" of freedom and a deck stacked more in favor of failure than achievement. The new life in freedom was also marked by hard labor; institutionalized discrimination; the threat of violence, death, and imprisonment; and the frustrations of tenancy with the often peripatetic existence it entailed. Evans wrote: "If economic failure, breakup of the family, and a desire to escape through travel resulted from these conditions, it is no wonder." Nor was it any wonder, in turn, that these concerns emerged as principal themes in the blues.[17]

Whereas others described the blues in terms of its matter-of-factness about suffering and social injustice, William Barlow found a spirit of rebellion in the blues, arguing that blues musicians presented a "ground-level view of southern society" and insisting that both their behavior and the content of their music represented a rejection of the values of the dominant white culture. Instead of an overt protest, however, the blues offered an alternative lifestyle in which rambling, hedonism, aggressive sexuality, and a general disregard for authority were the norm. Barlow sensed within the blues "an ethos of revolt" that he attributed to "the emerging consciousness of a young generation seeking personal freedom, social mobility, and better compensation for their labor." He insisted that the blues were "not the result of a few isolated incidents of individual genius, but rather a broadly based cultural movement occupying the time and energy of large numbers of black agricultural workers in the South's cotton belt."[18]

The black workforce in the Cotton Belt was anything but stable as the twentieth century began. The large-scale movement of blacks into the Delta was part of a regionwide, east-to-west, north-to-south flow of workers responding to the greater demand for their services in a region where the soil was fertile but difficult to clear and cultivate. Unfortunately, the wages or terms offered in the Delta, while often better than elsewhere in the rural South, were still much less attractive than those available in other parts of the nation. At the same time, the treatment of black labor, while perhaps superior to that in many other areas in the South, was decidedly inferior to that afforded elsewhere in the nation. As the farm wage gap between states like Mississippi and Ohio widened from twenty cents a day in 1880 to eighty cents a day in 1914, bright promise soon dissolved into bitter frustration, especially as centralized, streamlined, and impersonal plantation management increasingly consigned sharecroppers to a lifetime of hard labor with little hope of achieving either economic or personal independence from whites. Meanwhile, the prospect of political equality embodied in black-white political fusion efforts gave way to the reality of disfranchisement, lynching, and the hate-mongering of James K. Vardaman. Given these developments, it is hardly surprising that the blues emphasized dissatisfaction and alienation as well as an ongoing struggle in the face of overwhelming odds.[19]

As the completion of the Delta's railroad system sealed the region's transformation from untamed frontier to modern plantation kingdom, it also ushered in an era of declining social, economic, and political prospects, one that called for tough decisions by Delta blacks. While Delta blacks had always found it difficult to ignore the contradictions between their own circumstances and prospects and those of their white employers, the Delta's expanded railroad network also exposed many more of them to the contrast between black life in the Delta and the rosy promise of life in the urban North. The vision of a promised land to the north dominated the pages of the *Chicago Defender*, borne southward and sold by railroad porters traveling through the Delta. In addition to its role as the conduit for letters from relatives and friends already gone, the Illinois Central Railroad itself became a seductive symbol of the superiority of northern life. Moreover, the Delta's new railroad system put the majority of the region's blacks within twenty-four hours of Chicago, thereby providing both the temptation as well as the means to leave the Delta. Not surprisingly, the railroad became a symbol of freedom and escape, as references to the Illinois Central permeated the Delta blues:

That I. C. Special is the only train I choose,
That's the train I ride when I get these I. C. blues.[20]

Linking the blues to the Great Migration, William Barlow saw "a clear historical connection between the rebellious and restless spirit of this new music and the Afro-Americans' mass exodus out of the cotton belt." For all the anger and dissatisfaction they may have expressed, however, with their emphasis on rambling and impermanence as well as escape, the blues were no more the music of those who had decided to leave than of those who had decided to stay or, perhaps more so, those who were unable to decide. Certainly, by the second decade of the twentieth century, Delta blacks found themselves confronting a difficult choice.

Should they uproot themselves and their families (perhaps for the second time in a relatively short period), leave friends and familiar surroundings, and depart for the golden streets of northern cities? Or should they hang on in the Delta, hoping for the big crop year that might free them from debt and give them the opportunity to become independent, landowning farmers? As Neil McMillen has written, "The decision to vote with one's feet, to leave in search of fuller participation in American life, was perhaps the clearest and most frequently exercised expression of black discontent. But it was a relatively costly and wrenching option beyond the reach of many and one that even some of the most alienated black Mississippians might not choose to exercise." For many blacks the blues conveyed better than any other medium available their agonizing struggle with the "wrenching option" of northward migration.[21]

For most who did remain in the Delta, there was anything but stability and promise in their existence. They became part of a forever shifting, essentially rootless farm labor force, more concerned about survival than advancement, their existence and outlook captured by the bluesman's resigned lament:

> Goin' no higher;
> Goin' no lower down.
> Gonna stay right here,
> Gonna stay right here,
> 'Til they close me down.[22]

Muddy Waters left the Stovall place in Coahoma County for Chicago in 1943 and seldom returned: "I wanted to get out of Mississippi in the worst way, man. Go back? What I want to go back for?" It was Waters who popularized the lines:

> If I feel tomorrow, the way I feel today,
> I'm gonna pack my bags and make my getaway.

Such lyrics suggested disappointment and might mean that the singer was at last ready to muster his courage for the trip north to the promised land of Chicago, or they might signal no more than a move to a nearby plantation. Such a move might not bring better economic conditions; indeed, it could well bring worse ones, especially if it primarily reflected a desire to escape the supervision and enforced regimen of efficiency that characterized the large "business plantations." Still, by changing plantations a black sharecropper could at least exercise what little control he retained over his own destiny. Moreover, merely "slipping" one plantation for another postponed a much tougher decision about a bigger move away from family, friends, familiar surroundings, and the assurance of at least minimal upkeep from a landlord. It was small wonder, then, that blues lyrics, while stressing movement often expressed mixed feelings about it:

> Gotta mind to move,
> A mind to settle down.[23]

As Joel Williamson explained, the early blues should be seen as "the cry of the cast-out black, ultimately alone and lonely, after one world was lost and before another was found." When the blues were emerging in the late nineteenth and early twentieth centuries, Delta blacks were still struggling to disengage themselves from the dreams of independence and prosperity that had brought them or their parents to the region in the first place. They were also beginning to wrestle with the temptation to embrace a new dream, that of a better life in the urban North.[24]

Not surprisingly, the ambivalence, uncertainty, and restlessness that permeated the lives of Delta blacks was readily apparent in their music as well. Conflict and contradiction and the agony of making tough choices were apparent throughout the blues, not just in songs about rambling or escape but in those that dealt with personal relationships as well. For example, Charley Patton sang:

> Sometimes I say I need you;
> Then again I don't. . . .
> Sometimes I think I'll quit you,
> Then again I won't.[25]

By focusing on transience, uncertainty, and rebellion, the blues seemed to offer a disturbing contradiction to the reassurances provided by the teachings of the church. Moreover, blues performances appeared to compete with church services for the affections of Delta blacks, not so much because of their secular orientation but because they possessed a certain spiritual quality of their own and therefore threatened to usurp the communal, cathartic role that was otherwise the function of organized religious activity. Lawrence Levine explained that, like "both the spirituals and folktales, the blues was an expression of experiences and feelings common to the group." Elsewhere, Li'l Son Jackson, a bluesman-turned-gospel singer, identified the "sinfulness" of the blues in terms of the sense of autonomy and individual responsibility for one's own fate that they projected: "If a man feel hurt within side and he sing a church song then he's askin' God for help. . . . If a man sing the blues it's more or less out of himself. . . . He's not askin' no one for help. And he's not really clingin' to no-one. But he's expressin' how he feel. . . . You're trying to get your feelin's over to the next person through the blues, and that's what makes it a sin." [26]

The flesh-and-blood realism of the blues gave them a relevance that many blacks found lacking in the scriptures or spirituals. Vicksburg bluesman Willie Dixon explained, "I was raised on blues and spirituals, but after you wake up to a lot of facts about life, you know, the spiritual thing starts to look kind of phony in places." [27]

Lawrence Levine linked the anticlerical implications of the blues to what he called the "decline of the sacred world view," a phenomenon he traced through black humor as well. One need only note the scorn and ridicule heaped on the stereotypical bed-hopping black minister in the Delta to make the connection. Bluesmen and the lyrics of the music they sang often expressed open contempt for preachers. When drunk or angry, Robert Johnson would even curse God openly, much to the consternation of his often frightened audience. Not surprisingly, Johnson had little time for religion in his songs:

If I had possession over Judgment Day. . . .
I wouldn't give my woman the right to pray.

In "Preachin' the Blues," Son House vowed cynically to "be a Baptist preacher and I sure won't have to work." House also placed the blues and religion squarely at odds when he sang:

Oh, up in my room,
I bowed down to pray;
Say, the blues come along,
And they drove my spirit away.[28]

For all such evidence of conflict between the two, however, the blues actually coexisted quite peacefully with organized religion and appeared even to complement it on occasion. Describing black tenant families, Jeff Titon wrote: "If values and behavior did not conform to white middle-class standards, they were well suited to the economic system and to the culture it carried. People moved frequently, if not easily, from Saturday night dances to Sunday services; structural and functional similarities made the transition more comfortable." Clifton Taulbert recalled Sunday afternoon sessions where Glen Allan blacks, many still wearing their church clothes, danced, drank beer, ate catfish, and "lost themselves in the blues." Taulbert added, "They sang the blues with the excitement of a Sunday church service. . . . They knew it would be Monday in the morning, but this was their time, their Sunday, and they let the blues express the life they lived." Titon explained that "the blues sermon often proved as therapeutic as Sunday morning worship. The large number of singers and listeners who have testified to feeling better after blues performances indicates that the ceremonies were effective, that people were renewed."[29]

Like his clerical counterpart, the bluesman was a key figure, symbolic of a communal culture. Moreover, like the preacher, the bluesman entertained his audiences by expressing deeply felt, shared emotions in a manner that made him more than an entertainer. The murmurs of reinforcement and encouragement that buoyed John Dollard as he spoke to a black congregation in Indianola bore a strong similarity to the give-and-take between audience and performer at a blues session. As Levine observed, "Black musical performances properly speaking had no audience, just participants."[30]

Another scholar saw both the preacher and the bluesman in terms of the "privileges of their office: more money, greater social prestige, finer clothes and an attractiveness to women not shared by the common man." Both preacher and bluesman filled their society's need for "entertainment, catharsis, recreation and ritual." Both promoted group solidarity and reinforced group values and traditions. Steeped in black culture, they represented "the two prime role models that have been generated within black society."[31]

Although the two worlds represented by the preacher and the bluesman seemed largely antithetical, they actually overlapped a great deal; many a bluesman moved into the pulpit, while not a few preachers found a second calling at the juke joint or country dance. Charley Patton not only recorded some religious songs but periodically renounced whiskey and women and turned to Bible study in preparation for a career in the pulpit. He reportedly fled via the back door of the church when he panicked at the thought of his first sermon, but he did preach successfully on several occasions. His conversions to the ministry never lasted, but he recorded a favorite sermon drawn largely from the book of Revelation and allegedly repeated it in a frenzy on his deathbed.[32]

Born into a deeply religious, "sanctified" Pentecostal family, Sonny

Boy Williamson claimed to have been a minister himself at one time. He soon abandoned the pulpit, however, for the life of an itinerant musician, performing under a variety of pseudonyms. Frederick Jay Hay saw in the early recordings of Williamson a tendency not just to secularize but actually to "sensualize" religion. "Eyesight to the Blind" described a woman whose sexual powers had all the healing capabilities of the Holy Spirit:

> You talk about your woman,
> I wish to God you could see mine. . . .
> Everytime she start loving,
> She brings eyesight to the blind.

Hay compared this message to that of "Amazing Grace": "I once was blind but now I see."[33]

In a sense the bluesman and the preacher may have also shared similar pressures to conform to widely held stereotypes. For the preacher this meant flamboyance, conviviality, and possibly an eye for women; for the bluesman it certainly meant an eye for women, but it demanded as well a reckless, rambling, hard-drinking lifestyle that made his music and his persona one and the same. The stereotype of the lazy, shiftless musician was hardly peculiar to the bluesman, but if they did not consciously cultivate this persona, Delta blues performers did nothing to dispel it. As Barry Lee Pearson explained, "The itinerant musician presented the image of being footloose and fancy free — a romantic alternative to the drudgery of sharecropping." Freddie Spruell's "Low Down Mississippi Bottom Man" depicted the bluesman stereotype to near perfection:

> Way down in the Delta, that's where I long to be,
> Where the Delta bottom women are sure goin' crazy over me.
> I'm lookin' for a woman who's lookin' for a low-down man.
> Ain't nobody in town get more low down than I can.[34]

When Tommy Johnson left Crystal Springs for the Delta, he was still a teenager and relatively innocent of the ways of the world. After a year or so of associating with Delta bluesmen, however, he was not only a compulsive womanizer but a hopeless alcoholic, so addicted that when whiskey was unavailable he would consume shoe polish or even Sterno or "canned heat." His "Canned Heat Blues," recorded in Memphis in 1928, was clearly autobiographical: "Canned heat don't kill me / crying babe I'll never die." Along with his degeneration into a "rambler" and a "rounder" came a surprisingly sudden maturity as a musician that Johnson attributed to a pact with the Devil. He repeated to anyone who would listen the story of his bargain at the crossroads:

> If you want to learn how to play anything you want to play and learn how to make songs yourself, you take your guitar and you go to where a road crosses that way, where the crossroad is. . . . Be sure to get there, just a little 'fore twelve o'clock that night so you'll know you'll be there. You have your guitar and be playing a piece sitting there by yourself. You have to go by yourself and be sitting there playing a piece. A big black man will walk up there and take your guitar and he'll tune it. And then he will play a piece and hand it back to you. That's the way I learned how to play everything I want.[35]

A similar and even more powerful legend grew up around bluesman Robert Johnson. Son House recalled that as an adolescent Johnson would slip away from home late at night to attend one of the "balls" where House and Willie Brown were playing. When the two took a break, Johnson would pick up one of their guitars and attempt to play it, although, according to House, the results were usually anything but satisfactory: "Such another racket you never heard! It'd make the people mad, you know. They'd come out and say, 'Why don't y'all go in there and get that guitar away from that boy! He's running people crazy with it.' I'd come back in and I'd scold him about it. 'Don't do that, Robert. You drive people nuts. You can't play nothing.'"[36]

Frustrated, humiliated, and unenthusiastic about farm work, young Johnson finally ran away from home and stayed gone for approximately six months. He surfaced again one evening when House and Brown were playing, a guitar swung over his back. House took up where he had left off taunting Johnson, "Well, boy, you still got a guitar, huh? What do you do with that thing? You can't do nothing with it." This time, however, Johnson responded self-confidently, "Let me have your seat a minute." House agreed, winking at Brown and warning Johnson that he "had better do something" once he was in House's seat. To House's and Brown's amazement, Johnson had mysteriously transformed himself into a guitarist par excellence. "He was so good. When he finished all our mouths were standing open. I said, 'Well, ain't that fast! He's gone now!'"[37]

One of Robert Johnson's relatives told a researcher that the suddenly gifted young bluesman had met the Devil at a certain crossroads in the Delta. "The Devil came there and gave Robert his talent and told him he had eight more years to live on earth." Almost certainly aware of the legend of Tommy Johnson's pact with the Devil, Robert Johnson did nothing to dispel the rumors or the reputation he developed as a dangerous, sinister but also melancholy and darkly romantic musical genius. Johnson sang frequently about the Devil and the supernatural and often projected a deeply troubling, menacing personal image. Muddy Waters timidly peeked into a crowd in Friars Point to catch a glimpse of a musician he thought might be Robert Johnson: "I stopped and peeked over, and then I left because he was a dangerous man."[38]

The figure who carried the association with the Devil to its obviously orchestrated extreme was William Bundy, who called himself "Peetie Wheatstraw," the "Devil's Son-in-law," or the "High Sheriff from Hell." Born near Memphis in 1902, Wheatstraw grew up across the river in the Arkansas Delta and doubtless influenced Robert Johnson as he did others, like Floyd "the Devil's Daddy-in-law" Council. Unlike Johnson's, however, Wheatstraw's attempts to link himself with the Devil became comical, little more than a caricature. In his "Peetie Wheatstraw Stomp," he bragged:

> Women all raving about Peetie Wheatstraw in this land. . . .
> I am Peetie Wheatstraw, the High Sheriff from Hell;
> The way I strut my stuff so well now you never can tell.
> He makes some happy, some he make cry;
> Well, now he make one old lady, go hang herself and die.

The "High Sheriff from Hell" even appeared in novelist Ralph Ellison's *Invisible Man:* "My name is Peter Wheatstraw, I'm the Devil's only son-in-law, so roll'em! . . . All it takes to get along in this here man's town is a little shit, grit, and mother-wit. And man, I was born with all three. . . . I'm a piano player and a rounder, a whiskey drinker and a pavement pounder, I'll teach you some good bad habits."[39]

A legendary element in the folklore of the blues, the musician's bargain with the Devil has roots in African religious beliefs that are also preserved in voodoo. Actually more like the trickster figure of Afro-American lore than the sinister Devil or Satan depicted in the scriptures, Legba was a black man traditionally associated with the crossroads. (Robert Johnson played the role of trickster to the hilt, carrying a large rabbit's foot and performing all manner of acrobatics with his guitar.) Known for his manual dexterity, Legba was also a personification of male sexual potency, and this characteristic, combined with his freedom of movement and free and easy way with words, left him an appropriate symbol for the bluesman himself. Thus Legba became, in the view of Steve West, a figure who "frequents shadows on the limits of civilization and waits for those so disillusioned with life and vastly victimized by false promise that they would carry a guitar down to the crossroads at midnight and wait for the devil to work his magic."[40]

Although the pact with Satan soon took on the aspect of a folk legend turned musician's promotional gimmick, the fabled willingness of bluesmen to strike such a deal not only reinforced the stereotype of the blues as the devil's music but was perhaps the ultimate symbolic expression of black alienation. William Barlow saw in the mythology of the deal with the Devil "a defiance of the dominant white culture that enforces its social constraints with the help of its official religion, Christianity." The significance of the relationship between the official, white-sanctioned Christian code of morality and the aims and wishes of local whites was by no means lost on Delta blacks, as indicated by the heroic status accorded Roy, the condemned murderer who refused to repent, as well as the popularity of a number of folk-hero black "badmen" like Stagolee.[41]

The bluesman, a rounder, drifter, drinker, and womanizer who disdained work and any restraints on his morality or behavior, was the antithesis of what Delta whites wanted their black workers to be. It was not just the music but also the lifestyle of the blues musician that presented a problem for the white power structure. Refusal to work for the white man could be evidence of laziness, or it could suggest rebellion. One bluesman asked, "A black man, if he didn't work out in the fields, he was called lazy, no good. But who was he working for? You figure out who the lazy one was!" One observer allowed that a planter would "rather see a dog than a guitar player." Certainly, the image of a man who survived without working for whites was a socially desirable one within the black community, and a bluesman was just as likely to boast, "I's Wild Nigger Bill frum Redpepper Hill, I never did work, an' I never will," as a white country musician was to cite long years of hard labor on the farm.[42]

In addition to obtaining the best possible labor at the lowest possible cost, Delta planters also hoped to convince blacks of their stake in a system that actually offered them minimal opportunity for advancement. As the personification of alienation, the bluesman put in time everywhere but put down roots nowhere and acknowledged no common interest whatsoever with white merchants or landowners. In many ways the image of the bluesman was comparable to that of the boll weevil, a destructive little bug who brought ruin to many cotton-growing areas of the South and set off near-panic among planters in the Delta. The popularity of songs such as Charley Patton's "Mississippi Bo Weavil [*sic*] Blues" suggested that, despite its potential for destroying them along with whites, the boll weevil's capacity to bring ruin to the white man won it the admiration of blacks, while its endless wandering in search of a home struck a familiar chord as well.[43]

The sense of restlessness that pervaded the blues was also evident in the prominent role accorded trains in many blues songs. Black firemen often used the train's whistle to spread a mournful blues note across the flat fields of the Delta:

> Mister I. C. engineer, make that whistle moan.
> Got the I. C. blues and I can't help but groan.[44]

One of the most famous "blues railroads" was the Yazoo and Mississippi Valley, known more commonly as the "Yellow Dog." This short-line railroad (which also figures prominently in Eudora Welty's *Delta Wedding*) earned its place in history when W. C. Handy recorded his initial contact with the blues and told of a young musician singing, "I'm goin' where the Southern cross the dog." This famous crossing, where the Yellow Dog intersected the Southern line, lay at Moorhead. Hence a bluesman wailed:

> If my baby didn't catch the Southern,
> She must've caught the Yaller Dawg. . . .
> The Southern cross the Dawg at Moorehead [*sic*]
> Man, Lawd on, she keeps through. . . .
> I swear ma baby's gone to Georgia;
> I believe I go to Georgia, too.[45]

As a means of escape for not only the individual but his or her lover as well, the railroad was simultaneously a source of both reassurance and anxiety. The "Pea Vine" was a winding little railroad that connected Dockery's plantation with the nearby towns of Cleveland and Boyle and with the river port city of Rosedale. Although it was confined wholly to Bolivar County, in Charley Patton's "Pea Vine Blues" even this little railroad seemed a tempting avenue of escape for a loved one:

> I think I heard the Pea Vine when she blows.
> Blowed just like my rider getting on board.[46]

The desire to move on, to escape mistreatment, and to be free was as pervasive in the blues as it was in the lives of Delta blacks. "I got rambling, I got rambling (all) on my mind," sang Robert Johnson, who played the role of rambler to the hilt. Johnny Shines recalled that Johnson "was a guy, you could wake him up any time and he was ready to go. . . . Say, for instance, you had come from Memphis to Helena, and we'd play there all night probably and lay down to sleep the next morning and hear a train. You say, 'Robert, I hear a train. Let's catch it.' He wouldn't exchange no words with you. He's just ready to go. We'd go right back to Memphis if that's where the train's going. It didn't make him no difference. Just so he was going."[47]

Bluesman Mott Willis described a similar lifestyle when he told of his own nomadic meanderings in the Delta: "I was just backwards and forwards, you know. . . . I moved around from place to place, you know; staying with different fellows playing. . . . Well, fact of the business, I've been all over that Delta just about." Delta sharecroppers were no strangers to moving themselves, but the apparently unrestricted mobility of the bluesman was as much the stuff of exotic fantasy for them as it was a source of irritation to white planters, who feared anyone or anything that stood to make their labor any more restless or dissatisfied than they already were.[48]

Another area in which the blues rejected prevailing white norms was that of sexuality. The double entendre of the blues was by no means difficult to decipher. Yet, despite their highly suggestive content, the lyrics of the blues flourished in a society where even the slightest hint of sexual aggressiveness on the part of black males could cost them their lives. Robert Johnson's "Terraplane Blues" was only one such song:

I'm gonna heist your hood, mama,
I'm bound to check your oil. . . .
I'm going to get deep down in this connection,
Keep on tangling with your wires,
And when I mash down on your little starter,
Then your spark plug will give me fire.[49]

Charley Patton's "Shake It and Break It (Don't Let It Fall, Mama)" suggested the joys of intercourse while standing and the potential enjoyment of sexual experimentation in general:

You can shake it, you can break it, you can hang it on the wall.
Throw it out the window, catch it 'fore it falls.
You can break it, you can hang it on the wall.
Throw it out the window, catch it 'fore it falls.
My jelly, my roll, sweet mama, don't you let it fall.[50]

"Jelly roll" was a common metaphor for sex (or the sex organs) in the blues, whose lyrics often associated eating and the preparation of food with lovemaking. A desirable young woman was a "biscuit," her lover a "biscuit roller." A light-skinned, "coffee"-colored woman might be paired with a good "coffee grinder." James "Son" Thomas promised:

When I marry, now I ain't gonner buy no broom.
She got hair on her belly gonner sweep my kitchen, my dining room.

Robert Johnson's "Come On in My Kitchen" carried the same culinary/sexual implications. Even a forlorn blues song like Johnson's "Stones in My Passway" offered a boastful sexual metaphor:

I got three legs to track on.
Boys, please don't block my road.[51]

The lyrics sung by male blues performers contained their share of posturing and exaggeration, but, when it came to attracting women, many bluesmen claimed a genuine advantage. One of them told Alan Lomax, "I got a home wherever I go." Another elaborated, "If I'd see a woman I wanted and she just absolutely — her husband couldn't carry her home. I'd pick that guitar hard and sing hard. And I've had women come up and kiss me and didn't ask me could they kiss me — kiss me right then. Just grab and kiss me."[52]

On his first recording trip, Robert Johnson seemed to confirm his image as a womanizing bluesman. Recording executive Don Law found Johnson a room in a boardinghouse and urged him to get some sleep in anticipation of the first day of recording. Law joined his wife for dinner at a hotel, only to be summoned to the police station, where Johnson, badly beaten and his guitar smashed, was being held for vagrancy. After bailing Johnson out, Law took him back to the boardinghouse, instructed him to stay in the house for the rest of the evening, and gave him forty-five cents for breakfast. Upon returning to the hotel, Law received another phone call. This time it was Johnson himself. When Law asked Johnson what was wrong, the bluesman replied, "I'm lonesome, and there's a lady here. She wants fifty cents and I lacks a nickel."[53]

After surveying numerous jokes in which blacks celebrated their sexual superiority to whites, Lawrence Levine examined this apparent embrace of what seemed to be a degrading white stereotype of blacks. Levine's commentary on this form of black humor might have been applied to the blues as well, because both reflected "an awareness that the pervasive stereotype of Negroes as oversexed, hypervirile, and uninhibitedly promiscuous was not purely a negative image; that it contained envy as well as disdain, that it was a projection of desire as well as fear." By personifying this stereotype, bluesmen only enhanced their status as black folk heroes, because their menacing sexual aggressiveness and self-assurance combined with their disdain for menial labor to make them a symbol of resistance to white authority.[54]

Son Thomas was not only a bluesman but a folk sculptor of some renown. Thomas explained why the clay faces he created presented blacks as poised and proud: "Tell me why if you see a statue of a man in a white person's yard it will be a black man. They make him black all over and have his lips red and his eyes white. Most of the time you see him, if he ain't got a fishing pole, he got a hoe. I reckon it's an invitation to work. Trying to make the colored folks work. When you see one with a hoe it's to let us know it's all we can do. Well, Old John did more than hoe-right around the house."[55]

William Ferris elaborated on Thomas's comments, explaining that "the theme of John, the yard boy, and his sexual relations with the white woman inside the 'big house' is widespread in Delta folktales, and like Thomas's clay faces, it counters the stereotyped white impression of blacks as depicted in their lawn statues."[56]

At its heart the assertive masculinity of the blues was often a matter of racial as well as personal pride. In "I Wonder When I'll Be Called a Man," Bill Broonzy asserted, "A Black man's a boy, I don't care what he can do." As he sang, Broonzy drew on his boyhood experiences in the Delta, his service in World War I, and his return to the plantation where the owner, instead of hailing him as a hero in the uniform of his country, merely said: "Boy, get you some overalls."[57]

Occasionally the blues suggested a direct relationship between racial and masculine aggression:

Killed that old grey mule.
Burned down that white man's barn. . . .
I want you to love me or leave me.
Anything you want me to do.
Well, it's strange things happening,
Someday might'a happen to you.[58]

By asserting masculine aggressiveness, the blues offered an outlet for the frustrations of the black male, whom Hortense Powdermaker saw "entangled in a mesh of contradictions. . . . He sees the whites, whose culture and concepts have been to a large measure imposed on him, breaking their own rules with impunity — or rather, evading them — choosing their wives from their own group, hedging them about by protections and taboos, and taking their mistresses from his. He sees women of his own group consorting with men of both races. He cannot keep them for himself, nor can he in turn take women from another group." [59]

In "Long Black Song," Richard Wright told the story of Silas, an enraged black man who whipped his wife because he suspected she had given sexual favors to a white traveling salesman in exchange for a reduced price on a phonograph. (Wright's use of the phonograph may reflect his sense of its popularity among Delta blacks.) A hardworking landowner, Silas exploded in rage, fought with two white men, and met his death after whites surrounded his house and burned it down around him. [60]

Blues lyrics sometimes suggested what seemed to be "senseless," uncontrollable violence and rage. Furry Lewis sang:

> I believe I'll buy me a graveyard of my own;
> I'm goin' kill everybody that have done me wrong.

Other lyrics were more indirect:

> I feel my hell a-risin' every day.
> Someday it'll burst this levee and wash the whole wide world away.

Such sentiments invite comparisons with the sinister figures of black outlaw folklore; they bring to mind the examples of Roy, the "unprepared man," as well as James Coyner, the cold-blooded mutilator-killer described by David Cohn. Like these "bad niggers," both mythical and real, the bluesman's heroic status derived, as William Barlow saw it, from the desire of Delta blacks "to negate the feelings of powerlessness and to avenge victimization by the white social order." [61]

The important linkage between racial and masculine pride seemed to cast the black female as little more than a helpless sex object utterly defenseless against exploitation, abuse, and abandonment at the hands of every selfish, fast-talking black stud who came along. In "Low Land Moon," Lonnie Johnson warned:

> I'm going to buy me a shotgun, long as I am tall.
> I'm going to shoot my woman, just to see her fall.

In "Me and the Devil Blues" Robert Johnson sang casually that he intended to "beat my woman, until I get satisfied." In other Johnson songs, women were depicted as phonographs or automobiles, mere mechanical conveniences meant to provide pleasure or diversion for males.[62]

Such rhetoric was less a commentary on the helplessness of the black female than on the frequent perceptions of male powerlessness that surfaced in the angry, violent behavior of black men in the Delta. In "Long Black Song," Wright's Silas expressed his rage toward his wife by whipping her, but the real source of his anger was the white-dominated caste system and the emasculating sexual double standard it imposed on him: "From sunup to sundown Ah works mah guts out to pay them white trash bastards whut Ah owe em, n then Ah comes n fins they been in mah house! Ah can't go into their houses n yuh know Gawdam well Ah can't. They don have no mercy on no black folks; we's jus like dirt under their feet!" Facing certain death, vowing to fight to the end but realizing the futility of it all, Silas concludes, "It don mean nothin'! Yuh die ef yuh fight! Yuh die ef yuh don fight! Either way yuh die 'n it don mean nothin'."[63]

The masculine perspective dominated the early Delta blues because, in the formative period of the music, the Delta itself produced only a few female blues performers. The dangers and uncertainty of life as an itinerant musician were such that many female singers chose church choirs or minstrel troupes over juke joints and house parties around the Delta. The handful of female blues artists who achieved prominence in the Delta, however, lived by the same rules—or with the same absence of rules—and projected feelings of rebellion, rootlessness, and alienation similar to those exhibited by their male counterparts.

An accomplished guitarist, Josie Bush was married briefly to another blues pioneer, Willie Brown. Bush's strong appeal to male audiences often led to violent arguments with her jealous husband while the two were performing together. Moreover, her attractiveness to her male listeners suggested that the sexual energy unloosed by the blues transcended gender. Such evidence abounds in the lyrics of the relatively small number of songs actually recorded by early female blues artists in the Delta. Louise Johnson's "On the Wall" urged women to "cock it on the wall," while Mattie Delaney claimed, "I asked him about it and he said all right, I asked him how long and he said all night." Delaney's "Down the Big Road Blues" was also a classic expression of rootlessness and alienation:

I feel like crying,
Ain't got no tears to spare,

I had a happy home,
And I wouldn't stay there.[64]

Blues singers often seemed reluctant to express commitments to places or people, but they also exalted the merits of an enduring male-female relationship and offered detailed descriptions of the pain and sorrow engendered by such a relationship gone sour. Hence Robert Johnson bragged about being a "Steady Rollin' Man" who rolled "both night and day," but he admitted that "you can't give your sweet woman everything she wants in one time." As a result, Johnson complained, "she get rambling in her brain, mmm some other man on her mind." In "From Four until Late," Johnson punned that a woman was "like a dresser, with a man always rambling through its drawers" but admitted, "A man is like a prisoner, and he's never satisfied." Meanwhile, from the female perspective, Louise Johnson moaned that "I never had no good man, I mean to ease my worried head," and Mattie Delaney, who sang about her "traveling mind," nonetheless conceded, "I can't go down that big road myself."[65]

If male-female relationships were treated much more casually and the deterioration of such relationships much more matter-of-factly in the blues than in mainstream American popular music, this seemingly cold-blooded realism simply acknowledged the economically marginal, emotionally debilitating circumstances that could easily undermine otherwise solid relationships between black men and women in the Delta. (Under such circumstances, it was surely no coincidence that a stable, monogamous relationship was a key to higher class standing among Delta blacks.) Moreover, to express a desire for companionship on one's journey down that "big road" was merely to give voice to a basic human need. In the case of Delta blacks, whose journey often promised little but deprivation, humiliation, and denial, that need was especially intense.

The blues presented a strong reflection of the everyday life experiences of Delta blacks. Blues songs dwelt on hard work, violence, poverty, despair, wanderlust, loneliness, drunkenness, and incarceration, which were so much a part of black life in the Delta that any performer might be fairly well assured of a knowing response from his listeners should he even allude to one of these experiences in song.

The physical influences that shaped the lives of Deltans on both sides of the color line also figured prominently in the blues. In "Dry Spell Blues," Son House sang of the devastating effects of a drought and the resulting hard times. Muddy Waters's "Flood" conjured up visions of a gloomy, rainy day in the Delta:

> Go look at the weather,
> I believe it's goin' to be a flood. . . .
> I believe my baby's gon' quit me,
> Because I can feel it all in my blood.[66]

As these lyrics suggest, however the appeal of the blues derived not just from their relevance to what was immediate and tangible but from their capacity to evoke a sentiment, a mood, a feeling that had to be experienced to be fully understood. In Robert Johnson's "Preachin Blues," the blues was a familiar but by no means welcome feeling:

> The blues, is a lowdown shakin' chill.
> You ain't never had them, I hope you never will.
> Well, the blues, is a aching old heart disease.
> Like consumption, killin' me by degree.[67]

Lonnie Johnson's "Devil Got the Blues" presented an even more intimidating portrait of the blues:

> The blues is like the devil,
> It comes on you like a spell.
> Blues will leave your heart full of trouble
> And your poor mind full of hell.[68]

Although the blues flowed directly from the life experiences of Delta blacks, the popularity of the music in the urban North, where successive generations of black migrants found alienation, frustration, and disillusionment in yet another promised land, suggests why the old bluesman made no reference to historical or geographical context when he explained that "it take a man that have the blues to sing the blues." Clearly the blues struck an affirmative chord with large numbers of people who had never seen a stalk of cotton or a mule, much less witnessed a lynching. Lawrence Levine insisted that "the rootlessness and alienation which were so well conveyed in the blues and work songs were not solely the reflection of Afro-American culture but of the larger society as well, which was at its heart rootless and deeply afraid of the rapid changes that were transforming it." Lawrence Goodwyn concluded that the discontented white farmers and tenants who rallied to the cause of Populism in the 1890s did so because "in an age of progress and forward motion they had come to suspect that Horatio Alger was not real." As we have seen, Goodwyn's observation was even more applicable to black farmers and farm laborers in the Delta at the turn of the century. Living on the "periphery" of American society, Levine explained, blacks had little reason to embrace its "dreams and myths." As a result, they were "more able to accept the fact of their alienation, their isolation, their fears, and give unambiguous voice to the anguish of modern man." [69]

Levine's comment is better understood when one realizes that, despite the music's identification with the cotton fields and levee camps of the Delta, the context in which the blues emerged was shaped in no small part by the Delta's ties to the modern urban-industrial colossus, whose investment capital, transportation network, and economic doctrines were already well established in the region by the turn of the century. Insulated from popular retaliation by the rigidly enforced rules of caste and the legally mandated system of disfranchisement, Delta planters eagerly followed the lead of their northern industrialist counterparts by implementing centralized, cost-conscious management and supervisory techniques that effectively transformed sharecroppers into wage laborers, separating them from the product of their labor and dashing their dreams of economic independence. As this process unfolded, the blues gave voice to the emotions of increasingly alienated workers who could do little but stand and watch as their dreams of self-determination and progress fell prey to the seemingly paradoxical convergence of economic modernization and social and political retrogression in the Delta.

When Ralph Ellison observed that black culture embodied a great deal more than "the relatively spontaneous and undifferentiated responses of a peep living in close contact with the soil," he went on to explain that "despite Jim Crow, Negro life does not exist in a vacuum, but in the seething vortex of those tensions generated by the most highly industrialized of western nations." Ellison's observation was especially pertinent to blacks in the Delta, where, significant contextual differences notwithstanding, the modernization of the plantation economy contributed to the disaffection of the workforce in much the same fashion as the rise of an impersonal urban-industrial economy produced a similar result north of the Mason-Dixon line. As Alan Lomax explained, "Years before the rest of the world, the people of the Delta tasted the bittersweet of modern alienation so that the blues of those days ring true for all of us now." [70]

The more or less universal contemporary relevance of blues themes was clear enough, but for much of the twentieth century the white listening audience for the blues consisted largely of academics and urban intellectuals. During the 1920s and 1930s, recording companies found a strong and expanding demand for the stylings of previously little-known southern blues artists. Companies such as Okeh, Columbia, and Victor played a key role in expanding and solidifying the popularity of blues music, but they made little effort to market the blues to white listeners. Country music was the medium of choice for working-class southern whites, regardless of whether they remained in Dixie or headed north. Country artists like Jimmie Rodgers and Bob Wills drew heavily on black instrumental stylings, but, ironically, it was changes in the listening habits and stylistic preferences of a younger, more urban-based black audience that led initially to the broader exposure of whites to blues influences.[71]

The Delta continued to produce accomplished blues performers, but the ongoing exodus of blacks to northern cities encouraged musical stylists to develop a more relevant and sophisticated music calculated to appeal to the tastes of an increasingly urbanized black population. Such a form was "rhythm and blues," an electrically amplified, dance-oriented music that had all but overwhelmed the older traditional country blues by the end of World War II. Among Delta bluesmen only Howlin' Wolf and Muddy Waters succeeded in making the musical and instrumental adjustments that seemed to be necessary for significant commercial success.[72]

Prior to the 1950s, the popularity of rhythm and blues performers within the United States was defined almost wholly in terms of their appeal to black audiences. At the end of the 1940s, however, it became apparent that the musical tastes of white Americans were shifting dramatically. This shift was particularly apparent in the Delta and elsewhere in and around Memphis. For some time the affluent white youth of the Delta had been hiring black bands for dances at schools or country clubs, and by the 1950s jukeboxes were usually well stocked with newly introduced 45 rpm versions of rhythm and blues tunes, or "nigger music," as they were known to white youths captivated by their lyrical and rhythmic sensuality.[73]

Ike Turner of Clarksdale played piano in a rhythm and blues group called the Kings of Rhythm and also worked as a disc jockey at a local radio station. Turner and his cohorts could play the Delta blues in traditional fashion, but they drew as well on the inspiration of the contemporary "jump blues" bands they heard on radio and records. In March 1951 they joined forces with producer Sam Phillips of Memphis to record "Rocket 88," which Robert Palmer described as "a rocking little automobile blues, squarely in the tradition of Robert Johnson's 'Terraplane Blues.'" Palmer also noted that Phillips and others decided in retrospect that "Rocket 88" was the first rock and roll record. Certainly by the time that "Rocket 88" was recorded, "rock and roll," once known primarily to bluesmen as a euphemism for sex, had become a familiar phrase in rhythm and blues. It was perhaps not totally coincidental that another big rhythm and blues recording of 1951 (by the New York-based Dominos) was the overtly sexual "Sixty-Minute Man":

I rock 'em and roll 'em all night long;
I'm a sixty-minute man.[74]

Meanwhile, in June 1951 as "Rocket 88" climbed the charts, Cleveland, Ohio, disc jockey Alan Freed began *The Moon Dog House Rock 'n' Roll Party*, where he played rhythm and blues records for both white and black listeners and called the music "rock and roll." At approximately the same time, "Sixty-Minute Man" became the first rhythm and blues tune to "cross over" to the pop charts, where it enjoyed a twenty-three-week stint. In the next few years, a number of rhythm and blues tunes captured the hearts of white youths, including Bill Haley's much more successful cover of Joe Turner's rhythm and blues hit "Shake, Rattle, and Roll." A few black performers like Fats Domino and Chuck Berry managed to establish themselves with white pop fans, but Sam Phillips realized that this new music would never reach its true commercial potential without white artists who could perform in what Bill Malone called "a convincing black style." A coworker recalled Phillips saying repeatedly, "If I could only find a white man who had the Negro feel, I could make a billion dollars."[75]

Phillips finally found such a man in Elvis Presley from Tupelo, a town in the hills some eighty miles east of the Mississippi Delta. Never before had the musical culture of blacks and lower-class whites been so closely conjoined as they were in the early stylings of Presley, whose music bore the imprint of country and gospel music as well as the blues. This remarkable synthesis was apparent on Presley's first single, released by Phillips's Sun Records, consisting of "Blue Moon of Kentucky," a bluegrass number written by Bill Monroe, and "That's All Right, Mama," an old blues tune learned from Arthur "Big Boy" Crudup. Presley explained that he "dug the real low down Mississippi singers, mostly Big Bill Broonzy and Big Boy Crudup," although his family often scolded him for listening to such "sinful music."[76]

Similar influences shaped the music of Carl Perkins. As a member of the only white tenant family on a plantation in Lake County, Tennessee (just north of the Yazoo Delta), Perkins grew up listening to Bill Monroe and the Grand Ole Opry on radio as well as to the gospel singing of his neighbors. He learned his guitar style from an elderly black man named John Westbrook:

I'd be so tired, chopping or picking cotton, whatever we was doin', and I'd take off for Uncle John's after we'd work hard all day. Looking back on it now, there's that old black man who was tired, much tireder than I was as a young boy, but yet he took time and sat on his porch and showed me the licks that he knew. I was dealing with a black angel. He didn't have to take time to show me anything. And under the circumstances of segregation back in those years, when he couldn't go get him a drink of water at the courthouse, he could have hated a little white boy like me, but he didn't. He loved me.[77]

Perkins's story and the experiences his family shared with the black families on the plantation suggested that the working-class white country music audience should have experienced little difficulty in relating to the blues. Although white tenant farmers and mill workers enjoyed advantages unavailable even to upper-class blacks, theirs was also a marginal world that offered little hope for economic or social advancement or meaningful political expression. Both groups suffered at the hands of an isolated regional labor market where limited opportunities for significant advancement engendered a perpetual restlessness of spirit and body that contributed to high rates of turnover in the cotton mill as well as the cotton patch. Surely no point of comparison between the blues and country music is so striking as the common emphasis on mobility, whether in the form of travel or aimless "ramblin'." Not surprisingly, country singers were as fascinated by trains as were bluesmen, and, more often than not, they were as ambivalent, longing for escape on the one hand, searching for a place to call home on the other. Although it was even less a music of overt protest than the blues, country music did provide a critical, alienated view of modern, urban-industrial society. Early country music stars like Jimmie Rodgers, and then later Hank Williams, personified the rootlessness and the overt sexuality, as well as the fatalistic and self-destructive genius, that were so readily associated with bluesmen like Robert Johnson.[78]

Like the blues, country music also reflected the tension between the teaching of the church and the temptations of the world. Jerry Lee

Lewis, cousin of evangelist Jimmy Swaggart, briefly attended the South-western Bible Institute in Waxahatchie, Texas, before being expelled for rendering a "rockin'" version of "My God Is Real" during a chapel performance. Lewis periodically renounced "the devil's music" throughout much of his early career, and Malone noted that Lewis "often acted as if he had walked out of the pages of Wilbur J. Cash's *Mind of the South:* He is the prototypical ambivalent southerner, embodying both hedonistic and puritanical traits." Malone was, of course, correct, but Lewis, who as a youth loved to play with black musicians around his Ferriday, Louisiana, home, was hardly more prototypically southern than a host of blues singers (not to speak of his rhythm and blues contemporary Little Richard) in this regard. Among the bluesmen, Charley Patton, Sonny Boy Williamson, John Lee Hooker, and Muddy Waters, to name but a few, also had strong religious upbringing; and, as we have seen, like Jerry Lee, several bluesmen succumbed repeatedly, albeit briefly, to the "call to preach," in the process renouncing the blues as the instrument of the Devil.[79]

These similarities are indeed striking, but despite the common economic and cultural terrain they occupied, both country music and the blues were thoroughly commercialized by the post–World War II era, and in the final analysis it was the prospect of increased record sales rather than the breakdown of racial barriers to communication and understanding that brought them together under the rubric of rock and roll. Certainly, commercial influences were primarily responsible for the fact that during the 1940s, as Charles Gillett observed, country music "probably absorbed more elements of black music than were accepted into the mainstream pop of the time." In addition to the country performers who drew on black gospel influences, Ernest Tubb modernized the "white blues" style of Jimmie Rodgers through his electrified, "honky-tonk" sound. Even the "mountain" music of Roy Acuff and Bill Monroe showed black influences, while the Delmore Brothers and several others served up offerings dubbed "hillbilly boogie." Then, as Gillett saw it, "when Hank Williams emerged on the new MGM label in the late forties, he shook all these black-influenced country styles together using as strong a beat as his recording supervisor would sanction." With young whites exhibiting a growing fascination with black music, country musicians not only began to perform rhythm and blues songs but sought as well to incorporate the distinctive, rocking beat into their country offerings.[80]

The exposure of young white "rockabilly" stars to black musicians came not only as a result of growing up within earshot of both the blues and black gospel music but by virtue of the fact that many of these white performers began their careers with small independent recording companies that were also producing the songs of various rhythm and blues artists. As William Barlow explained: "Given the proliferation of R&B through independent record labels and disk jockeys in the postwar era, little wonder that young white musicians like Elvis Presley, Bill Haley, Jerry Lee Lewis and Buddy Holly began to copy the new black musical styles they heard all around them." [81]

Bill Malone observed that the early stars of rockabilly performed with a style that expressed "the macho complex so deeply imbedded in southern working class culture" and violated "conventional middle-class standards" as well. Clearly, then, the bluesman and the rockabilly star shared a great deal when it came to the styling and the imagery of their music. Moreover, if the early white southern rock and roll stars did succeed in implanting "much of the culture of the working-class South in the nation at large," this cultural implant was actually a hybrid, one that tapped a sense of alienation that flourished on both sides of the gaping chasm of misunderstanding and fear that continued to separate the races in the South.[82]

Youthful white rock and roll fans were hardly more aware than their concerned parents of the social and historical significance of the blues. Yet, the bluesy stylings — as well as the emphasis on sexuality, the physical and often ephemeral aspects of love, and the general rejection of prevailing community norms — that permeated early rock and roll won the hearts of white teenagers drawn to the ill-defined but undeniable sense of rebellion that it conveyed.[83]

As the true substance of rock and roll's appeal to American youth became apparent, guardians of the public morality sounded the alarm. In the spirit of the McCarthy era, some critics saw the music as part of the "Communist conspiracy." A Florida minister flayed Elvis Presley for reaching "a new low in spiritual degeneracy," although Elvis enjoyed the reputation of the proverbial choirboy compared to what Nick Tosches described as the "hellish persona" of "the Killer," Jerry Lee Lewis, whose behavior taxed the vocabulary of the most articulate minister and rendered similarly speechless the terrified parents of teenagers of either sex. The subversive, even revolutionary implications of rock and roll and its link to the blues was by no means lost on the defenders of the racial status quo. Throughout the South leaders of the massive resistance movement condemned rock and roll as "jungle music" and charged that it was part of an NAACP plot to pull white youths down to the level of blacks.[84]

That a music so potentially subversive in its social and political implications could succeed in threatening the Cold War decorum of the 1950s seems less surprising if one considers the interactive roles of technology, marketing, and, of course, the profit motive, in the rock and roll explosion. Richard Petersen argued, for example, that the adaptation of network radio programming to television that occurred during this period simply led radio stations to adopt the "Top Forty" format as the least expensive way of filling airtime. Because Top Forty charts were calculated on the basis of not only record sales but radio airplay and jukebox selections as well, a great many rhythm and blues records appeared on the charts, thereby demonstrating their popularity with transistor-radio- and jukebox-listening, 45-rpm-record-buying white teenagers, who represented the primary audience for rock and roll.[85]

Once they recognized the tremendous profit potential of the new music, the recording industry's management elite moved in and took rock and roll from the margins to the mainstream, where the unmistakable market appeal of its rebellious essence could be exploited. In the process, however, they quickly took steps as well to bring both the content and the packaging of the music under their control. As big-name firms regained control of the music distribution market, they muscled out the smaller labels that had launched rock and roll and sustained it through the early years of the rock and roll revolution. By the end of the 1950s, as Barlow wrote, "the primal 'roots' rock and roll of Little Richard, Fats Domino, Chuck Berry, Bo Diddley, Elvis Presley, and Jerry Lee Lewis was being replaced by the sanitized 'schlock rock' of Fabian, Paul Anka, and Frankie Avalon — or the clean-cut, white buck cover versions of Pat Boone." Charles Gillett agreed that recording-industry leaders "killed off the music but kept the name."[86]

Just when it seemed, however, that the blues influences in rock and roll would fall victim to the conservatism of the music industry, the raw, revolutionary, blues-derived elements that had initially made rock and roll so appealing to American youth resurfaced during the "British invasion" of 1963. Ironically, it was only with the British invasion that rock music became the medium through which a small group of blues (rather than strictly rhythm and blues) performers actually became known to large numbers of American whites. Rock musicians from Great Britain, where whites far more readily accepted and appreciated the blues, gratefully acknowledged the influence of these Delta bluesmen, who thereby gained considerably greater recognition among American whites than they might otherwise have achieved.[87]

The Rolling Stones, the Animals, and the Yardbirds were among the British groups influenced by Muddy Waters. ("If it had not been for you, we would never be where we are today," telegraphed the Rolling Stones to Waters on his birthday in 1975.) Waters's appeal to American whites seemed directly related to the fact that these groups, particularly the Rolling Stones (who took their name from one of his songs), began recording his songs and praising his music. "Before the Rolling Stones," explained Waters, "people over here didn't know nothing and didn't want to know nothing about me. . . . If they'd buy my records, their parents would say, 'What the hell is this? Get this nigger record out of my house!' But then the Rolling Stones and those other groups come over here from England, playing this music, and now, today, the kids buy a record of mine, and they listen to it."[88]

Sonny Boy Williamson not only recorded with several British artists but also influenced the music of an American group called Levon and the Hawks, who went on to win almost universal acclaim as The Band. Unfortunately, Williamson died before a tour or a joint recording session could be arranged. Elsewhere, the distinctive guitar stylings that marked the recordings of Howlin' Wolf deeply affected a host of rock performers on both sides of the Atlantic. Wolf accompanied the Rolling Stones on their first appearance on the television show *Shindig,* and their popular recording of his "Little Red Rooster" further affirmed rock and roll's debt to the blues.[89]

The linkage between rock and roll and the blues became more apparent at the end of the 1980s as the blues finally achieved significant popularity among middle-class white adults, who found in them the energy and grit that contemporary, mass-produced rock music appeared to have lost. A Grammy-winning album reissue of every known Robert Johnson recording quickly hit the Billboard Top Pop Album chart in 1990 and carried tributes to Johnson from Keith Richards ("Everybody should know about Robert Johnson") and Eric Clapton ("I have never found anything more deeply soulful than Robert Johnson"). A *Newsweek* writer's exuberant assessment of Johnson's musical legacy as "a powerful concentrate which, when diluted, became 35 years of rock and roll" merely indicated broader public appreciation of a relationship long acknowledged by rock pioneers such as Big Joe Turner, who conceded, "For a fact rock 'n' roll ain't no different from the blues, we just pepped it up a lot. Man, that music was in the blues bag all the time."[90]

One can hardly escape the irony in the fact that the blues, a music born of the incessant toil and demolished dreams of impoverished Delta blacks, exerted such a formative influence on rock and roll, a music that not only tapped the alienation and wanton energy of the relatively advantaged white youth of the 1950s but, despite the best efforts of the American economic and moral establishment to thwart it, continued to reflect and shape the sensibilities of succeeding generations. This irony was compounded by indications that as the blues gained a new audience with whites they seemed to lose their appeal among younger blacks who found rap, rhythm and blues, and other more contemporary forms of musical expression more attuned to their lifestyles, aspirations, and concerns.

There is precious little evidence that the commercially inspired fusion of black and white music that lay at the heart of rock and roll has made a significant contribution to interracial understanding or that the new generation of white blues fans has much appreciation of the context of human suffering from which this suddenly trendy music evolved. Still, as they see the promise of socioeconomic advancement that was once assumed to be nothing less than their national birthright give way to diminished hopes and frustrated expectations, a number of Americans of every race in every region may one day come to appreciate the difference between *hearing* the blues and *feeling* them. If so, just as the blues once so clearly chronicled the failure of Delta society to live up to its ideals (or to celebrate ideals consistent with the life experiences of the majority of its members), their remarkable musical legacy may eventually transcend geographic boundaries and racial barriers to focus critical popular attention on the discrepancies between the real and ideal in not only regional but national life as well.

Searching
for
Southernness

Community and Identity in the
Contemporary South

Two, four, six, eight,
We don't wanna integrate.
Eight, six, four, two,
We don't want no jigaboo!

Clearly, the white students who massed outside the University of Georgia's Center Myers Hall on the evening of January 10, 1961, were not there to showcase either their facility with mathematics or their gift for poetry. Rather, they sought to defend their exclusionary version of the southern community from any and all would-be black invaders and from two invaders in particular. Meanwhile, inside Center Myers, an exhausted Charlayne Hunter, one of the alleged intruders in question, drifted off to sleep to the rhythms of what she later called those "peculiar southern lullabies." Although her white antagonists insisted on seeing her as a trespasser and in subsequent months and years treating her as an alien in their midst, Hunter's presence on the campus represented not an invasion from without but the early intermediate stages of a revolution from within, one aimed not at demolishing a community but at redefining it and establishing within it the legitimate place and identity historically denied to black southerners.[1]

Twenty-seven years after her arrival at Georgia had triggered a riot, Charlayne Hunter-Gault came back to address the graduating class of 1988. Though not nearly so dramatic as her first appearance on campus, her return on this occasion was in some ways no less significant. Although she was speaking at commencement, her remarks would have been equally appropriate for homecoming as she took this opportunity to join other southern blacks who, as journalist Peter Applebome wrote recently, "in a logical extension of the civil rights battles of the past, are staking claim to their vision of the South — not as background figures on the mythic landscape of moonlight and magnolias, not as victims of oppression dragged here from Africa, but as Southerners, with as much stake in the region as any Mississippi planter or Virginia farmer."[2]

Hunter-Gault established this theme at the outset, noting, in language that contrasted starkly with the hateful rhetoric that had greeted her on her initial visit to the campus, that it was "good to be back home again. In a place that I have always thought of as 'our place.'" She went on to praise the South as the nation's only "true melting pot" and observe that "through the events of our toil and our tumultuous history," southerners have become "a definable people."[3]

If on the one hand, the tenor of Hunter-Gault's talk was gracious and even conciliatory, it was also remarkable in the matter-of-factness with which she not just acknowledged but celebrated her southernness. When Hunter-Gault first arrived on the Georgia campus in 1961, W. J. Cash's *Mind of the South* had recently surfaced in paperback and was just beginning to make its presence felt among students, scholars, and activists obsessed with the South's problems and determined to do something about them. Certainly, the mob violence that attended Hunter-Gault's enrollment at Georgia merely confirmed Cash's distinctly unflattering portrait of an emotionally dysfunctional white South given to schizophrenia, violence, and "attachment to fictions and false values," and an especially exaggerated "attachment to racial values and a tendency to justify cruelty and injustice in the name of those values." Had Cash not done himself in some twenty years earlier, he would not have been surprised that Hunter-Gault's presence at Georgia had set off a riot. Indeed, he would have expected no less and probably a lot more. On the other hand, Cash would have been stunned by the fact that Hunter-Gault had survived and then returned willingly to the university where she received a warm welcome from a predominantly white audience and actually claimed kinship with the sons and daughters of some of those who had once taunted and threatened her. Certainly, the only actors in the entire drama who would have been recognizable to him as southerners were those who had hurled rocks and racial epithets at her window on that evening in 1961.[4]

Cash had conceded that southern whites and blacks maintained a relationship that was "nothing less than organic" because "Negro entered into white man as profoundly as white man entered into Negro — subtly influencing every gesture, every word, every emotion and idea, every attitude," but having offered this insight, one truly perceptive by the standards of 1941, Cash went no further. Though clearly sympathetic to southern blacks, he just as clearly had only white males in mind as he picked his way through the maze of contradiction, delusion, and irrationality that, for him, at least, constituted the tortured southern psyche. In succeeding years, even considerably more racially enlightened observers followed Cash's exclusionary example by identifying southern whites as "southerners" and southern blacks as "blacks."[5]

Thus it was that southern blacks were denied their regional identities both by the antagonistic defenders of a southern way of life that rendered blacks not only identityless but invisible and by their would-be liberators who had undertaken the challenge of dismantling the barriers to fuller black participation in American life. There are some at least partial explanations for this curious state of affairs. Focused on the suffering and injustice imposed on blacks by the Jim Crow South, external critics found it logical and easy enough to conclude that the last thing that any black would crave would be an identity as a southerner. The term was not only reserved for whites, but, for much of the twentieth century, when nonsoutherners employed it, they seldom did so with complimentary intent. Beyond that, to the assertion of white southerners that the blacks who toiled in their fields were satisfied and happy, many observers simply posed the counterfallacy that all southern blacks were hopelessly, totally, and eternally alienated from the place where they had seen so much injustice and hardship.

Recognition of black southerners' ties to the South also ran counter to the emerging black power/black pride movements and their focus on the roots of black culture in the African homeland rather than in the slave South to which Africans had been dragged against their will and in which they were subjected to brutal, dehumanizing treatment at the hands of their white oppressors. Not surprisingly, many black intellectuals insisted that their African (rather than their southern) heritage was the true source of the strength, dignity, and sense of purpose that lay behind the resolve of black southerners to confront the mobs, police dogs, and firehoses that stood between them and their full rights as American citizens.

Viewed against this backdrop, no phenomenon of the post–Civil Rights era, save perhaps for the reverse migration of blacks to the South, is more striking than the strong and apparently still strengthening inclination of blacks in the South to identify themselves as southerners. In fact, these two trends are most likely related. Thadious M. Davis observed recently that "while anthropologists and sociologists may see the increasingly frequent pattern of black return migration as flight from the hardships of urban life, I would suggest that it is also a laying claim to a culture and to a region that, though fraught with pain and difficulty, provides a major grounding for identity."[6]

C. Vann Woodward agreed, concluding that "the attractions of the South for those returning were mainly old cultural constants . . . the values of place and past, the symbols and traditions of region rather than race." Like country music and the blues, the South's autobiographical and literary tradition clearly stresses the importance of place. From William Faulkner to Will Percy to Ben Robertson to Richard Wright to Willie Morris to Anne Moody to Albert Murray to Eudora Welty, to name but a few, southern writers have consistently emphasized their connection with or desire for connection with place as a central theme in their lives. For example, Harry Crews subtitled his vivid childhood reminiscence *A Biography of a Place.* Charlayne Hunter-Gault called her 1992 memoir *In My Place* because it focused on her resolute decision to abandon the "place" to which the white South's rules of caste conformity sought to confine her and claim for herself and other black southerners their rightful "place" as Americans judged by their energies and talents and as southerners entitled by birth and struggle to claim the South as home. Hunter-Gault also found comfort and inspiration, however, in a physical and sensory South that was her "place" as well. Attending summer school in a "hot sultry Athens," she received "an unexpected gift" when she encountered "the evocative sights, sounds and smells of my small-town childhood, the almost overpowering sweet smell of honeysuckle and banana shrub seducing buzzing bumblebees and yellow jackets; the screeching cries of crickets emanating from every shrub and bush; clouds of black starlings producing shadows wherever they flew over the dusty red clay haze. This was the part of the South that I loved, that made me happy to be a Southerner, that left me unaffected by the seamier side, which would deny I could have pride in anything but Aunt Jemima."[7]

Elsewhere, as she reflected on her childhood experiences there, Nikki Giovanni realized that Knoxville was "a place where no matter what I belong" and that in turn "Knoxville belongs to me." Determined that her son "must know we come from somewhere. That we belong," Giovanni penned her autobiographical *Gemini,* in which she reflected on her youthful experiences in Knoxville and her grandparents' neighborhood, which had been destroyed by urban renewal. Giovanni observed poetically that white biographers would "probably talk about my hard childhood / and never understand that / all the while I was quite happy." She addressed this concern recently in *Knoxville, Tennessee,* a beautifully illustrated children's book, which recalled the pleasures of fresh vegetables, barbecue, buttermilk, church socials, and mountain picnics with her beloved grandmother.[8]

Likewise, Maya Angelou retained an intense, if somewhat more ambivalent, connection with her grandmother's store in Stamps, Arkansas, a gathering place for black cotton pickers, who came in early, still sleepy, but expectant and hopeful, and filled the lamplit store with "laughing, joking, boasting and bragging." By the end of the day, however, "the sounds of the new morning had been replaced with grumbles about cheating houses, weighted scales, snakes, skimpy cotton and dusty rows. In cotton-picking time," recalled Angelou, "the late afternoons revealed the harshness of Black Southern life, which in the early morning had been softened by nature's blessing of grogginess, forgetfulness and the soft lamplight."[9]

David R. Goldfield noted that the Civil Rights movement went a long way toward removing "the public obsession with race" and thereby "enabled" white southerners "to regain contact with other cultural elements such as past, place and manners." Goldfield's observation was no less applicable to black southerners, especially black writers. Novelist Alice Walker observed that the history of her family, "like that of all black Southerners, is a history of dispossession" and that when she came of age in the early 1960s, she awoke "to the bitter knowledge that in order just to continue to love the land of my birth, I was expected to leave it." Describing the South of her birth as "a beloved but brutal place," Walker explained that "it is part of the black Southern sensibility that we treasure memories for such a long time, that is all of our homeland those of us who at one time or another were forced away from it have been allowed to have."[10]

This realization led Walker to recognize from her first observation of him that Rev. Martin Luther King Jr. was "The One, The Hero, The Fearless Person for whom we had waited." Struck by King's serenity and courage, Walker knew immediately that she would resist the forces that sought to "disinherit" her and that she would "never be forced away from the land of my birth without a fight." In her 1972 tribute to King, she thanked him for leading this fight: "He gave us back our heritage. He gave us back our homeland, the bones and dust of our ancestors, who may now sleep within our caring *and* our hearing. . . . He gave us continuity of place, without which community is ephemeral. He gave us home."[11]

Walker assessed the importance of this restored heritage to her and other southern black writers when she expressed sympathy for her "Northern brothers" who "have never experienced the magnificent quiet of a summer day when the heat is intense and one is so very thirsty, as one moves across the dusty cotton fields, that one learns forever that water is the essence of all life. In the cities, it cannot be so clear to one that he is a creature of the earth, feeling the soil between the toes, smelling the dust thrown up by the rain, loving the earth so much that one longs to taste it and sometimes does."[12]

Walker did not intend, she wrote, "to romanticize the Southern black country life." Yet, as she saw it, "No one could wish for a more advantageous heritage than that bequeathed to the black writer in the South: a compassion for the earth, a trust in humanity beyond our knowledge of evil, and an abiding love of justice."[13]

Whereas Richard Wright and his contemporaries of an earlier generation had struggled with a society dominated by the pervasive and confining realities of color, Walker and her post–Civil Rights movement contemporaries felt somewhat less compelled to focus on the effects of white antagonism. Hence, they could explore the strengths and soft spots, complexities and contradictions of African American life. Walker's fiction reflected her desire to look beyond (though certainly not ignore) white oppression and explore themes of community, identity, and gender in her writing. Walker had journeyed to Africa in search of her proverbial "roots," and in her short story "Everyday Use," a young woman named Dee, who, thanks to having her African consciousness raised, now calls herself "Wangero," comes home to visit her impoverished mother. Wangero begs her mother to give her some handmade quilts that are already promised to Maggie, her disfigured and inarticulate sister, who is about to marry an ignorant, mossy-toothed country black man. Having refused the offer of these "old-fashioned" quilts when she went away to college, Wangero now wants them to hang on display. "Maggie can't appreciate those quilts!" she argues with unintended irony. "She'd probably be backward enough to put them to everyday use."[14]

In *The Color Purple,* Walker went on to explore male-female and female-female relationships within the black family and community, stressing the strength and courage of her female characters as they struggled for fulfillment in a world dominated not just by whites but by males as well.

Elsewhere, before the Civil Rights movement came to Greenwood, Mississippi, playwright Endesha Ida Mae Holland was unaware of any African American literary tradition whatsoever. By the end of the 1960s, however, Holland was immersed in black studies, which taught her that "it was okay to be black." From that point on, she began to use memory to "rescue and reconstruct — to search, document, and celebrate — my Mississippi Delta's community of Black people" and her "community of black women in particular." More recently, black writer Tina McElroy Ansa offered an irreverent look at black women and the cult of matriarchy in *Ugly Ways,* a novel that reaches a riotous conclusion as the ever-combative Lovejoy sisters fall to scuffling at the funeral home, accidentally dump their mother's corpse on the floor, and proceed to deliver a series of recitations on her shortcomings as a parent.[15]

If the Civil Rights movement allowed blacks to reclaim their homeland and more readily explore the complexities and nuances of their own lives and communities, it also produced some unanticipated consequences that lent a perceptible sense of urgency to efforts to reclaim their regional identity. Writing in 1970, when the echoes of the Civil Rights crusade had scarcely died away, Alice Walker exulted that "what the black Southern writer inherits as a natural right is a sense of community." More than two decades later, however, for many black southerners, the long-awaited, much-suffered-for destruction of Jim Crow with its barriers to educational, social, and economic advancement actually seemed to have led to the erosion of this cherished sense of solidarity and belonging.[16]

Born and raised in Glen Allan, Mississippi, and gone on to a successful business career, Clifton Taulbert admitted: "Even though segregation was a painful reality for us, there were some very good things that happened. Today I enjoy the broader society in which I live and I would never want to return to forced segregation, but I also have a deeply-felt sense that important values were conveyed to me in my colored childhood, values we're in danger of losing in our integrated world. As a child I was not only protected, but also nourished, encouraged, taught, and loved by people who, with no land, little money and few other resources, displayed the strength of a love which knew no measure. I have come to believe that this love is the true value, the legitimate measure of a people's worth."[17]

Reflecting on her experience at all-black Williston High School in Wilmington, North Carolina, Linda Pearce recalled that "we were in a cocoon bathed in a warm fluid, where we were expected to excel. . . . and then something called desegregation punctured it. We went from our own land to being tourists in someone else's. It never did come together, and I think it's on the verge of falling apart altogether now."[18]

With integration and expanded opportunities, increasing numbers of blacks moved up and out, and once-thriving black enterprises struggled to remain competitive in an integrated marketplace. Returning to Clarksdale, Mississippi, after a thirty-year absence, Helen O'Neal-McCray was shocked by the boarded-up black businesses and the signs of community deterioration and decay: "Black people used to live all together, shacks and nice houses. . . . Now they're divided. . . . drugs have succeeded in doing what slavery and all the white people in the world could not — destroy the black family."[19]

Clearly, such sentiments were not meant to advocate a return to racial segregation any more than historians who argued for the viability of black culture and community life under slavery were touting the merits of human bondage. In fact, the sense of lost community among many black southerners who had lived in the South before and after Jim Crow merely confirmed, as historians had long argued, that black southerners had managed to retain a viable culture and family life and a sense of their own worth in a society where color barriers had confronted them at every turn. They seem now to reflect so wistfully on this accomplishment precisely because they feel increasingly hard-pressed to sustain it in a post–Jim Crow era where color counts for less but, apparently, so do family, religion, community, and other affirmative institutions that had helped to unite them in the face of oppression and restriction.

Even reflective, remorseful white southerners who readily acknowledged that the community that once nurtured them was secured by ugly and impenetrable barriers rooted in both color and class sometimes found it no easy matter to resist the memories of the comfortable and protected lifestyle that it had offered them. As a seventeen-year-old, Willie Morris had dreamed of living the tranquil good life as a member of the Delta's landed elite. He fantasized about attending Ole Miss — "as all my friends planned to do" — and then returning to the huge plantation where his girlfriend lived "to preside there on the banks of the Yazoo over boll weevils big enough to wear dog tags, pre–Earl Warren darkies, and the young squirearchy from the plantations abutting on Carter, Eden, Holly Bluff, Sidon and Tchula."[20]

"I saw no reason to leave," Morris recalled, "I knew Mississippi and I loved what I saw. . . . In Yazoo I knew every house and every tree in the white section of town. Each street and hill was like a map on my consciousness; I loved the contours of its land, and the slow changing of its seasons. I was full of the regional graces and was known as a perfect young gentleman. I was pleasant, enthusiastic and happy. On any question pertaining to God or man, I would have cast my morals on the results of a common plebiscite of the white voters of Yazoo County."[21]

A former Ole Miss sorority girl whose social and political awakening led her to work in the congressional campaigns of black legislator Robert Clark, Melany Neilson offered this insider's retrospective on what it had meant to her to be a youthful member of the Delta's white elite:

> The best of us were from fine families. We were bright, the star students, teachers' favorites. Our fathers were farmers, professionals, businessmen, young to middle aged, hopeful, full of promise. Our mothers were attractive, members of the Garden and Bridge clubs, Den Mothers, some of whom paid weekly visits to the beauty parlor and had their names written up in the *Holmes County Herald* society column. We had comfortable homes, cars, memberships at the local country club. We were the best because we expected to be; our privileges were granted, not earned, by an accident of birth.[22]

Like Neilson, Chalmers Archer also grew up in Holmes County, Mississippi, but as part of another community. In *Growing Up Black in Rural Mississippi,* Archer recalled Holmes County and "how horribly and how wonderfully it treated me." As a youngster, Archer witnessed beatings and knew the grief caused by white violence firsthand. After a gang of whites threatened to kill him, Archer's parents — in a move rendered deeply ironic by contemporary realities — had packed him off to Detroit for safekeeping. Yet, recalling his life in Holmes County, Archer remembered many more good things than bad in a childhood where hard work and ever-present racial anxieties were offset by a sense of belonging — to a family, to a community, and to a place. As he explained, "I have many good memories of my experiences growing up in Tchula. After all it was 'home.' And it's just human nature to want to look back kindly on a place of which you were once so much a part."[23]

Archer's nostalgia for a place where he had suffered both repression and poverty reflected a yearning for what Alice Walker called "the solidarity and sharing a modest existence can sometimes bring." Voicing similar sentiments from a poor-white perspective, Harry Crews recalled, "The world that circumscribed the people I come from had so little margin for error, for bad luck, that when something went wrong, it almost always brought something else down with it. It was a world in which survival depended on raw courage born out of desperation and sustained by a lack of alternatives." Yet, for all the hardships he and his people had known there, Crews was by no means alienated from his South Georgia roots. For example, he recalled with genuine affection the one-Saturday-a-month pilgrimages his family made to Alma, Georgia, where around the square,

> the dusty air would be heavy with the pleasant smell of mule dung and mule sweat. . . . Farmers were everywhere in small groups, talking and chewing, and bonneted women stood together trading recipes and news of children. . . . Sometimes I would have as much as a dime to spend on penny candy, but better than the taste of the candy was finding a telephone in a store and standing beside it until somebody used it. I never talked on one myself until I was almost grown, but I knew what a phone was, knew that a man's voice could be carried on a wire all the way across town. No film or play I have ever watched since has been as wonderful as the telephones I watched as a boy in Alma, Georgia.

Crews denied that he was "singing a sad song for the bad good old days, wishing he was back barefoot again traveling in wagons and struck dumb by the mystery of telephones. . . . What I am talking about here is a hard time in the shaping of the South, a necessary experience that made us the unique people we are." Few southerners experienced harder times than Dorothy Allison, who spun a dismal tale of white trash life in her novel *Bastard Out of Carolina,* but Allison's abused and neglected protagonist, Ruth Anne "Bone" Boatwright, recalls "Greenville, South Carolina, in 1955" as "the most beautiful place in the world." "Bone" remembers especially the weeping willows that "marched across the yard, following every warding stream and ditch, their long whiplike fronds making tents that sheltered sweet-smelling beds of clover."[24]

Born to economic circumstances similar to Allison's, Will D. Campbell cited the custom of bringing food to a bereaved family as evidence of the intertwined sense of place and community that prevailed in the Mississippi of his youth: "Somehow in rural, Southern culture, food is always the first thought of neighbors when there is trouble. That is something they can do and not feel uncomfortable. It is something they do not have to explain or discuss or feel self-conscious about. 'Here, I brought you some fresh eggs for your breakfast. And here's a cake. And some potato salad.' It means, 'I love you. And I am sorry for what you are going through and I will share as much of your burden as I can.' And maybe potato salad is a better way of saying it." [25]

The recent outpouring of such reflections from once economically deprived southerners of both races probably comes as no surprise to Robert Coles, who reminded us more than a quarter century ago that: "The poor . . . regardless of race, also love the land; love the pinewoods, love the promising sunrises and flaming sunsets; love the wideness of the countryside, the elbowroom, and sounds of chickens or pigs, the sight of birds and bushes and wildflowers, the feel of feet touching pine needles or grass. . . . We tend to overlook the attachment, even reverence, a sharecropper can feel for the earth he doesn't own and often fails to subdue." [26]

If their common desire to reestablish their sense of place and identity seemed to hold the potential to bring black and white southerners together, it was fraught with divisive possibilities as well. Nowhere are these more obvious than in the widespread and still-developing conflicts over the Confederate flag. At the institutional level, the refusal of a black cheerleader to carry the flag at Ole Miss sporting events in 1981 set off a more-than-decade-long dispute that finally led university administrators to disavow the flag as the official symbol of the university and attempt with little success to get white students to wave a new banner bereft of Confederate insignia or implication. [27]

Meanwhile, at Virginia Military Institute, administrators set off a storm of protest when they decreed that the Confederate insignia should no longer appear on the school's class rings. The flag controversy even spread from the Kudzu Belt to the Ivy League as the dispute over the right of a white Harvard student from Virginia to hang the Stars and Bars from her window led a black student from Kentucky to display a swastika in hers. [28]

At the state level, disputes over the Confederate flag flared from Texas and Oklahoma to Florida. In South Carolina and Alabama, angry blacks assailed the practice of flying the Confederate battle flag over their state capitol. In Mississippi and Georgia, controversy arose over the presence of the Stars and Bars on the state's flag itself. In the latter case, Atlanta's role as the host of a recent Super Bowl and the 1996 Olympic Games gave the conflict a special intensity. [29]

Adopted in 1799, Georgia's first state flag consisted of the state's coat of arms on a field of blue. A new post-Reconstruction banner resembled the first flag of the Confederacy and featured a vertical blue stripe and horizontal bands of red and white. The state's coat of arms was added to the flag in 1905. This banner flew over Georgia until 1956 when the legislature moved to incorporate the familiar stars and bars of the Confederate battle flag into the state flag.[30]

Defenders of this flag insisted that the modification was meant to honor Confederate soldiers, but it came at a time of confrontation, when the state's white political leaders were flocking to the banner of massive resistance to the 1954 *Brown v. Board of Education* decision and vowing last-ditch defiance of any and all desegregation efforts. Flag critics also pointed out that the day before the state House of Representatives approved the flag-change bill, it had passed by a vote of 179–1 the so-called Interposition Resolution, which declared the U.S. Supreme Court's school-integration decrees "null, void and of no effect" in Georgia. Expressing similar sentiments, state representative Denmark Groover of Macon insisted that the new flag would "show that we in Georgia intend to uphold what we stood for, will stand for, and will fight for." A former member of the legislature who had opposed adding the Stars and Bars to the state banner remained absolutely convinced that the intent of the bill's supporters was to affirm their support for segregation. He offered an analogy that anyone familiar with Georgia could readily understand: "There was only one reason for putting that flag on there. Like the gun rack in the back of a pickup, it telegraphs a message." (The association of the new state flag with the "southern way of life" was pervasive indeed. As an elementary- and high-school student in the late 1950s and early 1960s and as a high-school teacher in the late 1960s, I recall that all classroom films acquired from the Georgia State Department of Education began with a vivid shot of the state flag accompanied by an exceedingly robust rendition of "Dixie.")[31]

After the passions of the Civil Rights era had cooled somewhat, several individuals and groups launched assaults on the flag, the most notable coming in 1987 after a widely publicized incident in which white supremacists waving rebel flags attacked civil rights marchers in Forsyth County. Finally, in May 1992 Governor Zell Miller announced that he would support legislation to restore the pre-1956 flag and called the current flag "the last remaining vestige of days that are not only gone, but also days that we have no right to be proud of." Miller's move against the flag reflected the changes that had swept across Georgia's political landscape in the last three decades. As an unsuccessful candidate for Congress in 1964, he had campaigned against the Civil Rights Act of 1964, which he deemed "neither constitutionally acceptable or fundamentally proper." In his January 1993 State of the State address, however, Miller asked the legislators, "Will you do the easy thing or the right thing? . . . If you're truly proud of the South, if you're truly proud of this state and all its 260 years, then help me now to give bigotry no sanction and persecution no assistance." Such a move would require "sheer guts," Miller acknowledged, but as the great-grandson of a Confederate soldier wounded at both Chancellorsville and Gettysburg, Miller found the flag a blemish on the state's image, and he added, "Frankly, I do give a damn."[32]

Not surprisingly, with its large population of blacks and non-native whites and its economic stake in projecting an image of enlightenment and harmony, the Atlanta area provided the strongest support for removing the Confederate battle flag from the state's official banner. Meanwhile, supporters of the flag feared that the next step might be a sandblasting of Stone Mountain, especially after a black clergyman admitted that his dream is that someday folks will look up at the world's largest stone carving and say, "Who are those Fellows?" Some observers saw the flag controversy pitting the "fergit" crowd (composed of black activists and a smattering of white liberals) against the "fergit, Hell" crowd (anchored by the UDC and the Sons of Confederate Veterans). In reality, the dispute was hardly that simple. Polling data from Georgia showed, for example, that a majority of the black respondents expressed no objection to keeping the state flag as it is. Meanwhile, though pro-flag partisans insisted that white southerners saw it as a memorial to their heroic Confederate forebears, a 1992 survey showed that fewer than 20 percent of the southern whites polled could even claim such an ancestry. On the other hand, even white southerners of the liberal persuasion were sometimes a bit testy where the flag was concerned. For example, when asked by an argumentative northerner why the South needed a flag when the North doesn't have one, even the affable Roy Blount Jr. wanted to respond, "That's because the North isn't a place. . . . It's just a direction out of the South."[33]

Such sentiments notwithstanding, southerners were only slightly more likely than other Americans to own a Confederate flag. Meanwhile, to make matters even more confusing, from Israel to Northern Ireland, individuals or groups seeking to defend or gain their independence often seemed drawn to the Confederate banner. John Shelton Reed tells of a visitor from Tblisi in then still Soviet Georgia who clutched the Confederate flag and swore, without apparent ironic intent, that "Some day this will fly in a free Georgia."[34]

As Reed observed, the complexity of the flag dispute arose from the fact that "a lot of people can't see any meaning other than the one they've attached to it." Hence, while the Sons of the Confederate Veterans and the United Daughters of the Confederacy manage to see the flag as the symbol of an honorable past, many black southerners see it as an emblem of white supremacy and racial oppression. Beyond these there is also, as Reed suggests, a small but hard-core "raise-hell, kick-ass boogie-till-you-puke crowd" of southern whites (and many whites elsewhere as well), who may attach no particular racial or ideological significance to the flag but simply object to being told that they cannot wear it or display it.[35]

Regardless of their racial views, the majority of southern whites who care about the flag see it as a crucial symbol that cannot be surrendered if their identity is to be retained. A somewhat cynical colleague of mine at Ole Miss once told me that he suspected that the real reason the school's alumni and administrators refused to let go of the flag was that it was the only thing that separated the school from any number of other third-rate institutions around the country. Ole Miss chancellor Gerald Turner put it somewhat more delicately when he explained, "If this university isn't Southern. . . . it's not anything."[36]

Meanwhile, for many black southerners the widespread assault on Confederate symbols went hand in hand with the consecration of a new set of icons and monuments venerating the crusade to free the South from the racial system founded on the ruins of the Confederate legacy. From the Civil Rights Memorial in Montgomery to the Civil Rights Museum in Memphis, stirring memories of the campaign for racial equality drew black tourists and visitors in huge numbers. Many of these also visited historic landmarks of the movement, including the Edmund Pettus Bridge in Selma and the Sixteenth Street Baptist Church in Birmingham. Many observers believed that Atlanta's two major tourist attractions were Stone Mountain, with its huge Confederate carving, and the Martin Luther King Jr. Center for Social Change. Public opinion polls reflected this curious juxtaposition of seemingly conflicting symbols as respondents consistently listed Dr. King and General Lee as the figures whom they believed best represented the South.[37]

Although black southerners were devoting considerable energy and attention to the matter of establishing their symbolic place in southern history and culture, they were by no means disinterested in more substantive matters. Black southerners had been raising critical concerns for generations, but by the 1990s they were speaking not as disaffected exiles in their own land but as legitimate insiders who felt a genuine sense of involvement in the affairs of state and society as a whole. Journalist John Head responded to the suggestions of a pro-flag partisan that "black people aren't really Southerners" with the insistence that "the South is my home. . . I am a Southerner." Head refused, he explained, "to allow others to say what that means," and he declined as well to "accept the Confederacy as the South at its best" or to "accept the Confederate battle flag as an emblem in which all Georgians can take pride. I criticize the South," Head went on, "not just because I believe it does not do well enough, but because I know it can do better. Love, not hate, is the basis for that criticism."[38]

Fearful that Olympic-inspired efforts to accentuate Atlanta's positives might lead to neglect of the plight of the city's poor and homeless, a number of whom might be displaced as a result of the games, novelist Tina McElroy Ansa proclaimed herself "a child of Atlanta" and "a daughter of Georgia," who wanted Atlanta "to look as spiffy to the world as any staunch city booster." Ansa was also concerned, however, with "Atlanta's well-earned image as a beacon of conscience . . . a place that forged the conscience of Martin Luther King, Jr., and W. E. B. Du Bois and *Constitution* editor Ralph McGill." The only way to show the world Atlanta's strength and conscience, Ansa believed, "is in how we treat the weak as well as the strong, the down-at-the-heel as well as the well-heeled, the slow as well as the swift." To Ansa, the big question was, once the games were over and the crowds had gone home, "how will we Georgians, we Atlantans feel about the Olympic image we presented to the world, and more importantly, to ourselves."[39]

Clearly, the Civil Rights movement had enabled black southerners not only to assert their southernness but to immerse themselves in the South's affairs. Like David Goldfield, C. Vann Woodward believed that in their crusade to free themselves, black southerners had done the same for white southerners. Woodward noted that "it was the whites, after all, who had abandoned the large parts of their tradition that they had sacrificed to their long obsession with race and to their fortress mentality of white supremacy. It was the blacks who got them moving away from their obsessions and toward a recovery of their more genial culture." Woodward's observation was insightful and inspiring, but, by and large, southern whites found it no easy matter to reconstitute a kinder, gentler version of their culture from the rubble of the old Jim Crow system. Indeed, many of them seemed hard-pressed to convince others and at times even themselves that there was more to their regional heritage than what Hodding Carter called a "wretched record of racial murders, political demagogues, separate rest rooms and school closings." For example, reflecting on his middle-class white childhood and adolescence in a small North Carolina town, Melton A. McLaurin clearly found it difficult to look beyond his onetime adherence to a Jim Crow system he now deplored in order to maintain his connections with a place where, for all their physical proximity, blacks and whites had led "separate pasts."[40]

Ironically, black southerners often found it easier to come back to the South and feel at home than did their white contemporaries. When white expatriate James Morgan returned to his native state to interview actor and fellow Mississippian Morgan Freeman, who had recently forsaken Manhattan to live near Charleston in the edge of the Mississippi Delta, he was more than a little uncomfortable. When the white interviewer finally summoned the nerve to ask Freeman whether his Mississippi experiences moved him to choose *Bopha!,* a film set in South Africa, as his first directing assignment, Freeman was incredulous: "Mississippi shaped me. . . . It absolutely shaped me. But this place is not South Africa. . . . Whatever we have in our history in Mississippi, we won't — I won't ever be able to equate with the emotions in South Africa." A tour of Freeman's place was punctuated by frequent interruptions as Freeman pointed out the beauty of the countryside and exulted of the sweet-smelling honeysuckle: "You don't have to plant that. That just grows. That's Mississippi." As the two parted company, the white writer told the black actor that he had expected him to fit into "the angry blackman box, the militant crusader container" only to discover that Freeman "may feel more warmly about our home state than I do." "I really am a product of the South," Freeman admitted, "easy-living, easy-going, quiet, gentle."[41]

Observers had long insisted that economic and educational progress would eventually cleanse white southerners of their racism and strip away many of their other distinctive regional traits as well. Income and years of schooling did eventually correlate positively with greater racial tolerance, but it seems that these same upwardly mobile white southerners who have benefited most from what Woodward called the "Bulldozer Revolution" are also those most likely to stress the importance of their identities as southerners. John Shelton Reed has documented this phenomenon most persuasively, comparing these white southerners to a host of other "ethnic" Americans who struggle to reach the mainstream of national life only to pull up short upon recognizing that they are about to surrender their identity at the altar of assimilation. Hence,

Reed contends that "it is the better educated, relatively affluent south-ern whites who are most likely to think in regional terms, to categorize themselves and others as 'Southerners and non-Southerners' and to be-lieve that they know what that means."[42]

Reed's self-consciously southern whites may well believe they know what southernness means, but viewed in the aggregate, much of their be-havior suggests considerable uncertainty. For many southern blacks, their regional identity was like a suit of clothes that the injustices of the white supremacy era had prevented them from wearing with dignity and pride. Yet, happily enough, when they were at last able to pull this identity out of the closet and don it for all to see, it seemed remarkably comfortable and appropriate. On the other hand, with the garments they wore as the defenders of Jim Crow decidedly out of fashion, white southerners awoke suddenly to find themselves desperately in need of a new, suitably distinctive, and appropriate cultural wardrobe to replace them.

Thus, in the wake of the Civil Rights movement, identity-challenged southern whites began a frantic scramble to cover their cultural naked-ness. For many of them, the most convenient fig leaf seemed to be *South-ern Living* magazine, which could claim over two million subscribers by 1990. *Southern Living* has come a long way since its inaugural issue in 1966 in which the editor's promise to help "urban and suburban families" live a more enjoyable life in the South shared the page with a recipe for a Frito chili pie made with corn chips, canned chili, and processed Amer-ican cheese. Today's version is a virtual guidebook to the upscale south-ern good life, and its essential message seems to be "Never miss an op-portunity to host a brunch and remember that a meal without cheese grits or a broccoli casserole is like a liquor cabinet without Jack Daniels or Maker's Mark." More than one observer was struck by the irony of New York-based Time-Warner's acquisition of *Southern Living,* but such a development was hardly surprising. It merely confirmed the growing perception that, having at last acquired the resources for full-scale par-ticipation in the national consumer culture, upwardly mobile southern whites were not only able but eager to consume their own regional cul-ture as rapidly as commercial marketers could commodify it.

Academic marketers also seized the opportunity to sell southern cul-ture. In 1989 the University of North Carolina Press published the *En-cyclopedia of Southern Culture.* An enormously valuable scholarly resource, the *Encyclopedia* was also, in a sense, as one pundit described it, "the in-tellectual equivalent of *Southern Living.*" Though it now boasts sales totals in excess of 100,000, the majority of these were to white southerners for whom it will serve, as I wrote a while back, "as a bible for the converted, an ideal coffee-table tome for those desiring to reaffirm their faith and be born again — perhaps in good Baptist fashion, again and again — in their own southernness."[43]

As the owner of one of the more ostentatious pickup trucks in Hart County, Georgia, and the not-the-least-bit-sheepish author of the *Encyclopedia*'s entry on Herschel Walker, I am hardly in a position to be condescending. The process I am attempting to describe and analyze is one in which I am at least a part-time participant. Yet, I am nonetheless inclined to share some of the concerns of Edwin M. Yoder, who worries that what he calls the "southernizing enterprise" or "the Dixiefication of Dixie" has very nearly degenerated into little more than "obscurantism and self-caricature." Writing in 1965, Yoder had given thanks for the "working mythologists" who seemed wholly dedicated to the proposition that "the South is and should remain 'a nation within a nation' and so much the better so." More than a quarter century later, most of Yoder's "working mythologists" now have computers, and many of them are connected via "the Bubba List" whose inhabitants seem to feed primarily on microscopically fine points of regional trivia and exotica. Upon returning after a recent four-day absence from my office, I discovered no fewer than 274 bulletins from fellow Bubbaites, most of them devoted to animated exchanges over the true nature of rabbit tobacco, the superiority of various subregional barbecue styles, and stirring tributes to okra, the South's most versatile vegetable. Meanwhile, in bookstores across the South, browsers searching for books brimming with fresh insights into the South are more likely to encounter a host of cutesy, one-sentence-per-page mini-books bearing titles such as *The Southerner's Instruction Book* and containing patently contrived pseudo-southernisms such as "Never drink the last diet Coke" and, worse yet, "Learn to say 'y'all' without feeling self-conscious." Apparently because of their low intellectual food value, these books are placed near the cash registers much as candy bars are situated near checkout lines in supermarkets.[44]

Like Yoder, I worry that this obsession with idiom and idiosyncrasy threatens to turn the South of popular perception into nothing more than a homegrown caricature of itself. This trend is readily observable in musical circles where youthful white urbanites and collegians flock to hear dozens of what I call "southern smart-ass" groups such as the Austin Lounge Lizards, whose offerings include the gospel favorite "Jesus Loves Me (But He Can't Stand You)." In Atlanta, young fans of both bohemian and preppy persuasion are drawn to Slim Chance and the Convicts, Redneck Greece Deluxe, and numerous other similarly trendy aggregations who specialize in raunchy rockabilly interspersed with parodied renditions of country classics and bawdy uptown takeoffs on down-home humor. The Atlanta scene even features a hyperactive all-female honky-tonker support group known as the "Dixie Hickies." The hottest such redneck chic group at present seems to be the (of all places) Chapel Hill-based Southern Culture on the Skids, a phenomenally popular college band whose name suggests both its repertoire and, quite likely, its social significance as well. This musical trend is actually merging with southern pop culture camp. Southern Culture on the Skids regularly performs with a group called Floyd Eats Mayberry, while another *Andy Griffith Show* spin-off band, the Fun Girls from Mt. Pilot, are actually four transvestites from Nashville.[45]

There may be less to this trend toward trivialization and superficialization than meets the eye, but it has led Harry Crews to observe that the South "has been corrupted all the way to quaint" and driven no less a professional southerner than Hodding Carter to complain that the South is now "at most . . . an artifact lovingly preserved in the museums of culture and tourist commerce." Hopefully, Carter will pipe down before he talks us all out of a job, but I suspect that he is quite likely correct when he suggests that so many white southerners now dote on the trivial and even the tacky aspects of southernness precisely because, as Carter says, "the South as South, a living, ever regenerating mythic land of distinctive personality" is "so hard to find in the vital centers of the region's daily life."[46]

Certainly, many of the South's most talented new literary figures seem to agree with Carter's assessment. When Mississippi novelist Richard Ford returned to his home state, he discovered, to his satisfaction, that he could "live here and treat the South as if it were any place else in the United States" without being overcome by the power of "southernness with a capital 'S' and all the baggage that goes with it." For nearly two generations, the widespread critical attention focused on the South's problems had imbued white southern writers with what Fred Hobson called a "rage to explain" about their region. In a post–Civil Rights, Sunbelt-era South, however, writers could and did follow the lead of Walker Percy in exploring the hollowness and superficiality of modern life as it affects not just southerners but all Americans. In Percy's words, "what increasingly engages the southern novelist as much as his Connecticut counterpart are no longer Faulkner's Snopeses or O'Connor's crackers or Wright's black underclass but their successful grandchildren who are going nuts in Atlanta condominiums."[47]

In reality, these grandchildren are probably going nuts in Atlanta traffic, trying to get to their condominiums, but Percy's example was particularly appropriate, for no residents of the South seemed to struggle more consistently to make sense of their sense of place than the movers and shakers of Atlanta. This much was glaringly apparent in the selection of the 1996 Olympic mascot, "Whatizit," which made its debut at the closing ceremonies of the 1992 Olympic Summer Games in Barcelona. To describe the debut as inauspicious would be an understatement of truly Olympic proportions. In fact, only "unmitigated disaster" will suffice. A computer-generated and wholly unendearing blue blob described by one commentator as "a bad marriage of the Pillsbury Doughboy and the ugliest California Raisin," Whatizit met with "international derision." Among the home folks, the reception was even less cordial. Stunned proponents of the nondescript mascot insisted that he or she (at birth the politically correct Whatizit was also "genderless") would grow on folks, but, stiff upper lip notwithstanding, they proceeded with a vigorous review of the steps that might be taken to improve the controversial creation's marketability.[48]

With an eye to an extensive line of products, including not only the standard stuffed toys but comic books, computer software, and beach towels, the committee consulted as final arbiters a group of 150 children. The transformed mascot was cuddlier and more expressive with bigger feet and now bore the nickname "Izzy." There was considerable irony here. Many of the mascot's Georgia-based critics, whose number was legion, found him objectionable precisely because his regionally neutral nerdiness seemed to stem from a desire to avoid any potential association of the Olympic Games with the South, particularly its racially objectionable past.[49]

Still, most white Georgians continued to find "Izzy/Whatizit" offensive because of the apparent pains that had been taken to make him inoffensive to those still inclined to be critical of the South. Said one, "I don't get where he's coming from. I don't really see how it represents anything specific to Atlanta, to the South — to the country, even. It ought to stand for something." A disgusted John Reed dismissed Whatizit as "a semiotic black hole that not only has no meaning itself but drains the meaning out of everything in its vicinity." Columnist Marilyn Geewax, a northern transplant to Atlanta, seemed to agree, noting that Atlanta was about to squander "a once-in-a-century opportunity to help reshape the image of the entire region." Columnist Bert Roughton had other ideas as to why some of the 57 percent of Atlantans polled in September 1993 found even the remodeled "Whatizit" objectionable:

Atlanta has been reinventing itself since it was reduced to ashes in the Civil War. . . .

Maybe that's why we all recoiled so much when we first laid eyes on Whatizit.

Maybe there was an uncomfortable recognition of something too familiar.

Maybe it's just the ugly truth: Izzy is us.[50]

As Roughton suggested, the reimaging of Atlanta has long been a favorite local pastime, but for all the efforts in this direction, as the 1990s unfolded Atlanta found itself facing yet another identity crisis. Ironically, after selling their city as the site of the 1996 Summer Olympic Games, the city's leadership wound up hiring a consultant (appropriately named Joel Babbit, no less) to select a slogan describing what it was they had actually sold. The search produced a flood of suggestions from the Henry Gradyesque "Atlanta: From Ashes to Axis" to the more candid but less inspiring "Atlanta: Not Bad for Georgia" to the also accurate but decidedly unpoetic "Watch Atlanta Transmogrify." Many feared that this search for a slogan was likely to culminate in the verbal equivalent of the insipid Izzy, something along the lines of "Atlanta: A southern city of great hospitality where the weather is generally fair, the business climate is positive, a number of large buildings exist, and you can have fun at Underground." The eventual winner, "Atlanta: Come Celebrate the Dream," was slick, suave, and suitably international, so much so that one cynical observer suggested replacing it with "Atlanta: Where the South Stops" or "Atlanta: It's Atnalta Spelled Backwards."[51]

As they struggle to recover their sense of themselves, white southerners might take note of George B. Tindall's observation that "to change is not necessarily to lose one's identity, to change sometimes is to find it." Readers of the *Atlanta Journal-Constitution* were treated to a case in point recently when the newspaper's management decided to offer its readers a new but no less southern perspective by choosing widely read syndicated columnist Rheta Grimsley Johnson as the successor to the phenomenally popular but duly departed Lewis Grizzard. Conservative — and sometimes reactionary — Grizzard had epitomized the ambivalence of many white southerners who have embraced the economic and material benefits that have come their way while remaining skeptical and sometimes resentful of some of the social and political changes that have accompanied these gains.[52]

Grizzard's small-town boyhood and adolescence in tiny Moreland, Georgia, provided him with a huge repertoire of stories about local characters (usually caricatures thereof). A master storyteller, he laced his stories with country colloquialisms such as "bad to drink" or "come up a real bad cloud." (The former is self-explanatory, the latter describes the onset of a severe thunderstorm.) His candid country-boy perspective shaped his reaction to all of his experiences. In a hilarious story entitled "There Ain't No Toilet Paper in Russia," he described Peter the Great's palace as "fifteen times bigger than Opryland."[53]

An unabashed participant in rat killings and other "redneck traditions" as a youth, Grizzard nonetheless confessed to having twice seen Pavarotti live — once in Paris and once in London—to having sat through at least the first act of *The Marriage of Figaro,* and to visiting the Louvre. To compound matters, Grizzard owned two pairs of Guccis, wore Geoffrey Beane cologne, and used the gun rack behind the seat of his truck to hold his golf clubs. Yet, although he had eaten caviar at Maxim's in Paris, Grizzard insisted that he liked pork barbecue better. He was also quick to remind "transplanted Yankees who deliver long diatribes about the South's shortcomings" that "Delta is ready when you are." As the foregoing suggests, Grizzard grew increasingly frustrated as he grew older and found the world changing too rapidly and in a direction of which he disapproved. Hence, in his next-to-last book, *I Haven't Understood Anything Since 1962 (And Other Nekkid Truths)*, he wrote, "I think there are a lot of other people like me . . . sick of being afraid to speak the truth, sick of groups like the Queer Nation, the ACLU, and the National Association of Women Who Would Just Like to Beat the Hell Out of Every Man They See."[54]

If it might have been — and often was — said of Grizzard that "he's bad to drink, but he's a good ol' boy," it was equally appropriate to say of Johnson, "She's a liberal, but she's a good ol' girl." Whereas Grizzard once claimed that his grandmother was the only person he knew who believed "the moonshot's fake and wrestlin's real," Johnson's Grandma Lucille also thought the lunar landing had been staged in the Arizona or Nevada desert. Grizzard would certainly have approved of Johnson's column, written in reflection on her first day at work on her new job in Atlanta, in which she recalled her family's Colquitt, Georgia, roots. Johnson remembered that even after her family had moved to Alabama (which is in the Central Time Zone), her mother insisted on keeping her schedule according to Eastern Standard, "Georgia time," and on maintaining a subscription to the *Miller County (Ga.) Liberal* so that she could keep up with the doings back in Colquitt. Grizzard would have been less than thrilled with Johnson's next column, however, which she devoted to an enthusiastic account of the life and promising career of a gay country singer from Tupelo, Mississippi. Like Grizzard, Johnson often bristles at condescending Yankee critics, but her approach to the South is considerably less defensive, more tolerant of change and diversity, but also more focused on such once-familiar regional staples as people, place, and memory.[55]

Jimmie L. Franklin stressed these themes in his 1993 presidential address to the Southern Historical Association. Only the second black scholar to preside over this organization, Franklin expressed his belief in a "shared past between black and white southerners." Earlier, he had insisted that "when we begin to test for the existence of common cultural values . . . we see reflected amid hardship and sorrow ingredients of southern life that often transcended race or ethnicity — matters of manners and morals, folk beliefs and foodways, blended musical forms, material culture and others." Ralph Ellison put it more succinctly when, shortly before his death in 1994, he insisted — in a statement strikingly reminiscent of the observation offered by W. J. Cash more than fifty years ago — that "you can't be Southern without being black and you can't be a black Southerner without being white." Such sentiments were heartfelt and appealing, but they also were more wishful than specific, much like the pronouncements of a host of other southerners, both black and white, who appreciated, as did white journalist Brandt Ayers, the "whole amazing pageant of southern history — the saga of migration from continent to continent and from farm to city, of wars waged and lost, of atrocities committed and borne, of loving and hating, of the long trek from poverty to better times — a journey that blacks and whites took together."[56]

Many years ago Richard Weaver insisted that "being a southerner is definitely a spiritual condition, like being a Catholic or a Jew, and members of the group can recognize one another by signs which are eloquent to them, though too small to be noticed by an outsider." At the time of Weaver's observation, however, "southerner" was a designation reserved for whites only. The fact that the term is no longer color-coded does not imply the resurrection of such a southern spiritual community held together by regional bonds rather than set apart by racial barriers, although the widespread longing among both black and white southerners for a renewed sense of kinship with people and place suggests that possibility is at least not as remote as it once seemed.[57]

Always able to see irony more quickly and clearly than many of his peers, C. Vann Woodward noted with obvious pleasure that, contrary to the warnings of the Citizens Councils, rather than destroy southern culture, the Civil Rights movement may have actually saved it. In reality, Woodward might have been a bit more accurate had he credited the Civil Rights movement with giving southerners the *opportunity*, or better yet, the *responsibility* to save southern culture.[58]

Hopefully, this is not another Lost Cause, but neither is it any piddling assignment. Edwin Yoder observed that during the Civil Rights era, "when so much of national importance was happening in and to the South . . . we southerners were studied hard, everywhere, like savages brought in from a newly discovered continent in the Elizabethan Age." These days, however, Yoder senses that many Americans simply react with "boredom and impatience" to pleas that the South remains a distinctive entity worthy of special attention, and he confesses to feeling a "certain burden and exertion in keeping it alive" himself.[59]

As Yoder's comments suggest, the struggle to solve the riddle of Southern identity once captivated the entire nation; now southerners confront that challenge by themselves and for themselves. For blacks and whites alike, the urge to affirm their southernness grows out of a need to resurrect a sense of community that seems very much endangered, both by their progress toward the mainstream of American life and by the loss of identity this progress seems to entail. This concern with regional identity is especially acute in an era when economic disparity, political polarization, a rising tide of violence, and other pathologies threaten to rip apart the social fabric, even as the new global economy is rapidly rendering distinctions among nations themselves increasingly obsolete.

Skirmishes over the Confederate flag and the playing of "Dixie" seem like pretty tame stuff compared to the tanks and mortars being used to settle questions of cultural identity elsewhere in the world. Still, the parallels are instructive and sobering. In a no-longer segregated South, two well-defined ethnic groups are struggling to coexist peacefully under a common cultural canopy. Endowed by their history with a distinctive regional heritage, they now face the challenge of recovering from that conflict-ridden past a common attachment to something meaningful and enduring. Whether or not black and white southerners will succeed in their efforts to reconstruct what Ayers calls a "composite culture of the South" may well depend less on their ability to agree than on their willingness to tolerate disagreement about an identity that, to preserve, they must first learn to share.

From
"New South"
to
"No South"

The Southern Renaissance and the

Struggle with Southern Identity

Novelist Walker Percy grew so tired of hearing about the "New South" that he once quipped, "My definition of a New South would be a South in which it never occurred to anybody to mention the New South." In its most recent incarnation, "New South" has implied a region thoroughly transformed and so totally discontinuous with its troubled past that it would in reality be not so much a "New South" as what George Washington Cable referred to as a "No South," fully assimilated and essentially indistinguishable from the rest of American society. In the late nineteenth century, the original "New South Creed," as Paul Gaston called it, promised economic change without the sacrifice of racial, political, and cultural continuity. Defeated and embittered, southern whites found inspiration and energy in the New South Creed's assurances of a golden age ahead and comfort and consolation in its carefully constructed vision of a golden age behind, a stirring, romanticized portrayal of an antebellum heritage to be preserved and celebrated rather than surrendered and forgotten. Espousing a powerful mixture of myths about the past, illusions about the present, and fantasies about the future, New South spokesmen succeeded in creating a new and enduring regional identity. As Michael O'Brien observed, "the New South helped to make permanent the very idea of a South."[1]

Daniel J. Singal has pointed to the pervasive and enduring influence of the New South Creed as the principal obstacle to the arrival of intellectual modernism in the region. In fact, the struggle to unravel the tangle of myth and contradiction that lay at the heart of the New South Creed was a central dynamic within the post–World War I Southern Renaissance. Ellen Glasgow and Frank L. Owsley were but two of the participant-observers who noted, in Owsley's words, "the intellectual and moral sterility" induced by the "'New South gospel'" and insisted that the literary and scholarly outpouring of the Southern Renaissance represented in large part "a revolt against the philosophy of the New South." Certainly, this was true of W. J. Cash's *Mind of the South*. A bold revision of the region's history, a sharply critical analysis of its contemporary condition, and a skeptical, even fearful, assessment of what lay ahead, Cash's book was also, in historian Richard King's words, "a quintessential expression of the regional self-scrutiny which marked the Southern Renaissance."[2]

Because, as Singal pointed out, "cultures typically take their shape from the culture being rejected," a clearer understanding of the origins and substance of the New South Creed can provide a useful starting point for a reassessment of the Southern Renaissance itself. Shaped by antebellum sectional conflict and hardened by the Civil War and Reconstruction, the concept of the South as "an object of patriotism" manifested itself in the postbellum white South's "savage ideal" of violence and intolerance in defense of the social and political status quo. It also permeated the New South's aggressive crusade for economic progress characterized by Cash as "a sort of new charge at Gettysburg which should finally and incontestably win for it the right to be itself for which, in the last analysis, it had always fought." In fact, "the New South meant and boasted of," Cash explained, "was mainly a South which would be new in this: that it would be so rich and powerful that it might rest serene in its ancient positions, forever impregnable." In support of his contention, Cash quoted an 1880 editorial from the *Raleigh News and Observer* arguing that "the South should . . . make money, build up its waste places, and thus force from the North that recognition of our worth and dignity of character to which that people will always be blind unless they can see it through the medium of material strength."[3]

As Cash saw it in 1941, the New South could best be understood as "not quite a nation within a nation but the next thing to it." In reality, of course, New South proponents were not aiming to establish an independent economic and political state but rather, in Gaston's words, to assure "the South's dominance in the reunited nation." Still, Cash's description of the New South as a quasi-national entity whose leaders were intent on utilizing new means to gain vindication of its ancient ideals is nonetheless helpful. Certainly, it can enhance our understanding of how the proponents of the New South Creed succeeded in constructing a new cultural identity through a process similar to the one typically employed to create the "imagined political community" that Benedict Anderson offered as his definition of a nation. Regardless of the process, the invention of a national identity is far from unusual. The Third French Republic, Bismarckian Germany, Pakistan, Israel, Khomeini's Iran, a number of states in the former Soviet Union, and the recent and distant pasts of many other societies in both hemispheres and a variety of latitudes present vivid examples.[4]

New national identities often come equipped with an appealing vision of the future, but an inspiring, emotionally charged past is an even more fundamental feature. As several scholars have noted, the first step in establishing the credibility of new identities is to assert their antiquity, or at least their ties to antiquity. The destruction of slavery as well as the decisiveness of the South's defeat in the Civil War clearly precluded any effort to revive the "Old" South as such. Moreover, the loss of slave capital (the primary source of capital in the antebellum era) and the challenge of reviving southern agriculture on a free-labor basis in an age of flagging world market demand for cotton soon demonstrated the wisdom of building a dynamic, diversified, modernized industrial economy modeled on that of the North. In the wake of the bitterly humiliating experience of Radical Reconstruction, however, white southerners would surely have rejected any effort at regional resuscitation that smacked of capitulation to the Yankees or a repudiation of the Confederate cause or their antebellum heritage.[5]

As a result, Gaston explained, the crusade to build a New South involved "more than a program of building on the ashes. Somehow the ashes themselves had to be ennobled." Consequently, even as New South apostle Henry Grady preached the merits of economic modernization, he paid unceasing tribute to the "exquisite culture" of the Old South and insisted that "the civilization of the old slave regime in the South has not been surpassed, and perhaps will not be equaled among men." Grady found a valuable ally in writer Thomas Nelson Page, the supreme glorifier of that old regime, who saw in the Old South "the purest sweetest life ever lived," one that "made men noble, gentle, and brave and women tender and pure."[6]

To be sure, neither Grady nor Page was starting from scratch with the invention of the myth of a glorious Old South. The notion of a genteel, refined plantation aristocracy had emerged in the colonial era and matured in response to the increasingly critical pressures of abolitionist attacks during the second quarter of the nineteenth century. According to Drew Faust, in the wake of secession the concept of a Confederate identity resulted from "a widespread and self-conscious effort to create an ideology . . . to unite and inspire the new nation." The Confederate South needed affirmation of "the conservatism and continuity of its revolution" that, in fact, "its new departure was, in reality, no departure at all."[7]

Hoping to offer similar reassurance of continuity to white southerners of the Redeemer Era, the architects of the New South not only emphasized the magnificence of the antebellum regime and the heroism of the Confederate "Lost Cause" but insisted on an umbilical connection between the New South and the Old. When he insisted that the New South was "simply the Old South with its energies directed into new lines," Page sounded remarkably like Grady when he insisted that the New South was simply "the Old South under new conditions." All of this seemed like so much doublespeak, but for the most part, these New South zealots seemed oblivious to the contradictions inherent in the creed they espoused. Responding to Georgian Charles C. Jones Jr.'s attack on the New South movement's perceived threat to Old South values, former Confederate general P. G. T. Beauregard simply reassured him that "we are already on the road to prosperity and ere long the South shall have regained the influence it once enjoyed in the Councils of the Nation."[8]

Such blurring of the distinctions between past and future glories is far from uncommon in other societies where the proponents of nationalism (who, not infrequently, are also the proponents of modernization) often seek support for their efforts through appeals to a sense of identification with and pride in a particular version of their nation's history. As recently as 1978, for example, Anwar Sadat praised his fellow Egyptians as "a people who are working for a modern civilization comparable to the one they erected thousands of years ago."[9]

As Sadat's comments suggest, nationalist movements often seek popular support by embellishing their own accomplishments as well as those of their ancestors. In the case of the New South, even as the region's first golden age was being venerated, its second one was declared to be already at hand. The New South crusade was hardly launched before its proponents were lustily, if implausibly, proclaiming victory. By mid-1886, Henry Grady was insisting that "we are entering upon an almost ideal era of progress," and by the end of the year as he prepared to deliver his famous "New South" address at Delmonico's in New York, he saw "a tidal wave of prosperity . . . rushing over this region."[10]

The creation of any new group identity typically requires the "invention of tradition," which, according to Eric Hobsbawm, is likely to occur wherever and whenever "a rapid transformation of society weakens or destroys the social patterns for which 'old' traditions had been designed." These invented traditions often secure the emotional allegiance of the populace at large through the veneration of a particular flag, symbol, song, significant historical event, or national hero (in the case of the New South, the leaders of the Confederacy, including even the once-despised Jefferson Davis, fit the bill nicely). As Charles R. Wilson has pointed out, the New South's invention of tradition even shaped architectural trends, spurring the postbellum resurgence of the Greek Revival style that had never been prevalent throughout the antebellum South and had even been on the decline by 1850. As Wilson put it, by the early twentieth century, "tradition dictated . . . that the southern legend needed not only high cotton but high columns as well."[11]

Invented traditions can be functional and pragmatic as well as symbolic. In the case of the New South, an obvious example of an invented tradition was racial segregation, which, as John Cell made clear, was "nothing less than an organic component of the New South Creed." Grady and his cohorts were quick to point out that a stable racial climate was the key to maintaining an attractive investment climate for northern capital. Accordingly, racial separation became a prominent theme in Grady's speeches as early as 1883, and by 1885, he was insisting that the doctrine of separate but equal should apply "in every theatre" as well as in "railroads, schools, and elsewhere."[12]

Segregation became one of the New South's invented traditions in response not only to the destruction of slavery but to the expansion of the region's railroads and the concomitant movement of the population into the region's urban areas and industrial workplaces. All of these developments increased the likelihood that the two races would come in contact — and into conflict — without the controlling presence or influence of slavery. As racial tensions rose and racial violence flared, the wisdom of both the federal retreat from Reconstruction and the transfer of northern capital to the South might well be called into question. In the long run, racial harmony and, hence, an attractive investment climate, could be insured, argued Grady and his associates, only by the white South's being allowed to handle the region's racial problems without fear of further interference from Washington. "Otherwise," Cell explained, "the tense divisiveness of the Reconstruction era might return."[13]

Because Grady and his colleagues blamed the unsettled racial conditions in the late-nineteenth-century South on its tragically misguided policies, the widely held perception of Reconstruction as a reckless social experiment that brought untold horrors and suffering to the white South became as crucial an element of the New South version of southern history as the genteel Old South and the heroic Confederate South. The New South's racial ethic found its ultimate literary expression in the novels of the Rev. Thomas Dixon, who painted horrific portraits of Reconstruction as he endorsed the resubjugation of blacks and embraced industrialization as the South's salvation.[14]

Meanwhile, Grady insisted that if his fate was left "to those among whom his lot is cast . . . the negro will find that his best friend is the southern democrat." What the New South's proponents actually sought, however, was the regional equivalent of white supremacist "home rule" in both social and political relations, the former through institutionalized racial separation and the latter through institutionalized denial of the vote to blacks. Disfranchisement quickly purged the electorate of almost all potential black voters and a great many lower-class white ones as well, thereby assuring the Democratic party's dominance and facilitating the invention of yet another New South tradition — one-party politics. Effectively insulated from lower-class insurgency, conservative white Democrats soon enjoyed a stranglehold on political power, returning to Washington year after year and capitalizing on their seniority in Congress to give southern political leaders a good measure of the political self-determination that New South advocates sought.[15]

As transparent and contrived as it may seem in retrospect, the New South Creed was one potent piece of mythology. It painted an almost seamless and undeniably seductive mural in which a glorious past, a reassuring present, and a glittering future were fully integrated and virtually indistinguishable. The Old South legend was the emotional and psychological cornerstone of the New South ideal, but where the antebellum Cavalier had been done in by forces beyond his control or even his comprehension, his New South descendants were firmly in command of their own destinies. As champions of past, present, and future, the New South crusaders were in an all but impregnable position while anyone who challenged them could be readily cast as the opponents of progress, tradition, and, for good measure, the status quo as well.

The New South Creed resembled nationalist ideologies both in its emotional and psychological appeal and in what Anderson might call its "philosophical poverty and even incoherence." Thus, like other architects of national or group identity, the ranks of the New South apostles included Henry Grady, Frances W. Dawson, Richard H. Edmonds, and a number of eloquent and persuasive orators, scribes, and unabashed propagandists but no critical, analytical "grand thinkers." This was hardly surprising; the New South Creed's attempt to create a sense of "deep horizontal comradeship" in the face of overwhelming evidence of inequality, exploitation, and even conflict simply required, as Hobsbawm put it, "too much belief in what is patently not so." [16]

Although the New South Creed clearly remained the dominant ideology among late-nineteenth-century southern white political, economic, and intellectual leaders, its contradictions, inconsistencies, and inaccuracies were too blatant and significant to escape challenge altogether. The first generation of postbellum southern intellectuals generally shared a belief that economic modernization was the answer to a multitude of the region's ills. Still, by no means all of them accepted the romanticized version of antebellum southern life, nor did all of them embrace the hyperbole and ballyhoo about the era of progress already at hand, or, beyond that, define progress solely in terms of factories and profits. In fact, as they challenged the New South Creed these early critics raised important questions and suggested crucial themes that would ultimately engage many of the leading figures of the twentieth-century Southern Renaissance.

Walter Hines Page could sound, at times, every bit as boosterist as Henry Grady. Yet, he showed nothing but disdain for the enduring traditions that held the South back, and he urged his fellow southerners to think more about building schools than erecting monuments to the Confederate dead. Insisting that his native state needed nothing quite so badly as a "few first class funerals," Page sounded remarkably like H. L. Mencken and his South-baiting minions three decades later when he described North Carolina as "the laughing stock among the states" and declared, "There is not a man whose residence is in the state who is recognized by the world as an authority on anything." A staunch proponent of economic progress, Page nonetheless expressed his doubts about what the New South had actually achieved. Describing Page as "a more effective critic of Southern sloth, poverty, and intellectual and cultural sterility than any southerner of his generation," Fred Hobson explained that when Page "looked at Dixie, what he saw was a problem South, the same South that Howard W. Odum and the social scientists would see and seek to remake thirty or forty years later."[17]

Like most his white contemporaries, Page saw the "Negro Problem" as essentially unsolvable and more of a problem for whites than for blacks. This was clearly not the case, however, with Charles Chesnutt, who, as Wayne Mixon points out, criticized the New South movement "from the perspective of the man most neglected by it, the Negro." Chesnutt's irony-laden short story "The March of Progress" posed the complex dilemma of a black community facing the decision of whether to appoint as teacher of their new grammar school a white woman, "Miss Noble," who had already given long years of service in the black schools and community or to hire "Mr. Williams," a young man who had once been one of her star pupils. One of Mr. Williams's supporters insisted that "the march of progress requires that we help ourselves," because despite the best efforts of blacks to educate their children, "the white people won't hire 'em as clerks in their sto's and factories an' mills an' we have no sto's or factories of our own." Lacking funds to educate their youths as doctors or lawyers and unable to elect them to office, blacks faced the reality that the "two things" these young black people could do were to "preach in our own pulpits and teach in our schools." Otherwise, "they'd have to go on waitin' on white folks, like their ol' fathers have done because they couldn't help it."[18]

After being shamed into acknowledging Miss Noble's many kindnesses and sacrifices in their behalf, however, the school committee votes unanimously to hire Miss Noble, but upon receiving the news, the frail white teacher collapses and dies. A suitable period of mourning ensues, and "two weeks after Miss Noble's funeral, the other candidate took charge of the grammar school, which went on without any further obstacles to the march of progress."[19]

Though he lived most of his adult life in Chicago, Chesnutt wrote as a southerner, and his concerns about the direction in which the New South was headed transcended racial lines. In fact, his final novel, *The Colonel's Dream,* directed considerable attention on the plight of the New South's overworked and exploited poor whites. In detailing the frustrated efforts of Colonel French, a chivalrous ex-Confederate, who sought to blend the best of Old South ideals with the economic benefits of New South progress, Chesnutt exposed the conditions confronting many white workers in the New South. When Colonel French asks citizens about conditions in the mill, a local liveryman fairly explodes: "Talk about nigger slavery — the niggers never were worked like white women and children are in them mills. . . . When I look at them white gals, that ought to be rosy-cheeked an' bright-eyed an' plump an' hearty an' happy, an' them po' little child'en that never get a chance to go fishin' or swimmin' or to learn anything, I allow I wouldn' mind if the durned old mill would catch fire an' burn down. They work children there from six years old up, an' half o 'em die of consumption before they're grown."[20]

Like Chesnutt, a few of his white contemporaries challenged the Jim Crow system within the context of a broader critique of the entire New South Movement. The son of a slaveholder and a Confederate veteran himself, George Washington Cable seemed an unlikely critic of southern racial practices, but in several novels and numerous speeches and essays Cable attempted to call forth a "Silent South" of humane, fair-minded whites who would challenge the region's racial code and restore the civil rights of black southerners.[21]

Across subsequent generations, southern liberals would repeatedly attempt to awaken and rally this potentially dominant though still slumbering constituency against the irrational, racist, and reactionary white masses and the demagogic politicoes who so crudely but effectively manipulated their prejudices and shortcomings, often with tragic effect. Cable's call for racial justice came within the context of his overall critique of the New South movement, and he offered some poetic mockery of Henry Grady's famous New South speech, which essentially ignored the region's racial problems. Cable was quick to praise the eloquence of "Grady" but equally quick to point out that "on MEN'S EQUAL RIGHTS, The darkest of nights, Compared with him wouldn't seem shady."[22]

Although Cable believed that economic development would benefit the South, he also shuddered at the materialism, rapacity, and almost delusional boosterism that characterized the New South movement. He conveyed these sentiments as well as the overall ambivalence and complexity of his feelings about the South in general in his 1895 novel, *John March, Southerner,* which unfolded against the backdrop of the corruption of the Reconstruction and Redeemer Eras and the blind boosterism and get-rich-quick greed of the New South mentality. As a young man John March is an orthodox, overly proud, and shallow professional southerner. Duped into cooperating with a shady developer who manages to swindle him out of his landed inheritance, March recovers most of his land and, seeing the light, devotes himself to the betterment of his community.[23]

In Cable's novel, mulatto politician Cornelius Legget asks that blacks be given their share of New South prosperity: "White man, ain't eveh goin' to lif hissef up by holdin' niggeh down." Such assertive and perceptive black characters were unknown in the fiction of Cable contemporaries such as Thomas Nelson Page. *John March* also resembled the work of several later southern writers such as William Faulkner, whose characters often struggled to reconcile their affection for the South with their distress at its problems and deficiencies. Seeming to anticipate Quentin Compson's explanation to Harvard roommate Shreve McCannon that "You can't understand it. You would have to be born there," March's future wife tells a northern friend that southerners' affection for the South "was simply something a North-ern-er can't understand," something as intangible and spiritual "as our souls in our bodies."[24]

Not surprisingly, Henry Grady and Cable's other critics accused him of favoring "social intermingling of the races." Despite his denials, the furor over Cable's writings and utterances played no small part in his decision to relocate permanently to New England, where he became an early prototype of the southern expatriate writer of the mid-twentieth century. Likewise, reform-minded southerners of the mid-twentieth century would echo Cable's call for the South to rejoin the nation and the world at large: "When we have done so we shall know it by this . . . there will be no South. . . . We shall no more be Southerners than we shall be Northerners." Cable cared little for preserving the separate identity of the South or its inhabitants. Instead of the "New South," he explained, "what we ought to have in view . . . is the No South."[25]

Page, Cable, and other early critics of the New South Creed raised a number of objections and concerns that would fuel critical discourse about the South for much of the twentieth century. This discourse took on a greater sense of urgency in the years after World War I as developments of the war era affirmed that, in Richard King's words, "the cultural superstructure to which educated and 'enlightened' Southerners gave their allegiance and by which they understood themselves was out of phase with the reality of southern life." As Gaston has argued, myths such as the New South Creed "arise out of complex circumstances to create mental sets which do not ordinarily yield to intellectual attacks." In fact, he added, "the history of their dynamics suggests that they may be penetrated by rational analysis only as the consequence of dramatic, or even traumatic, alterations in the society whose essence they exist to portray." As a consequence, "the critique and dissipation of myths becomes possible only when tension between the mythic view and the reality it sustains snaps the viability of their relationship." By the 1920s, tensions between the New South's myths and its realities seemed to be approaching the snapping point.[26]

Events such as the Leo Frank lynching, the resurgence of the Ku Klux Klan, and the wave of post–World War I racial violence helped to draw unprecedented attention to the South's enduring problems and deficiencies and spurred a multitude of observers within the region and without to reassess more critically the New South version of the status quo in the region. Published in 1924, Frank Tannenbaum's *The Darker Phases of the South* only reaffirmed growing perceptions of southern benightedness. In the same year, expatriated former Alabama Populist William H. Skaggs stepped forward in *The Southern Oligarchy* to focus the attention of Americans at large on the plight of "the great mass of white and colored citizens of the Southern States, who are held in political subjection and economic serfdom." Meanwhile, Oswald Garrison Villard repeatedly deplored the barbarity of lynching in the pages of the *Nation,* while W. E. B. Du Bois assailed southern racial customs in the NAACP's *Crisis.* H. L. Mencken's mockery of a New South that "for all the progress it babbles of" was "almost as sterile, artistically, intellectually, culturally, as the Sahara Desert" won him a corps of slavish imitators among young journalists in Dixie, including Gerald W. Johnson, Nell Battle Lewis, and Wilbur J. Cash.[27]

Within five years after the appearance of Mencken's famous "Sahara of the Bozart" essay, contemporary observers were beginning to speak of the "renaissance" that was by then well under way in southern thought and letters. The most notable explanation for the timing of this flurry of intellectual activity came from Allen Tate, who declared in 1945 that "with the war of 1914–1918, the South re-entered the world — but gave a backward glance as it stepped over the border; that backward glance gave us the Southern renaiscence [*sic*], a literature conscious of the past in the present." Earlier, Tate had alluded to a postwar economic transformation in the South, characterizing the Southern Renaissance as "a curious burst of intelligence that we get at the crossing of the ways, not unlike on an infinitesimal scale, the outburst of poetic genius at the end of the sixteenth century when commercial England had already begun to crush feudal England."[28]

Tate's interpretation has been questioned by a number of latter-day critics, including C. Vann Woodward, who described Tate's "backward glance" and "crossroads" theories as perhaps "necessary conditions" but not "historical explanations" for the Renaissance. Likewise, Michael O'Brien expressed doubt that the South was any more a part of the modern world in 1920 than in 1910. Both O'Brien and Singal challenged Tate's effort to link the Renaissance to economic and social modernization, the latter arguing that the really significant changes in the South's economy and society did not even begin until the New Deal and World War II era when the Renaissance was already well under way.[29]

On the other hand, as Reinhard Bendix has pointed out, in many modernizing societies "changes in the social and political order were apparent before the full consequences of the industrial revolution were understood." Certainly, there is no disputing Richard King's contention that many of the key participants in the Renaissance shared "a pervasive, subjective sense that *something* fundamental had changed in and about the South." Thomas Wolfe would eventually set his classic novel *Look Homeward, Angel* against the backdrop of Asheville's tumultuous emergence as a tourist mecca. Asheville's rapid growth brought prosperity to Wolfe's hard-charging, fast-trading mother but left Wolfe decrying, on the other hand, the New South definition of "Progress" as "more Ford automobiles [and] more Rotary Clubs" and admonishing his mother that "Greater Asheville" did not necessarily mean "100,000 by 1930" and that "we are not necessarily four times as civilized as our grandfathers because we go four times as fast in our automobiles," or "because our buildings are four times as tall."[30]

Elsewhere, although Alabama remained overwhelmingly rural and agricultural in 1930, Clarence Cason expressed concern "with the changes which the inevitable industrial development is making on the social and economic landscape of Alabama." Cason recalled that "fifteen years ago in the town where I lived the important names were invariably those of families who had held their land for generations." Yet it seemed to Cason that "the moment that cotton as a commodity passed from the agricultural to the industrial stage, there were signs of unnaturalness and unfamiliarity on the part of the people." Noting the construction of a "$2,000,000 cotton mill" in his hometown, Cason worried that "our local grocery stores are in imminent danger of being supplanted by chain companies; our drug and dry goods dealers face a similar hazard. We shall have five- and ten-cent emporiums. We shall have new professional men in the town; new doctors, new lawyers, new Ford dealers, new radio men; a new and expanded country club. The owner of our golf club land expects to sell her property to a Kraft paper mill. And we shall have new odors." Extrapolating from his hometown's experience and surveying the South as a whole, Cason concluded that "the old order — which placed living before livelihood — is losing its social and economic grip in many sections of the South."[31]

Finally, writing in 1933 from a still sleepy Oxford, Mississippi, William Faulkner bemoaned the passing of the traditional, communal South that he pronounced "old since dead" at the hands of "a thing known whimsically as the New South." This, he was quite certain, was "not the South" but "a land of immigrants" intent on rebuilding Dixie in the image of "the towns and cities in Kansas and Iowa and Illinois" complete with filling station attendants and waitresses saying "Oh yeah?" and speaking with "hard r's" and once quiet intersections that now boasted "changing red-and-green lights and savage and peremptory bells."[32]

Wolfe, Cason, Faulkner, and a great many other southern writers of the post–World War I era seemed much like their counterparts who lived in modernizing societies in the nineteenth century and, according to Robert A. Nisbet, "exhibit the same burning sense of society's sudden convulsive turn from a path it had followed for millennia." Steeped in the New South's mythology of a glorious past but confronted everywhere with overwhelming contemporary evidence of their region's backwardness, southern intellectuals of the Renaissance Era did in fact have much in common with their counterparts in other "developing" societies. Certainly, in the 1920s the South appeared to reach a point where, as Dewey Grantham put it, "the earlier equilibrium between the forces of modernization and those of cultural tradition could no longer be sustained."[33]

A case in point was the Scopes trial, described by Fred Hobson as "the event that most forcefully dramatized the struggle between Southern provincialism and the modern, secular world . . . the event that caused Southerners to face squarely the matter of the South and their own place in it." A determined proponent of southern progress, Vanderbilt professor Edwin Mims insisted in *The Advancing South* that the Scopes trial did not portray accurately a region where "reactionary forces" actually found themselves besieged by a "rising tide of liberalism." Mims even foresaw a "not far off" time "when scholarship, literature and art shall flourish, and when all things that make for the intellectual and spiritual emancipation of man shall find their home under Southern skies."[34]

Hobson declared that Mims's book was "in most regards a romanticizing of the New South just as surely as Thomas Nelson Page's work was a romanticizing of the old," and, predictably, a disgusted H. L. Mencken dismissed Mims as "the worst sort of academic jackass." Ironically, however, Mims's most strident critics proved to be a group of his colleagues and former students at Vanderbilt. John Crowe Ransom, Donald Davidson, and Allen Tate had, prior to the Scopes trial, shown no particular inclination to challenge either the New South ideal of progress or the steady stream of criticism leveled by Mencken and his disciples. In fact, the founders of and contributors to the literary magazine *The Fugitive* were said to be fleeing the sentimental, romantic "high-caste Brahmins of the Old South," and they even won praise as exemplars of New South enlightenment and progress. The *Nashville Tennessean* remarked, for example, that "*The Fugitive* is an advertising instrument for this city and this state, which reaches a public that could be reached in no other way and by no other means," and the publication actually received a subsidy from the Associated Retailers of Nashville.[35]

As the rabidly boosterist "Atlanta spirit" threatened to infect the entire region, however, the Fugitives began to sense that their real enemies were not the South's literary romanticizers but its economic and cultural modernizers. In 1930 Ransom, Davidson, and Tate joined forces with several of their current or former Vanderbilt colleagues, including historian Frank L. Owsley, English professor John Donald Wade, political scientist Herman C. Nixon, psychologist Lyle Lanier, and Vanderbilt alumnus Robert Penn Warren to publish *I'll Take My Stand: The South and the Agrarian Tradition*. Identifying themselves collectively as *Twelve Southerners,* the authors produced essays that varied widely in subject matter, emphasis, and quality. In general, these essays featured consistently vague tributes to the virtues of "agrarian" life and consistently severe condemnations of "industrialism."[36]

In reality, however, the contributors to *I'll Take My Stand* were less intent on defining agrarianism or even deriding industrialism than rallying their fellow white southerners to rise in revolt against what they saw as the ongoing New South effort to northernize their society. As New South advocates sought to beat the North at its own game by emulating and even surpassing the North's economic achievement, the Agrarians insisted that the South's way of life was already superior to that of the North, and, therefore, the effort to northernize the South's economy was more likely to pull the region down than lift it up. In 1927 Tate announced to Davidson that he would no longer attack the South in any fashion "except in so far as it may be necessary to point out that the chief defect the Old South had was that it produced, through whatever cause, the New South." An enthusiastic Davidson replied, "You know that I'm with you on the anti–New South stuff. . . . I feel so strongly on these points that I can hardly trust myself to write."[37]

In essence, the Agrarians sought in their erudite but diffuse treatises to discredit the dynamic, appealing, economically and politically pragmatic New South doctrine by emphasizing the threat that it posed to southern cultural autonomy. Twenty years after the appearance of *I'll Take My Stand,* Agrarian Frank L. Owsley explained that "much of the bitter resentment of backward peoples in the Orient against, what they term 'Yankee imperialism' is similar to that felt by the contributors to *I'll Take My Stand* in 1930." Expanding on Owsley's comment some thirty years later, John Shelton Reed insisted that "if we ask what else the Agrarians had in common with those backward but anticolonial peoples in the Orient, if we examine *I'll Take My Stand* in the light of nationalist manifestoes from around the world, the similarities are obvious."[38]

Reed explained that

when nationalists come from a nation that is economically "peripheral" in the world economy, one like the South of the 1920s that produced raw materials and supplied unskilled labor for a more "advanced" economy, they often adopt the same stance the Agrarians did, rejecting the western science and technology that, in any case, they do not have, and insisting that their very backwardness in "western" terms has preserved a spiritual and cultural superiority. From the nineteenth-century Slavophils, to the Hindu nationalists of early-twentieth-century India, to the apostles of *negritude,* today, it is easy to find cases of westernized intellectuals assuring the masses of peripheral nations of their superiority to those who dominate them economically and threaten to do so culturally.

Reed's analysis suggested the words of Mohandas Gandhi, who, as he lamented the incursions of western culture and technology into India, insisted "we consider our civilization to be far superior to yours."[39]

New South proponents sought to build an "imagined" cultural community organized around an identifiable and appealing economic and political agenda. The Agrarians, on the other hand, found it more difficult to create an alternative imagined cultural community whose political component was exceedingly obscure and whose only discernible economic program seemed to imply a return to subsistence farming. Some critics hastily pointed out that if it involved subsistence farming, a return to the region's agrarian tradition was both impractical and improbable in the dire economic circumstances of 1930. Others argued that the South actually had little in the way of such a tradition to return to in any event. Ironically, the efforts of the "Twelve Southerners" to invent an anti–New South agrarian tradition was in no small sense a by-product of the modernization effort against which they protested so vehemently. Social scientist Reinhard Bendix provided a useful comparative framework for understanding the historical setting from which the Agrarians emerged and, for that matter, the context in which the larger intellectual awakening of the Southern Renaissance occurred. Observing that in backward nations governments typically play a major role in instigating efforts to promote economic modernization, Bendix also cited the tendency of such nations to emphasize education in the hope of finding a shortcut to bridge the gap between themselves and more advanced societies.[40]

In the late nineteenth century, a number of prominent southern journalists and other observers had begun to tout education as the key to individual and societal economic progress. In the early twentieth century, progressive and business-progressive reformers had installed economic development as a legitimate responsibility of state government and had also advocated fundamental improvements in education. Although per capita spending per pupil was still barely half the national average in 1920, total expenditures for the public schools had increased by 630 percent in the southern states during the first two decades of the twentieth century.[41]

In the model advanced by Bendix, expanded support for education enhances the influence of a society's intelligentsia. This intelligentsia, in turn, generally participates in the initial efforts to free the society from its backwardness, but as time passes, some of its members may become critical of these efforts or even reject them altogether. Citing the Westernizers and Slavophils of Tsarist Russia as examples, Bendix described the schism that is likely to occur "between those who would see their country progress by imitating the more advanced countries and those who denounce that advance as alien and evil and emphasize instead the wellsprings of strength existing among their own people and in their native culture." Educated and well traveled (as the Agrarians certainly were), these latter intellectuals may actually feel somewhat alienated from the masses of their contemporaries, but as the beneficiaries of modernization, they also possess "the ideological vocabulary to interpret their alienation and to defend their culture" and, ironically enough, as Reed notes, "modernization itself is what they protest."[42]

Certainly when the Agrarians looked about them they had ample reason to fear that their efforts to derail the New South crusade had come too late. "Delegations go here and there over the North and East seeking new industries," observed Clarence Cason, who concluded in 1930 that "in desperation the South has taken up the cry that industry, a heathen god, alone can save its people." Clearly, this uninhibited fervor for factories was nothing short of abhorrent to the Agrarians, but just as they scorned the unthinking or not-thoughtful-enough boosters like Mims who embraced the New South concept of progress too wholeheartedly, as southern cultural supremacists they also attacked those southerners who occupied themselves with documenting and publicizing the South's defects and working tirelessly to help the region "catch up" with the rest of the nation.[43]

Thus one of the principal targets of the Agrarians (within the South, at least) was University of North Carolina sociologist Howard W. Odum, who led his "regionalist" disciples in unloosing an avalanche of statistics and social research data pointing to the need to modernize the South's economy and institutions through a scientific, planned effort to promote both industrial development and agricultural revitalization. Odum's insistence on a realistic, candid appraisal of southern problems led him to reject the Agrarians' treatises as fanciful and vague, but it likewise set him squarely at odds with "the gross spirit of materialism" and the self-serving optimism that characterized the New South Creed. Established in 1922, Odum's *Journal of Social Forces* became the principal outlet for discussions of the South's deficiencies and failures and the inadequacies of southern leadership and institutions. Odum boldly proclaimed that the South needed "criticism and severe criticism," and H. L. Mencken, who had certainly done his share of criticizing, cited Odum as the key figure in getting the Southern Renaissance "in motion."[44]

As historian Mary Matossian has pointed out, intellectuals in non-Western societies facing the challenge of "Westernization" often adopt a position that is "ambiguous, embracing the polar extremes of Xenophobia and Xenophilia." The post–World War I South's intellectual polarization over "northernization" or "Americanization" manifested itself in the conflict between the Nashville Agrarians and Odum and his disciples, who became known as the Chapel Hill Regionalists. Beyond that, however, as did a host of other key figures in the Southern Renaissance, Odum struggled on a personal level with the intense emotional divisions and anxieties that could also be wrought by the prospect of wholesale changes in an intellectual's society and culture. Bendix observed that as intellectuals search for a means of overcoming their country's backwardness "a typical part of this search consists in the ambivalent job of preserving or strengthening the indigenous character of the native culture while attempting to close the gap created by the advanced development of the 'reference society or societies.'" Bendix's observation could hardly have described Howard Odum better.[45]

While Mencken saw the Scopes trial as nothing short of a laugh riot, at Dayton Odum saw "more pathos than joke, more futility than fighting, more tragedy than comedy." Odum's ambivalence toward his own region permeated his *American Epoch,* which appeared a month before *I'll Take My Stand.* He explained, somewhat oxymoronically, that his approach in *American Epoch* represented a "new romantic realism," and he described the book itself as a "critical analysis based upon sympathetic understanding of facts." In successive chapters, "The Glory That Was the South" and "The Grandeur That Was Not," Odum offered a contrasting and thoroughly confusing portrait of erudite, genteel, and benevolent planters and loyal slaves on the one hand and the "extreme snobbishness" of an "imitation-aristocracy," as well as violence, and racial and social injustice on the other.[46]

As Wayne D. Brazil explained, although Odum "intended his exploration of the region's past to help explain its current condition," he failed generally to "define the specific lines of influence" or evaluate the relative importance of key historical factors. Still, as a partly fictionalized history of Odum's own family over four generations (the two principal characters, the old Major and Uncle John, were Odum's own grandfathers), *American Epoch* also amounted to an ambitious social, economic, political, and cultural history of the nineteenth-century South. Despite its ambivalence and imprecision, Odum's book anticipated the efforts of later writers who proved more effective in exploring the ties between the South's past and present. In fact, Odum's approach in *American Epoch* suggested the direction of some of the best writing of the Southern Renaissance, including that of Odum protégés C. Vann Woodward and W. J. Cash, as well as that of William Faulkner, whom Odum admired for daring to ask whether the South might well have both a "barbaric past" and "a flowed and cherished past."[47]

Unlike Odum, many of the critical commentators on the South in the 1920s seemed too astonished by the ongoing panorama of ignorance and depravity it presented to reflect seriously on the historical context from which this sorry state of affairs had evolved. H. L. Mencken's contempt for the claims of New South progress was obvious enough, but he was at times an all but uncritical admirer of the Old South, at one point even bemoaning the "Calamity of Appomattox" that led to the demise of "a civilization of manifold excellences . . . undoubtedly the best that These States have ever seen." To Mencken the "philistinism" of the New South "town-boomer southerner" seemed "inconceivably hollow and obnoxious" and "positively antagonistic" to "the ideals of the Old South." Embracing what was at best only a simplistic and superficial historical perspective, Mencken saw the New South as simply the Old South reduced to rubble. For him, the period of southern history since Appomattox could be summed up succinctly: "It would be impossible in all history to match so complete a drying up of a civilization."[48]

Mencken's disciples largely spurned the historical approach as well. In 1929 North Carolina journalist and Mencken devotee Wilbur J. Cash offered his perspective on "The Mind of the South" in Mencken's *American Mercury*. Essentially a prospectus for the book he would finally complete eleven years later, Cash's article ridiculed the contemporary reality of a New South that was "a chicken-pox of factories on the Watch-Us-Grow maps," dismissed "the New South formula" as "scarcely more than wind," and rejected the New South's leaders as "a handful of parvenus" who had "begotten no new cultural noblesse" and were in fact the "sworn enemies" not only of the arts but of "all ideas dating after 1400." Under their misguidance, Cash believed, the South would simply repeat "the dismal history of Yankeedom" and "exchange the Confederate for that dreadful fellow, the go-getter . . . the Hon. John LaFarge Beauregard for George F. Babbitt."[49]

Cash's article devoted little attention to the region's antebellum class structure or, for that matter, the larger historical setting from which the New South identity had emerged. In fact, Cash wrote largely in the shadow of Mencken, who had insisted that "in the great days of the south [*sic*] the line between the gentry and the poor whites was very sharply drawn." Shortly after his article appeared, Cash sent Howard Odum a synopsis of his proposed book in which he seemed simply to echo Mencken in his facile generalizations about the Old South's "static and paternal order" with its "landowners on the one hand, and the slaves and poor whites on the other." In response, Odum gently cautioned him not to "draw the lines very closely between the different cultural groups of the South," because "many of the beautiful old homes and great families grew up from log cabins in the pioneer wilderness, enlarged and rebuilt and then entirely transcended by the big house." Cash expressed great interest in Odum's suggestion and explained that he had "ploughed through all the histories I know," but save for U. B. Phillips's *Life and Labor in the Old South,* he had found little discussion of "the lack of distinct lines between classes in the Old South."[50]

Cash's admission was hardly surprising, given the uncritical, almost hagiographic approach that prevailed among New South historians. Reacting to the regional chauvinism that dominated and shaped the contributions of those who sought to chronicle the South's past, historian William E. Dodd had pointed out in 1904 that certain lines of investigation or argument were best avoided by historians of the South. For example, "to suggest that the revolt from the union in 1860 was not justified, was not led by the most lofty minded of statesmen, is to invite not only criticism but an enforced resignation."[51]

The romance of the Lost Cause was not the only ideological challenge confronting historians of the South. There was also the uncritical boosterism of the New South creed with its insistence on miraculous achievement, thoroughgoing progress, and racial and class harmony. As Dodd observed, "According to Southern public opinion, the whole race question is finally settled, never to be opened again, and in matters further removed from the field of politics, such as literature and art, it is exceedingly dangerous to give voice to adverse criticism of the South's attainments in the South or of her present status."[52]

As Paul Gaston summarized it, the "central theme" of the writings of New South historians was "the concept of triumph over adversity, of steel will and impeccable character overcoming staggering problems, often against what seemed impossible odds. The South depicted in most of these early histories rose from the extraordinary devastation of Reconstruction to a glorious plateau of achievement." The preface to Phillip Alexander Bruce's *The Rise of the New South* praised the volume as "a vital narration of the progress of a mighty people, who, from adversity which as no other section of North America has ever experienced" had risen and "won the race with adverse fate and become the pride of the Union."[53]

In the hands of many writers, the history of the New South was as romantic as that of the Old. In *The Rise of the Cotton Mills in the South,* Broadus Mitchell even promised readers that his story was "not only an industrial chronicle, but a romance, a drama as well." Mitchell proved as good as his word, as he consistently presented the nineteenth-century southern cotton mill builders as "philanthropists of the first order" who were "far-seeing, public-minded, generous-natural leaders" and whose motivation for building their mills stemmed "as much from altruism as any other cause." True to the New South myth, Mitchell presented his mill builders as direct descendants of the antebellum cavaliers who brought their instinctive paternalism direct from the plantation to the factory. Mitchell eventually broke with the New South tradition of venerating the Lost Cause, even proposing to melt down all of Richmond's Confederate monuments and turn them into "splendid gutters and downspouts," but his continuing insistence on portraying the original mill builders as philanthropic paternalists helped to demonstrate, as Singal explained, "the extraordinary power that could be wielded by the New South ideology over one of the most intelligent, learned, and compassionate southerners of his era."[54]

The New South identity's roots in a romanticized and strikingly nationalistic version of the region's history affirmed Eric Hobsbawm's insistence that "history is the raw material for nationalist or ethnic or fundamentalist ideologies, as poppies are the material for heroin addiction. The past is an essential element, perhaps *the* essential element in these ideologies." Hobsbawm might have been referring specifically to the New South historians both when he noted that "if there is no suitable past, it can always be invented" and when he observed that "the past legitimizes" by giving "a more glorious background to a present that doesn't have much to show for itself." Hobsbawm's comments may well suggest why the real flowering of the Southern Renaissance came in the 1930s as southern intellectuals of all sorts began to focus more of their critical attention on the historical raw material that went into the construction of the New South identity, attempting to understand how such a genteel, glorious past could have degenerated into such a dismal, defective present and developing what Louis Rubin described as the distinctive "two-way pull, the past-and-present perspectives that existed simultaneously in the writers of the Southern Renaissance."[55]

In the absence of a critical historical tradition, the intensifying focus on the relationship between the South's past and present meant that a great many southern intellectuals were practicing history without a license in the 1930s. Donald Davidson observed in 1937 that "The Historian's question — What the South was? — and the related question — What the South is? — underlie every important literary work or social investigation of the past fifteen years." Davidson's observation applied not only to his Nashville Agrarian colleagues but to their Regionalist adversaries Howard Odum and Rupert Vance in Chapel Hill as well.[56]

Vance's contributions to the study of southern history were particularly significant. Heavily influenced by U. B. Phillips's treatments of the antebellum South, Vance shared Phillips's respect for the influence of the frontier on southern history, but he broke with Phillips on the interaction between plantation and frontier. Where Phillips saw the planters' gentility imposing a countervailing influence against the rugged individualism and rough-and-tumble folk culture spawned by the frontier, Vance saw the plantation reinforcing, perpetuating, and passing on the problematic influences of the frontier to the New South. Largely anticipating the argument that W. J. Cash would make several years later, Vance insisted that "while they were formative, the folkways of the South got the stamp of the frontier. From the frontier, part of the area passed to the plantation, but the plantation area retained many of the frontier traits." Odum had seemed to be saying much the same thing when he noted that the southeast reflected "a sort of arrested frontier pattern of life." As Singal observed, "Almost everywhere he turned in surveying the modern South, Vance discovered that the basic patterns of the frontier still prevailed. The region continued to make its living by exploiting its natural resources heedlessly, applying little capital, skill or technology, with dramatically low levels of income and living standards the result."[57]

Whereas Phillips had stressed the importance of environmental influences in shaping the southern (white) character, Vance insisted that "history, not geography, made the solid South." Like Odum's, Vance's work was cited and quoted again and again by southern historians, and he frequently reviewed books for the *Journal of Southern History*. Vance was known for his encyclopedic grasp of southern history and held informal tutorials for graduate students at Chapel Hill. The editors of the Louisiana State University Press's "History of the South" series even invited Vance to write the volume in that series that was to follow C. Vann Woodward's *Origins of the New South, 1877–1913*. Vance eventually abandoned that project, but such a connection with Woodward would have been fitting, for Vance exerted a profound influence on Woodward, encouraging and challenging him as a graduate student at Chapel Hill and continuing to read and critique Woodward's work well into the 1950s.[58]

One of the first professional historians to attack the historical foundations of the New South identity, Woodward joined Vance and the other southern intellectuals of the 1930s who were intent on making the past more accountable to the present. When he arrived at the University of North Carolina in 1934, Woodward expected to be caught up in the same "surge of innovation and creativity" that was sweeping the southern literary scene, but the zealous young graduate student was sorely disappointed as he surveyed his own chosen field, where he found "no renaissance . . . no rebirth of energy, no compelling new vision." Far from "making waves," the masters of southern history were "united not so much in their view of the past as in their dedication to the present order, the system founded on the ruins of Reconstruction called the New South."[59]

Already inclined to liberal activism, the young historian plunged into a career that over the next two decades would help to revolutionize the study of southern history. As a fledgling scholar, however, Woodward proceeded with caution and indirection: "To attack the ramparts of the establishment in Southern historiography head-on would obviously have been unwise. Especially so when its views commanded such universal popular support as they did in the 1930s. . . . What was needed was a subject in Southern history and a means of writing it that would expose what seemed to be the fallacies, omissions, and long silences that characterized the New South school."[60]

Actually, Woodward already had such a subject in hand because he was committed to writing a biography of the flamboyant Populist Thomas E. Watson. As Woodward explained, "Not only was it a fascinating story in itself, but it plunged the historian into all the dark, neglected, and forbidden corners of Southern life shunned by the New South school." Because Populism had been an "embarrassment" to New South doctrines and contradicted historians' "pet themes of white unity and black satisfaction, it was generally shunted aside, minimized, or silently passed over." The Populists had even dared to challenge Henry Grady and other New South icons, and, beyond that, "the New South double-think of worshipping the symbols and myths of the Lost Cause and simultaneously serving the masters of the new plutocracy was too much for Populist critics. So was the reverence demanded for the Redeemers, the South's new rulers who overthrew and succeeded the Reconstruction reign."[61]

Woodward sharpened his attack on both the Redeemers and the New South version of Southern history in his *Origins of the New South, 1877–1913*, a book that he actually began at the end of the 1930s but with the interruptions brought on by World War II did not complete until 1951. In *Origins* Woodward took a more straightforward approach, repeating "the orthodox creed backward" in what amounted to "a sort of historical black mass in the eyes of the believers." First, he disputed the Redeemers' ties to the old planter regime, thus undermining their claims — and those of their New South descendants as well — to ancestral legitimacy through their roots in the old mythical cavalier order. Having challenged their pedigrees, Woodward proceeded to impugn their character as well, exposing their thievery and corruption and their willingness to serve up the South's people and its natural resources to the highest bidders among a group of greedy, exploitive Yankee capitalists.[62]

A few years later, as the Supreme Court mulled over the Brown decision, Woodward set out in his *Strange Career of Jim Crow* to show that, contrary to New South mythology, segregation (in his words) "did not appear with the end of slavery but toward the end of the century and later" after a period "of experiment and variety" in race relations "in which segregation was not the invariable rule." By attempting to expose segregation and disfranchisement as two of the New South's invented traditions, Woodward sought, as King explained, "to demythologize the existing social and legal institutions that regulated race relations."[63]

In his career retrospective that appeared in 1986, Woodward recalled that "the intellectual present in which I came of age was the peak and crest of the Southern Literary Renaissance. No southern youth of any sensitivity could help being excited by the explosion of creativity taking place during the early 1930s — in fiction, in poetry and drama." The writers to whom Woodward referred were indeed turning out impressive works of fiction, but as they too struggled to sort out the myths and inconsistencies of the New South doctrine, the major literary figures of the Southern Renaissance also had little choice but to grapple with what Louis Rubin called "the impossible load of the past." Coming to maturity in an age of such rapid change where old and new collided so frequently and often so violently, they acquired an almost unique "two way vision" that, as Rubin explained, "translated what they saw in terms of what *had been* as well as what was now. . . . They could both believe, with the old Army of Northern Virginia kind of belief, and yet share the self-consciousness, the skepticism of postwar America and the world."[64]

A major figure in the Southern Renaissance in her own right, Ellen Glasgow cited this move to the middle ground between sentiment and skepticism as the key to the emergence of a new breed of southern writer. What distinguished the new generation of writers from their predecessors, Glasgow believed, was "a detached and steadfast point of view." For Glasgow, however, detachment from the myth of the Old

South was no more crucial than detachment from that of the New. She had begun to exhibit this detachment herself well in advance of some of her Renaissance Era contemporaries. In the first decades of the twentieth century, Glasgow, whose father had been the manager of Richmond's Tredegar Iron Works, began in her novels to criticize both the intellectual stagnation bred by the Old South and the rampant materialism unloosed by the New South crusade. Much of Glasgow's writing seemed to anticipate the extent to which the key figures of the Southern Renaissance would be forced to confront simultaneously both the Old South legend and the New South reality. In her novel *The Romance of a Plain Man* (1909) and even more so in her 1913 *Virginia,* Glasgow raised questions about both the Old South and the New.[65]

Virginia was set in the Virginia of the 1880s, where "the smoke of factories was already succeeding the smoke of the battlefields and from the ashes of a vanquished idealism the spirit of commercial materialism was born." This New South materialist ethos was personified by tobacco manufacturer and railroad builder Cyrus Treadwell, who was "at once the destroyer and the builder — the inexorable foe of the old feudal order and the beneficent source of the new industrialism." Meanwhile, the Old South found its embodiment in Miss Priscilla Batte, headmistress of a female academy and the daughter of a fallen Confederate general: "Today, at the beginning of the industrial awakening of the South, she (who was but the embodied spirit of her race) stood firmly rooted in all that was static, in all that was obsolete and outgrown, in the Virginia of the eighties." The ultimate provincial, Priscilla is also the ultimate booster, every bit as indisposed to critical thinking as the South that would eventually be depicted by W. J. Cash. She admires Cyrus without understanding the threat he poses to the ideals of the Old South she claims to venerate. Actually, much as Cash would later suggest, Priscilla and Cyrus — Old South and New — had much in common. They shared a suspicion of art and ideas and ignored the racial and other problems their society faced, choosing instead to worship "the illusion of success."[66]

In 1928 Glasgow lamented the New South's ambition not simply "to be self-sufficing but to be more Western than the west and more American than the whole of America." She believed that this New South zeal for Americanization threatened to reduce southern life to "a comfortable level of mediocrity" and had therefore driven into revolt "an impressive group of Southern writers" who had broken away "from a petrified past overgrown by a funereal tradition" but had also recoiled from "the uniform concrete surface of an industrialized South."[67]

By 1943 Glasgow included in this group of literary rebels not only Thomas Wolfe and William Faulkner but Margaret Mitchell as well. This designation is actually less surprising than it seems. Although Mitchell's *Gone with the Wind* is often cited as irrefutable evidence of the lingering regional, national, and even global appeal of the Old South myth, she insisted on several occasions that she "had no intention of writing about cavaliers." As Mitchell pointed out, "practically all my characters, except the Virginia Wilkes, were of sturdy yeoman stock."[68]

Mitchell certainly captured the humble origins and meteoric ascent of many an antebellum Georgia planter in her depiction of the largely untutored, short but swaggering, "loud mouthed and bull headed" Irishman Gerald O'Hara, who longed with "a ruthless singleness of purpose" for "his own house, his own plantation, his own horse and his own slaves. And here in this new country . . . he intended to have them." Chafing in the employ of his brothers in Savannah, Gerald capitalized on two of his prime assets, his facility at poker and his "steady head for whiskey," to become the owner of a gone-to-seed plantation. Clearing fields and planting cotton and borrowing more money and buying more slaves and land, "little, hard-headed blustering Gerald" soon occupied his dream house and even won grudging social acceptance when the lordly Mrs. Wilkes conceded that despite his "rough tongue . . . he is a gentleman."[69]

Although Gerald does not survive long after the war, it is his genes that sustain his daughter Scarlett as she claws her way back to material comfort if not quite full-fledged social respectability. Meanwhile, the once high-and-mighty Wilkeses flounder and fail, especially the wonderfully grand but woefully inept Ashley, who clearly lacks the grit and gall that Scarlett possesses in abundance. If Mitchell's challenge to the cavalier myth was largely lost in Hollywood's ensuing rush to romanticize the Old South on film, the same was truer still of her more subtly critical treatment of life in the New South captured in Scarlett's rise to postbellum economic prominence. Amazed at the determination of other white women of her class to retain their dignity in the face of the defeat and economic devastation of the war, Scarlett observes, "The silly fools don't seem to realize that you can't be a lady without money." Pursuing that end, and the more immediate goal of saving Tara by paying off its back taxes, Scarlett marries the steady but older and uninteresting Frank Kennedy, an Atlanta businessman. Shortly thereafter, she realizes that the price of saving her beloved Tara is her permanent exile in Atlanta. (Symbolically, she can only save the Old South by resigning herself to life in the New South.) Determined to make the best of this situation, however, she realizes that in the rebuilding of Atlanta there was "still plenty of money to be made by anyone who isn't afraid to work — or to grab."[70]

Soon Scarlett is nagging poor Frank about his lax business habits, especially his reluctance to collect debts from friends and acquaintances. Shocked by her head for business and figures, Frank actually finds it "unbecoming." In the New South, manhood and material success go hand in hand. Scarlett, however, believes that "money is the most important thing in the world," and she determines to prove that she is "as capable as a man" by making "money for herself, as men made money." Securing a loan from Rhett Butler, she buys a lumber mill and proceeds to lie, cheat, and just plain outcompete many of her male counterparts, brazenly associating with common laborers and other such rough company. Not surprisingly, the whole town is scandalized by Scarlett's insistence on "conducting her affairs in a masculine way." Thus, by becoming a businesswoman, and, worse yet, a successful one, Scarlett manages to "unsex herself" in the eyes of the community. She stoops to employing convict labor and turns her head to the way her foreman abuses them because her mill is operating so profitably. She realizes that her behavior would have scandalized her genteel, aristocratic mother, Ellen O'Hara, but this Old South image gives way to a New South "impulse," one "hard, unscrupulous and greedy, which had been born in the lean days at Tara and was now strengthened by the present uncertainty of life."[71]

While *Gone with the Wind* was a considerably more complex literary effort than many of its critics perceived, Margaret Mitchell's struggle with the "impossible load" of the southern past paled in comparison to that of William Faulkner. Ambivalence about the New South legend permeated Faulkner's personal and literary world. A dashing Confederate cavalier who became an aspiring postbellum railroad developer, Faulkner's great-grandfather, the "Old Colonel," William C. Faulkner, personified the New South legend. Although Faulkner himself mocked the materialism and social pretentiousness of the New South's nouveau riche, he overextended himself severely to acquire a badly run-down antebellum estate and later in life loved to don the ostentatious garb of the Virginia hunting set and regale members of this group with embellished accounts of his ancestry.[72]

In *Sartoris* Faulkner drew heavily on both personal feelings and family experiences, presenting the ineffectual struggle of a venerable southern family confronting the unfamiliar realities of life in a rapidly changing post–World War I South. He went on to explore in grimmer and more complex detail the decline of a family, a society, and a tradition in *The Sound and the Fury*. In Faulkner's story, the once patrician Compsons have reached the point of seemingly irreversible degeneration and decay, and the entire clan is dwarfed in courage, wisdom, and integrity by their black servant Dilsey. The promiscuous daughter Caddy is the ultimate lost soul, and the obsessive son Quentin outstrips even the self-destructive Bayard Sartoris on his way to his suicidal demise. Ultimately, the only sane surviving Compson is the cold-blooded, mercenary Jason. Insisting, "I haven't got much pride, I can't afford it," Jason embodies the most sinister aspects of the materialistic and corrupt New South and bears no small resemblance to the Snopeses, whose sinister ascent Faulkner would soon begin to trace.[73]

A few years later in *Absalom, Absalom!* Faulkner explored the antebellum adolescence of the South's aristocratic tradition and in the process exposed the fundamental weaknesses that would make this tradition so susceptible to postbellum decay. In the chilling story of the rise and fall of the relentless single-minded parvenu Thomas Sutpen, Faulkner forced readers to consider the darker underpinnings of the Old South tradition. As Irving Howe summed it up: "Sutpen is a latecomer, an interloper who, in order to compress into his lifetime the social rise which in other families [such as the Sartorises or the Compsons] had taken generations, must act with an impersonal ruthlessness . . . which the Sartorises have learned to disguise or modulate." Ironically, if Sutpen was meant to offer some insight into the aristocratic tradition exemplified by the Sartorises or the Compsons, he also represented a decidedly darker version of Mitchell's Gerald O'Hara, and like Scarlett, who knew that "it took money to be a lady," Sutpen equated material success with social standing as well.[74]

If he was ambivalent about the underpinnings and the unexplored inner reality of the South's aristocratic tradition, Faulkner was repulsed outright by what he saw replacing it. In *The Hamlet*, he began to trace the rise of the odious Flem Snopes and his soon-to-be ubiquitous clan. "It is the historical perspective that renders this the more tragic," wrote Louis Rubin, who uncovered the essential contradiction confronting Faulkner and his literary contemporaries when he pointed out that "the South has not always been this way; it has become this way. The image of the heroic past renders the distraught present so distasteful, just as it is this very same heroic past that has caused the present." For Faulkner, the process of social displacement and decay that brought down the Sartorises and Compsons and replaced them with the Snopeses went hand in hand with the emergence of "a thing known whimsically as the New South," a society transformed from a rural, agrarian folk-based economy and culture to one increasingly characterized by factories and cities and depersonalized social relations, one where who or what a man or woman was mattered less than how much he or she was worth.[75]

The paradox of social and cultural decline intertwined with economic and material progress was a dominant theme for many other writers of the 1930s, including Thomas Wolfe, who seemed at different stages in his life and career to embrace conflicting perspectives on the South's past, present, and future. In an early playwriting effort, Wolfe sought to tell the story of Colonel Tasher Weldon, "a typical Southern aristocrat" who dotes on the good old days while his fortunes crumble down around him. After his death, when the Colonel's old manor is torn down, however, his son Eugene and his fiancée, "glorious forerunners of the New South," make a fresh start determined to succeed where the old Colonel had not so much failed as not even tried. Wolfe soon abandoned this literary effort as "naive and simplistic," and a subsequent Wolfe play, "Welcome to Our City," satirized the Babbitry that gripped the New South. In Wolfe's "Altamont," one booster bragged that "we have eight schools, one of which cost over a half a million dollars, six banks, nine bit hotels, over two hundred inns and boarding houses, and twenty-three churches, one of which cost half a million."[76]

Chapel Hill's influence on Wolfe was apparent enough in his identification with "a new generation of southerners who refuse to share in the beautiful but destructive conspiracy of silence of their fathers" about the shortcomings of the South. In his autobiographical 1929 novel *Look Homeward, Angel,* Wolfe anticipated Faulkner's focus on the paradox of family and community decline in the midst of New South progress. Eugene Gant's brother Luke "could sell anything because, in the jargon of salesmen, he could sell himself." A "hustler," he sold not just real estate but "patent wash boards, trick potato peelers, and powdered cockroachpoison" door-to-door. To his black customers he sold hair straightener and religious lithographs featuring black and white angels and cherubs "sailing about the knees of an impartial and crucified Savior" and bearing the caption: "God Loves Them both." At the novel's end, Eugene's mother, Eliza, has grown totally obsessed with real estate trading, and as she amasses more wealth, she grows even more niggardly, refusing even to spend money on food. Meanwhile, she seems largely oblivious to her dying husband and her quarreling children and their incessant "ugly warfare of greed and hatred."[77]

David Donald observed that the Nashville Agrarians considered *Look Homeward, Angel* "the most powerful southern novel of the decade," and Wolfe was flattered by their interest in his work. Ultimately, however, he grew disenchanted, describing Agrarianism as "a form of high toned fascism" and dismissing the "lily-handed intellectuals" who, having retreated to the security of the ivory towers of academe, sought to convince others of "the merits of a return to 'an agrarian way of life.'" Actually, Wolfe's characters seemed equally contemptuous of the South's mythically glorious past and its sordid and materialistic present. In *The Web and the Rock,* George Webber mocked a Charleston that "produced nothing" but "pretended to so much." This, Webber recognized, was "the curse of South Carolina and its 'Southness' . . . always pretending you used to be even though you are not now."[78]

In addition to a swirl of literary activity, the 1930s and early 1940s saw other thoughtful southerners such as Clarence Cason, David L. Cohn, William Alexander Percy, and Ben Robertson produce thoughtful personal reflections on the South's past, present, and future. After publishing his "Mind of the South" article, W. J. Cash spent the ensuing decade struggling to complete the book that he had discussed with Howard Odum in 1929. Cash's writings began, as the 1930s unfolded, to shed some of their shallow, mocking Menckenesque quality and take on a more historical perspective. Conceding in 1935 that the southern "cracker" could be neurotic, sadistic, even homicidal — "in brief, everything that William Faulkner and Erskine Caldwell have made him out to be, and perhaps something more" — Cash nonetheless sought to set this sad and unattractive portrait within a historical context marked by the "always narrowing conditions of life" that had traditionally confronted southern poor whites.[79]

When it finally appeared in 1941, Cash's long-awaited book began by emphasizing the South's "peculiar history" as the source of the "fairly definite mental pattern" that characterized white southerners in general. At one point, Cash had apparently planned to devote a chapter to a critical attack on both the Agrarians for their romanticized depiction of life in the Old South and Edwin Mims for his similarly rose-colored portrait of the New. The completed book gave these ostensibly contradictory (but actually complementary) myths even greater attention, and Cash suggested at the outset that in order to understand how the South had become "not quite a nation within a nation but the next thing to it" it was necessary to disabuse oneself of "two correlated legends — those of the Old and the New Souths."[80]

Having treated the Old South myth almost perfunctorily in his 1929 article, Cash went to great lengths to ridicule it in his book as a "sort of stage piece out of the eighteenth century" replete with gallant "gesturing gentlemen" and "lovely ladies, in farthingales." Taking Odum's suggestion to heart, Cash further insisted that, rather than descendants of "the old gentlefolk who for many generations had made up the ruling classes of Europe," the Old South's planters were little more than "superior farmers" scarcely distinguishable from — and actually, in many cases, risen from — the frontiersmen who inhabited "the vast backcountry of the seaboard states."[81]

To support this contention, Cash afforded "a concrete case," the story of "the stout young Irishman," a character based loosely on Cash's great-great-grandfather and one who was also strikingly similar not only to Odum's "the Major" but to Margaret Mitchell's Gerald O'Hara, who had appeared in print in 1936. (Odum's "Uncle John" meanwhile corresponded to Cash's "man at the center.") Cash's Irishman arrived with his bride in the Carolina upcountry in 1800 and used his life savings of $20 to buy 40 acres of land, toiling round the clock with his wife's help to clear and plant cotton on it. As the years passed, he acquired slaves and more land, abandoning the family's log cabin first for a "wide-spreading frame cottage" and then building a "big house," crude and boxlike but large and fronted by huge columns so that when it was eventually painted white, it stood out from the fields and pinewoods as an impressive edifice indeed. (In *American Epoch,* Odum had described the process whereby the "log house" became the "big house," and the "farm" became the "plantation.") At his death in 1854, the Irishman's estate included 2,000 acres of land, more than a hundred slaves, and four cotton gins, and, of course, the fledgling county-seat newspaper eulogized the Irishman as "a gentleman of the old school" and "a noble specimen of the chivalry at its best."[82]

If the Irishman's ascent seemed miraculously rapid, Cash insisted that in areas like Mississippi "because of the almost unparalleled productivity of the soil" the same thing happened "in accelerated tempo." (Such an observation underscored the similarities between Cash's Irishman and Faulkner's Sutpen, although the latter met with a considerably less glorious fate. Certainly, Sutpen, who had made his fictional appearance some five years earlier, was an example of a would-be planter aristocrat who exhibited what Cash described as the "cunning . . . hoggery . . . callousness . . . brutal unscrupulousness and downright scoundrelism" that, like the Irishman's industry and thrift, were also often rewarded in the antebellum South's plantation frontier.) [83]

Disputing both Henry Grady and H. L. Mencken in ridiculing the notion of antebellum southern cultural superiority, Cash sounded much like Walter Hines Page when he asked of the Old South: "What ideas did it generate? Who were its philosophers and artists?" Perhaps the most penetrating question of all was "What was its attitude toward these philosophers and artists?" Again sounding like Page, Cash answered his own queries: "One almost blushes to set down the score of the Old South here." [84]

Cash attributed this cultural barrenness to a host of factors, including the generally modest social origins of white southerners at large, as well as a simple, uncomplex, unvarying human and natural environment: "here everywhere were wide fields and blue woods and flooding yellow sunlight. A world, in fine, in which not a single factor operated to break up the old pattern of outdoor activity laid down on the frontier . . . a world in which horses, guns, not books and ideas and art were his [the planter's] normal and absorbing interests." [85]

Cash's argument here was hardly original. A similar one had been advanced more than a decade earlier by Ellen Glasgow, who insisted that "from the beginning of its history the South had suffered less from a scarcity of literature than from a superabundance of living." In the South, "soil, scenery, all the color and animation of the external world, tempted a convivial race to an endless festival of the seasons." Life was pleasant enough, but it was also "deficient in those violent contrasts which unkindle the emotions while they subdue the natural pomposity of man." As a result, Glasgow explained, "philosophy, like heresy, was either suspected or prohibited." [86]

Not only did Cash's book thoroughly debunk the myth of an aristocratic and cultured Old South, it displaced soothing New South myths of harmony and restraint with the shocking realities of schizophrenia and excess. His dismissive treatment of the Populists notwithstanding, unlike New South apologists who insisted on the fundamental unity of spirit and purpose among white southerners, Cash understood that southern white society seemed so ostensibly unified precisely because the southern color line was so rigid and inviolable. As he explained it, the "Proto-Dorian convention" assured common whites that, whatever their circumstances might otherwise lack, their skin color guaranteed them that they would never be at the bottom of the social pyramid so long as they remained supportive of their more prosperous but pragmatically folksy and cunningly manipulative white superiors.[87]

If Cash blamed Radical Reconstruction for turning the white South into a quasi nation and engendering the intolerance and conformity that formed the basis of the "savage ideal," he likewise argued (as Woodward did a decade later) that for all their supposed benevolence and foresight, the Redeemers and their New South descendants had done little to make things better. Cash was not immune to all aspects of the New South version of southern history, however. Borrowing heavily from the writings of Broadus Mitchell, he noted the benevolence of the captains of the cotton-mill crusade, praising their paternalistic effort to create jobs and build schools for the region's pathetic and downtrodden poor whites. Still, even as he lauded the intentions of the early mill builders, Cash deplored the long-term results as the mills fell into the hands of a new generation of greedy owners on whom he blamed the prevailing low wages, deplorable working conditions, overcrowded living situation, and, worst of all, the exploitation of six- and seven-year-olds — "baby labor," as Cash called it.[88]

In the final analysis, *The Mind of the South* was a book with the potential to offend practically everyone. Not only did the downtrodden but ambitious New South not have a grand aristocratic past that could be invoked whenever the region's critics or its self-evident ills became too unpleasant to bear or contemplate, but if the past looked far less rosy than most white southerners wanted desperately to believe, the myths of the present-day progress and future prosperity were largely hollow and false as well. As Singal noted, Cash's book "represented a complete reversal of the region's history once offered by the New South writers — it read like a compendium of those aspects of the South they had deliberately screened out." Despite its potential to offend, however, the responses to *The Mind of the South* in the southern press were overwhelmingly positive. A reviewer for the *Houston Post* called the book a "magnificent study," while the *Baltimore Evening Sun* found it "persuasive" and "charming." In the *Birmingham Age Herald,* John Temple Graves praised Cash's "objectivity" and saluted his "extraordinary" accomplishment.[89]

In Singal's view, the very publication of *The Mind of the South* symbolized "the triumph of Southern modernism," while the warm reception it received in the South attested to the "firm hold the modernist viewpoint had gained among the South's educated elite." In reality, the positive reception accorded Cash's book seems less remarkable in light of the fact that much of what he said about the South had actually been said before and, in many cases, more than once by a number of southern writers stretching from Page and Cable through Glasgow, Odum, Vance, Mitchell, and Faulkner, to name but a few. It was not only the keenness of Cash's own insights or the boldness with which he presented them but his skill in synthesizing and summarizing the views of other thoughtful southern whites of his and previous generations that established *The Mind of the South* as the "quintessential expression" of the spirit of the Southern Renaissance and the culmination of a revolt against a New South identity that had held sway in the region for half a century.[90]

By exposing the roots of an imperfect present in an imperfect past, the key figures of the Southern Renaissance played a major role in toppling one New South identity and clearing the way for the emergence of another. Many observers agree, in general terms, however, that the Southern Renaissance had largely run its course within a decade after *The Mind of the South* appeared. The New South Creed's inaccuracies and distortions had been laid bare by the Great Depression, and they seemed all the more egregious in the context of World War II, which focused particularly critical attention on the region's undemocratic and repressive racial practices. The 1940s also saw a number of black writers make major contributions to exposing the ugly realities of Jim Crow's New South. Ralph Ellison produced several noteworthy short stories suffused with the irony of black soldiers ostensibly fighting for democracy but unsure whether its worst enemies were abroad or at home. The most influential writing in this area, however, came from Richard Wright, whose *Black Boy* received a five-page, illustrated spread in *Life* magazine, which described it in June 1945 as "not only a brilliant autobiography but a powerful indictment of a caste system that is one of America's biggest problems." American aspirations to free-world leadership at the onset of the Cold War only made the southern racial situation seem even more intolerable, and it was fair to say that by the middle of the twentieth century Grady's South of harmony and progress had largely dissolved into Cash's South of "conflict and depravity."[91]

Instead of disappearing, however, the term "New South" quickly resurfaced, albeit in much transfigured form, as the cliché of choice among would-be reformers pursuing an agenda of dramatic change, especially along racial lines. As Cash's South supplanted Grady's, the "southern way of life" became, to defenders and detractors alike, largely synonymous with white supremacy and segregation. (Walker Percy actually came to dread the phrase because he knew that "in New Orleans, which has a delightful way of life, the 'Southern Way of Life' usually means 'let's keep McDonough No. 6 segregated.'") Consequently, the Renaissance Era's sensitive, tentative probings of the relationship between past and present and anxiety about the changes that seemed to lie just ahead quickly gave way to the moral absolutism and scorched-earth rhetoric of what Hobson called the school of "shame and guilt." Personified by Lillian Smith, the writers of the shame and guilt school saw little worth saving in "a way of life so wounding, so hideous in its effect upon the spirit of both black and white."[92]

Instead of worrying about (to recall Bendix) "the ambivalent job of preserving or strengthening the indigenous character of the native culture" as they sought to help the South find a way out of its backwardness, writers such as William H. Nicholls began to insist that if the region was ever to overcome its social and economic woes, "many of those still strong qualities of mind and spirit which have made the South distinctive must largely disappear." The post-Renaissance, "shame and guilt" writers were not entirely free of ambivalence about the wholesale transformation they advocated. Conceding that the change he sought could be "accomplished only at the expense of the qualities that made the South distinctive," Harry Ashmore nonetheless appended to his "Epitaph for Dixie" the hope that "a generation from now when the last shovelful of earth is patted down on the grave, we shall be able to see the vanishing age more clearly, to examine its virtues without being distracted by its faults." Still, former Mississippi congressman Frank E. Smith spoke for many of his colleagues when, all but echoing George Washington Cable, he insisted in 1965 that "what is needed is not a New South but a South that is inextricably and indefinably a part of the United States." Smith conceded that "in the mainstream of American life, much of the Southern identity will be lost, but if 'Southern identity' is the price to be paid for removal of the racial scar which has been the mark of things Southern, both the South and the country will have gained thereby."[93]

By 1990 it appeared to no less a professional southerner than Hodding Carter III that Smith's wish had at last come true. As he offered his own somber declaration of "The End of the South," Carter pointed to economic and political changes, but his focus was primarily on race: "In the South of the late 20th century, segregation by law has been destroyed, and segregation in fact is no more peculiar to Jackson, Miss., than it is to Jackson, Mich. On the other side of the coin, there is more school integration in the South than in any other section. Racism remains, but the nation now understands that race is the *American* dilemma." Carter took pains to assure readers that his was not "yet another fatuous proclamation of yet another New South." Instead, what was "lurching into existence in the South" seemed to him "purely and contemporaneously mainstream American for better or worse."[94]

Five years after Carter's definitive pronouncement, Louisiana State University Press issued the final volume in its "History of the South" series. While the immediately preceding titles in the series had explored first the "origins" and then the "emergence" of the New South, Numan V. Bartley's 1995 contribution, covering the years 1945–1980, was titled simply *The New South*. Bartley's New South, however, was less a work in progress than a finished product, a South that had, for better and worse, finally experienced "fundamental changes in the way southerners lived their lives, earned their livelihoods, and interpreted the events around them."[95]

Surveying essentially the same contemporary scene analyzed by Bartley, Leslie W. Dunbar asked in 1998 if this was "The Final New South" or at least "the end of the South as we've heretofore known it?" Whether Bartley's and Dunbar's New South amounted precisely to Cable's "No South" or not, the "sweeping transformation" and the "fundamental changes" that created it were possible only after the destruction of the New South identity that Henry Grady and his cohorts so painstakingly constructed more than a century ago. Ironically, just as Grady and company sought to build their New South on the ruins of the Old South, many southerners are now laboring to construct a new regional identity amid the rubble and reminders of the New South.[96]

Whatever the outcome of these efforts, they are unlikely to yield anything like the white-dominated, culturally and politically monolithic "not quite a nation" Cash described in 1941. In fact, many of the most energetic and purposeful participants in the process of constructing a new southern identity are black southerners whose spirited attacks on the Confederate flag, "Dixie," and other symbols of the New South's racial order complement their efforts to establish monuments to their own crusade to overturn that order. Meanwhile, finding little else of substance in which to ground their claim to a distinctive identity, many white southerners continue to cling to "Dixie" and the Confederate banner, insisting that they represent more than a sordid history of slavery and racial repression.[97]

The preoccupation of so many contemporary southerners with monuments and symbols confirms their involvement in what Hobsbawm calls the "politics of identity" through which "groups of people today ... try to find some certainty in a shaken and uncertain world." Beyond that, the current controversies illustrate the power of historical imagery and point once again to the past as the indispensable base tissue, the virtual DNA-equivalent from which a sense of group distinctiveness must be teased and nurtured. As Hobsbawm notes and as we certainly have seen, however, once it is caught up in the process of identity building, history as fact often gives way to history as "myth and invention." Ernest Renan has even insisted that "getting its history wrong is part of being a nation" and suggested that "the essence of a nation is that its people have much in common and have forgotten much."[98]

Hodding Carter pointed to the major obstacle to the creation of a new racially inclusive regional identity when he observed that "if the South once venerated a past that would not die, it now has a more recent past that must be denied or ignored." In the case of identity-challenged southerners who seem at this juncture a people more divided than united by their common past, a little selective amnesia or cosmetic historical adjustment might seem relatively harmless and even beneficial. On the other hand, as the suffering inflicted by contemporary disagreements over cultural and ethnic differences elsewhere in the world all too vividly attests, the misrepresentations of the past that often sustain the politics of identity can have serious and even terrible consequences. Closer to home, the abuses of history that were so integral to the New South Creed also bear considerable responsibility for its tragic legacy, summarized by Woodward as "caste, paternalism and segregation" and "juleps for the few and pellagra for the crew." At the end of the nineteenth century, the New South Creed promised white southerners a bright and appealing future, but its actual legitimacy rested on a carefully fabricated version of southern history. At the end of the twentieth century, the bitter fruits of this distortion of the past remain a formidable obstacle to the creation of yet another regional identity to which all southerners, white and black alike, may legitimately subscribe.[99]

Modernization and the Mind of the South

Bertram Wyatt-Brown was surely correct when he suggested in 1991 that the South's physical and institutional features had changed "much more" since Cash's *Mind of the South* appeared than they had changed between 1865 and 1941. Cash was obviously not the only one troubled by his region's resistance to change. Nor was he alone in believing that the roots of the South's recalcitrance lay in its "peculiar history" that had "so greatly modified it from the general American norm." This "profound conviction" was typical of a generation or more of scholars who saw the tradition-bound South locked in a death struggle with the forces of modernization.[1]

Because the North's response to modernization was supposedly the classic example, the South's failure to replicate that response marked it as an aberration whose deviation from the norm demanded some explanation. Consequently, instead of treating the region's experience with modernization as a discrete phenomenon worthy of study in its own historical context and in all of its complexity, a number of scholars simply concentrated on finding an explanation for the South's divergence from the northern example. The result, as Edward L. Ayers put it, was a tendency "to define Southern history by what failed to happen. Our questions are not *why*, but *why not*." (Italics mine.)[2]

Students of southern history and politics effectively blamed the South's political and economic elite for steering the region off the expressway to modernity and onto a back road that was exceedingly steep and circuitous with more than its share of clip joints, potholes, and dead-end turns. A prominent case in point was Woodward's sharply critical account of the misdeeds of the post-Reconstruction Redeemer leadership who sold the South into colonial subjugation at the hands of greedy northern financiers and industrialists.[3]

Would-be revisionists eventually disputed Woodward's contention that the Redeemers were decidedly probourgeois business types who had "little but nominal connection" to the antebellum planter class. Even Woodward's critics, however, generally accepted his basic premise that reactionary post-Reconstruction political leaders had stunted the South's growth and social development, causing it to lag well behind the North. Stressing the similarities between persisting postbellum planters in Alabama and the Prussian Junkers, Jonathan Wiener concluded that "although the New South was undoubtedly new, its socioeconomic structure was nevertheless distinct from that of the North. This was a consequence of postwar planter domination, which weakened the genuinely bourgeois classes and moved the South closer to the Prussian Road than to the democratic capitalist one." Wiener's comparative study added a new wrinkle to the study of southern political economy in the late nineteenth century. Still, instead of using the Prussian analogy as a point of departure for considering the South's experience within a larger genuinely global context, Wiener appeared to fall in step with his ostensibly more provincial predecessors by using the similarities between the South and Prussia simply to explain the differences between the South and the North.[4]

Certainly, the South's state and local political and economic leaders might have made other, better, and less self-interested decisions about strategies for economic development. Yet, the presumption that the South's political, business, or agricultural leaders were primarily responsible for its failure to modernize according to the classic "northern" pattern ignored a number of crucial differences between the historical, technological, and structural contexts in which the modernization of the two regions occurred. When William H. Nicholls insisted that the South "must choose" between "tradition" and "progress," he apparently assumed that such a simple, clear-cut choice was actually possible. Both David Carlton and Gavin Wright have warned against falling prey to such ruling-class determinism or at least "the misconception that 'ruling classes' are normally in position to control matters at this aggregate level." Karl Marx made much the same point when he observed that "while men make their own history, . . . they do not make it just as they please."[5]

Reinhard Bendix also rejected the presumption that elites have the power and wherewithal to "industrialize whole societies." Bendix argued as well that the dominant "Western" (for our purposes, read "northern") model of modernization imposed a "deterministic view of the future," because it presumed a "uniform process of industrialization in which countries entering upon this process at a later time will repeat in all essentials the previous industrialization of some other country." Bendix pointed out that as it unfolds in a variety of historical, cultural, technological, and geographic contexts, modernization actually affects each society in ways that are profoundly different. Moreover, each society's experience with modernization influences the subsequent experience of other societies undergoing modernization. In essence, these latter "follower" societies may benefit from the experiences of their modernizing predecessors, the "leader" societies.[6]

In many cases, the innovations and advances established by more modern societies — in communication and technology, for example — can provide shortcuts for those who lag behind on the journey to modernity. Sizing up what he saw as a menacing cold war adversary in 1951, David L. Cohn pointed out that the Russians "have performed the feat of jumping from the oxcart into the airplane within one generation" because "Western technology enabled them to skip the transitional processes that the West itself endured." Consequently, Cohn observed, "this enemy, telling the centuries upon his beads, . . . goes with the secrets of nuclear fission in his head and a piece of black bread in his hand." (Years later humorist Lewis Grizzard would view the other side of this paradox, pondering how the Russians could send a man to the moon but fail so miserably in trying to manufacture toilet paper.)[7]

To suggest an analogy to dining, for those coming to the table for the first time, modernization offers not a fixed menu but a cafeteria line. Although not all the options are adaptable to the tastes or the pocketbooks of all the would-be diners, ironically, the later one arrives, the more items are available.

As a latecomer to the modernization feast, the South seemed to have a variety of options, but the limited capital available ultimately dictated a moderate, mundane diet drawn from some of the offerings that had actually been on the table for some time. For example, the South's heavy dependence on the textile industry where many of the technological innovations had already been developed put less pressure on the pocketbooks of the region's investors but also gave them little incentive to invest in the development of new technology and processes. Analyzing what appeared to be the "uninventive South" circa 1920, David Carlton and Peter Coclanis explained that "its technological problems were either already solved (at a low level, thanks to a huge underemployed population available at bargain wages) or could be solved by established firms in the manufacturing belt, sufficiently close at hand to provide daunting competition to local entrepreneurs. Its industrialization was conditioned as well on access to northern markets and business techniques." Consequently, Carlton and Coclanis concluded, "Southern entrepreneurs, conservative legatees of a society deficient in business or technological skills, were perfectly willing to become, in effect, franchisees of the already developed technological community of the manufacturing belt."[8]

Carlton and Coclanis have also shown that the difficulties faced by southern entrepreneurs in mobilizing investment capital forced them to rely on small-scale, risk-averse investors who preferred industrial ventures that were mature and stable but offered "little developmental potential." This reality, in turn, "worked to confine the entrepreneurial impulse, by and large, within limited and unimaginative channels." Thus, the overrepresentation of slow-growth, low-value-added industries in the South's industrial mix was symptomatic of a "structural problem" rather than an ill-intentioned or irrational resistance to innovation or, as they put it, "some peculiar southern conservatism inherited from the slave regime."[9]

A central tenet of the traditional model of modernization was the belief that industrialization would draw southerners from the land into large industrial cities. Urbanization as an agent of change had been the subject of a famous 1938 essay in which sociologist Louis Wirth argued that an urban environment could dramatically alter human behavior. For Wirth population heterogeneity distinguished the city: "The personal traits, the occupations, the cultural life, and the ideas of the members of an urban community may therefore be expected to range between more widely separated poles than those of rural inhabitants." Population diversity provided opportunities for a variety of experiences, while the city's faster-paced, more economically oriented exchange of goods and services not only led to impersonality but also freed residents from the strict social conventions of rural life.[10]

This model was clearly more appropriate to England, where, as Bendix pointed out, the labor force in the early factories was effectively separated from the land, than to a "follower" society (such as the South), where the workforce often "retains its familial and economic ties to the land." Bendix noted that "the permanent separation of workers from their ties to the land obviously facilitates the growth of class consciousness," while preservation of these ties may result, among other things, in "a weak commitment to industry." Beyond that, Bendix admitted, "We do not know after all what forms modernization might take where separation between town and countryside fails to occur at least for a considerable period of time."[11]

Embracing many of Wirth's assumptions, William H. Nicholls saw the "persistence of agrarian values" as the major obstacle to the South's economic, social, and political progress. Nicholls cited the relative weakness of the South's urban middle class, attributing this to the "glacial slowness of Southern urbanization," which, in turn, meant the continuing dominance of the region's "overall social structure" by its "rigid rural substructure." Like many of his contemporaries, Nicholls invested far too much faith in the transformative potential of urbanization and industrialization. He did offer a key insight, however, when he pointed out that so much of the South's industrial development was, at best, "semi-rural in character" and therefore "carried over many values and many similarities in social structure from the old rural pattern."[12]

Nicholls was definitely onto something here. One structural characteristic accounting for the distinctive nature (relative to the North) of the South's industrial growth was the dispersal of its manufacturing plants in small-town and rural locations. In the late nineteenth and early twentieth centuries, textile manufacturers built mill villages adjacent to small and medium-sized towns in locations with waterpower and an abundance of cheap white labor. With the introduction of electricity such operations could be even more widely dispersed to take advantage of a growing surplus of labor fed by the mechanization of southern agriculture. In the post–World War II years, federal acreage-reduction subsidy programs encouraged continued farming on a reduced scale even after southern farmers made their move into the factory. In 1969 nearly 40 percent of the South's manufacturing plants were in rural or small-town areas. Consequently, rather than relocating to large and distant cities, many southern industrial workers remained on the land interacting with family and friends in much the same fashion as had their parents and their parents before them.[13]

In recent years, scholars have pointed out that, over time, a surprising degree of class consciousness actually emerged among southern textile mill workers. Having grown up among farmers forced to take their first jobs in industry in the 1950s, however, I am struck by Ben Robertson's insight into his South Carolina upcountrymen who had just moved into the mills:

> In the cotton fields they had conducted their dealings with the landowner as one independent man with another. Their relationship was individual and personal, and at the mill in town they still were inclined to deal with the overseer as they had with the owner of the cotton field. It still had not fully dawned on these men that the overseer in their mill was not the mill, that he was only an agent. It was difficult for them to realize that they were not working for any individual as an individual — that they were working for a corporation, complicated and technical and highly organized and involved. These men were individuals, they were cotton farmers who had moved into town.[14]

The rise of the South's metropolitan economies and the recent heavy losses of textile and apparel jobs notwithstanding, the pattern of relatively decentralized manufacturing employment persists. Home to a number of carpet plants, Murray County, in rural Northwest Georgia, enjoyed the distinction in 1980 of being the nation's most industrialized county in terms of the percentage of its labor force employed in manufacturing. A total of eleven nonmetropolitan Georgia counties appeared on the list of the nation's top seventy-five counties in this category. With seventeen North Carolina counties and ten from South Carolina also on the list, these three southern states accounted for roughly half (thirty-eight) of the nation's seventy-five most industrialized counties. Even in 1990 both the percentage of total manufacturing employment concentrated outside metropolitan areas in these three states and the percentage of the nonmetropolitan labor force employed in manufacturing were still far higher than the national average.[15]

The experience of the American South demonstrates that the process of modernization is never precisely the same from one context to another (even on the same continent and, beyond that, within the same nation). It likewise suggests that rather than a simple, fight-to-the-death, winner-take-all slugfest, the interaction between what we call "tradition" and what we call "modernity" may take on a variety of shapes and yield a variety of outcomes.

Sensing that in the wake of World War II the South could no longer postpone its long-deferred confrontation with the forces of modernization, a generation of scholars and pundits believed that this confrontation would ultimately mean the end of the South as a distinctive regional entity. Although C. Vann Woodward welcomed many of the changes accompanying what he called the "Bulldozer Revolution," even Woodward worried about the demise of "cherished old values" and empathized with southern traditionalists who felt "helpless and frustrated against the mighty and imponderable agents of change."[16]

William H. Nicholls saw the forces of traditionalism giving a better account of themselves in the struggle with the forces of modernity. Still, Nicholls believed that southern traditions were "irreconcilably at war with regional economic progress," and for him the triumph of progress "inevitably" meant "the destruction of many of the traditions my ancestors held dear."[17]

Because the forces of modernization seemed both immutable and irresistible, most observers made no allowance for an outcome in which the South changed but remained by any means recognizably or distinctively southern. In fact, however, the South's experience largely affirms the contention of Lawrence Levine and others that, in Levine's words, "Culture is not a fixed condition but a process: the product of interaction between past and present. Its toughness and resiliency are determined not by a culture's ability to withstand change, which may indeed be a sign of stagnation not life, but by its ability to react creatively and responsively to the realities of a new situation." Where cultural identity is concerned, Levine pointed out, "The question . . . is not one of survivals but transformations."[18]

Ironically, what Cash had identified as the "mind" of the South was essentially, to borrow Levine's words, "the product of interaction between past and present." In Cash's view, however, by bringing southern white society into contact with a variety of forces for change, this process of interaction had actually played the primary role in shaping the hardened, self-destructively defensive mind-set that he described. Cash did not foresee that as this interaction continued it might also eventually help to shape a different southern mind, one more open, sensitive, and self-critical, a mind that was in fact already emerging in the 1930s as Cash struggled to finish his book. Writing near the end of the longest period of relative continuity in southern history, Cash could not perceive that the mind he saw (and believed had persisted for roughly a century) could actually be only a stage in an ongoing process of interaction with — and ultimately adaptation to — the forces of change.

Daniel J. Singal pointed out that the major problem with Cash's book may have been his insistence that the South possessed "a permanent mind impervious to the forces of historical change." As Singal put it, Cash unfortunately employed the "relatively static concept of *mind*" instead of the "more fluid and modern notion of *culture*" in order to "describe the most deep-rooted assumptions and values of southerners over the centuries." Consequently, Singal explained, Cash was unable either "to trace the continuities that so preoccupied him" or "to stay sensitive to the very real changes that have occurred in the way southerners view their world."[19]

Across the late twentieth-century South's cultural landscape there was evidence in abundance that southerners were not so much either resisting or surrendering to change as *adapting* to it or, in many cases, adapting *it* to their viewpoints and lifestyles. For example, despite warnings and predictions to the contrary, increasing affluence and sophistication have not necessarily been totally at odds with the South's reputation as the "Bible Belt." Marshall Frady cited the example of a luxury auto in an upscale Atlanta neighborhood bearing a bumper sticker that insisted, "People of Distinction Prefer Jesus." Meanwhile, elsewhere in the Georgia capital, the message board of the Peachtree Baptist Church read on one occasion: "Being Born Again Means Being Plugged Into A New Power Source."[20]

For thousands of somewhat less affluent southerners, the symbol of a changing South was not a skyscraper or a sleek new jetport or a station wagon beside a split-level but a satellite dish beside a double-wide mobile home. Modular living and multichannel viewing seemed to carry revolutionary implications, but many southerners quickly clasped these innovations to their cultural bosoms. Cash would have nodded knowingly as he watched those southerners who did not get enough fire-and-brimstone, swift-and-certain-damnation preaching on Sunday mornings using their satellite dishes to tune in any number of high-energy televangelists. Later, when their hedonistic impulses kicked in, they could simply switch to any number of "adult" programming options. In fact, rustic jokesters even took delight in claiming that they could tell by the angle of a neighbor's dish whether he was watching the Playboy Channel.[21]

Meanwhile, the double-wide trailer quickly permeated southern music and humor. One popular song celebrated the charms of "the queen of my double-wide trailer," while another more obscure one bemoaned the actions of a fed-up wife who

left me and took my home sweet mobile home.
She took the patio. Lord the concrete slab is gone. . . .
I don't know how she hitched it up or put them damn wheels on.
She left me and took my home sweet mobile home.[22]

Likewise, the notorious susceptibility of mobile homes to high winds spawned jokes such as "How is an Alabama divorcée like a tornado?" The answer: "They both wind up getting the double-wide." Though they represented real upward mobility to a great many southerners, mobile homes became synonymous with a lack of education or sophistication. "Did you hear about the fire at the Alabama Governor's Mansion?" The answer: "Yep, they lost everything but the axles!"

For some time, economists and sociologists have watched with interest as certain commercial franchises "invaded" the small-town South. McDonald's is a classic example, but none of these enterprises has had a more profound effect than the Wal-Mart Discount Department Store. More so than even the opening of a McDonald's restaurant, a Wal-Mart store invariably brings major changes to a small town and its hinterland. Once a center of social as well as economic activity, especially on Sundays, downtown streets or the courthouse square stand nearly empty because shoppers have already made their purchases at Wal-Mart, which not only offers lower prices and wider selections (plus a snack bar), but also stays open late on weeknights. The result is a fundamental alteration in traditional patterns of economics and social interaction at the community level. Rather than resist such potentially disruptive changes, however, many southerners seemed not just to embrace them but claim them for their own. When consulted by interviewers, for example, 68 percent of a recent *Atlanta Journal-Constitution* poll's respondents reported that Wal-Mart was "very" or "somewhat important" to their definition of "today's South."[23]

Not surprisingly, Georgia writer Mary Hood discovered that, depending on its location, a Wal-Mart could be a metaphor for either continuity or change and sometimes for both. Hood observed this phenomenon firsthand in the fast-growing Atlanta suburbs of Cherokee County, where "the past, present and future are simultaneous." In a more rural section of the county Hood found a Wal-Mart where the clerks had names like "Delma or Edna or Frony or Bud, Jr., and they call me m'am or honey." In this store's electronics department, the radios play country music and announce obituaries and car washes, while customers pay in cash, renew old acquaintances, and part company with "that country benediction, 'Y'all come to see us sometime.'"[24]

Nine miles away, Hood visited a second Wal-Mart, reflective of the local community's transition from small town to suburb. At this establishment, the pace is faster and the snack bar nonexistent. "These are busy people, involved in PTA and soccer and tennis camp . . . everyone has somewhere else to be and soon." Here the radios blare "96 Rock," and most of the shoppers pay with "designer checks." The more youthful customers bear names such as Brandon and Angie and Kim and Scott and Amber, and among them, "orthodontia is epidemic."[25]

Curiously enough, it was on the fast-moving frontier of development where the apartments and subdivisions have actually bypassed the little towns and reconfigured the pasturelands that Hood got a chilling taste of the future. Here, neither street signs nor billboards bore any relation or reference to the locality itself, and everything was cloaked in the impersonal, cutting-edge flash of fast-lane trendiness. In this area's Wal-Mart, Hood shopped in that "anonymity attained more often in large cities," and the clerks seemed more "worldly" and "chic." Though only a few miles from the cozy pay-cash ambiance of the first store, here Hood felt not just anxious and alienated but "underdressed" and had to remind herself "that my plastic's as good as theirs: I can owe for anything in this store."[26]

Southern foodways also reflect this process of adaptation to change quite well. My hometown of Hartwell, Georgia, affords some prime examples. The progression of fast-food establishments mirrors both a community's growth and the increasing affluence of its inhabitants. In the 1960s Hartwell offered a Dairy Queen and a local establishment called the Chic 'N Burger. As it grew, it attracted first a Tastee Freeze, then, in a major surge forward, a Hardee's (whose primary appeal to the local folk lay in its excellent biscuits) and then a Pizza Hut. Kentucky Fried Chicken arrived shortly thereafter, but the big news — the real signal that Hartwell had established itself as a genuine tricounty trade center — was the arrival of McDonald's. Arby's showed up just recently, locating defiantly in the very shadow of the golden arches, and Burger King is on the way.

On the higher end, Vickery Parke offers cuisine best described as "continental southern with a flair," with the meals prepared by trained professional chefs. Its survival in a town of approximately six thousand clearly says something about changes in palates and pocketbooks in the area, but even as Vickery Parke patrons savor their veal scallopini with wild mushrooms, scarcely a mile away the Swamp Guinea is, in fact, literally swamped with diners downing deep-fat-fried catfish, shrimp, and chicken.

Even the outlying rural areas are caught up in this process of foodways in transition. The Reed Creek community, once known for its bootlegging and brawling rather than its gastronomic delights, has experienced a significant in-migration of retirees and affluent professionals who live full- or part-time on a nearby lake. At present these newcomers seem to be locked in a seesaw struggle for dining dominance with the longtime residents of the community. A few years back, I drove through Reed Creek for the first time in several years and encountered a restaurant called Reed Creek Trattoria, a pleasant little establishment sharing a crossroads with a combination gas station and grocery and hardware store. A sign beside the restaurant's door offered diners the following definition: "Trattoria — A place to eat; restaurant; casual, informal cafe. Fresh, simple food found throughout Italy and Reed Creek!"

On a subsequent visit to the same location, however, I found not the Reed Creek Trattoria but Me-Maw's, which offered diners no self-definition (why would they need one?) but the traditional "meat and two" (vegetables) plus bread and dessert for $3.99 (beverage not included). Me-Maw's flourished for a while, especially during deer season when hungry hunters sought out her hearty (and heavy) offerings, but before long the familiar gave way to the exotic as Gumbo Charlie's, specializing in Cajun dishes, made its appearance in Reed Creek. The Louisiana cuisine seemed strange to many local folks, but Gumbo Charlie's offered the undeniably novel and entertaining spectacle of live lobsters in an illuminated tank. In the long run, however, she-crab soup or crawfish étouffée somehow proved unsatisfactory fare for folks who spent their workdays on tractors and backhoes, and Gumbo Charlie's was soon gone from the Reed Creek scene, lock, stock, and lobster tank. In the wake of its demise, the pendulum swung back in the direction of more traditional palates as the same location became the home of Country Bumpkin's, whose menu ranged from $1.99 breakfast specials to plate lunches and hamburger steak combo plates.

This culinary schizophrenia is hardly confined to the small-town South. Atlanta offers a variety of such juxtapositions. For example, diners can go from cornbread with cracklin's at Harold's Barbeque (near the Federal Pen) to caviar at Nikolai's Roof (atop the Hilton downtown).

Elsewhere, from the Last Resort in Athens to Crook's Corner in Chapel Hill to City Grocery in Oxford, the South sports a number of restaurants featuring "nouveau southern" dishes combining the familiar staples such as grits with shrimp and salmon, catfish with remoulade sauce, black-eyed peas with risotto (actually a Tuscan import), field peas with penne pasta, or sweet potatoes with leeks — and you would be surprised at what they're doing with turnips these days.

In addition to its foodways, the South's cultural identity has traditionally been defined by its music. Viewed over time, the development of country music offers an excellent example of southern culture as an evolving product of adaptation to the forces of change. Technology, especially the phonograph and the radio, seemed on the one hand a threat to the region's traditions and values, yet both of these not only served as the vehicle by which southern music would reach listeners around the nation and ultimately the world but brought other forms of music into the South and encouraged the lyric and stylistic intermingling and cross-fertilization that marked southern music from the beginning.

As early as the turn of the century, Harvard archaeologist Charles Peabody was disappointed to find black workers singing not only hymns but "ragtime" tunes, "undoubtedly picked up from some passing theatrical troupes." By the time folklorists began their field recordings in the South, as Francis Davis put it, "a supposedly authorless and uncopyrighted song learned by ear for generations might be in reality a song once featured in a vaudeville revue, or written or recorded by some long-forgotten professional entertainer." Noting the "tangled genealogy" of southern musical styles, Edward L. Ayers insisted that southern music became *more* rather than *less* "southern" in the late nineteenth and early twentieth century as "older styles and newer fashions mixed and cohered, as musicians of both races learned from one another." Ayers clearly had both early country music and the blues in mind when he observed that "what the twentieth century would see as some of the most distinctly Southern facets of Southern culture developed in a process of constant appropriation and negotiation. Much of southern culture was invented, not inherited."[27]

For southern whites, the nostalgic and melancholy Victorian parlor songs popular throughout the nation at the turn of the century were particularly appealing, and songs such as the "Pale Amaranthus" were soon southernized into the famous Carter Family classic "Wildwood Flower." Early recordings of southern rural musicians, black and white, proved so commercially successful that recording companies quickly dispatched talent scouts who fanned out across the region in search of new singers and new songs. The quest for fresh material soon exhausted the available reservoir of folk, spiritual, gospel, and dance tunes and encouraged performers such as Fiddlin' John Carson and Ernest V. "Pop" Stoneman to try their hand at songwriting. Although these early country composers retained the old Anglo-Saxon ballad format, their subject matter was often taken directly from recent headlines. Ironically, many of their songs expressed some significant misgivings about the impact of modernization. Stoneman's "Sinking of the Titanic" deplored the sin of human arrogance and stressed the limits of human capability in pointing out that although the *Titanic* was billed as an unsinkable ship, "God, with his mighty hand, showed the world it could not stand."[28]

Elsewhere, the automobile mobilized courtship by rendering it less susceptible to parental scrutiny, and the repeal of prohibition combined with the new, ultrapowerful V-8 engines to further enhance humanity's ability to inflict physical and moral injury on itself. Dorsey Dixon's "Wreck on the Highway" depicted a chilling scene of destruction and death (precedent, of course, to eternal damnation) where "whiskey and blood ran together" and emphasized the linkage between advancing technology and receding morality by adding, "But I didn't hear nobody pray."[29]

Country music pioneer Uncle Dave Macon seemed to be making a similar statement when he vowed: "I'd rather ride a wagon and go to heaven / than go to hell in an automobile." (It is worth noting in passing that at this point Uncle Dave's wagon freight company had recently been driven out of business by a trucking line.) As Charles Wolfe pointed out, however, "Uncle Dave was able to make his peace with technology" once "he was able to integrate it into his life." As soon as traveling by auto became vital to Macon's performing career, he began to sing the praises of the Model T in "On the Dixie Bee Line (In That Henry Ford of Mine)." Uncle Dave kept abreast of developments by recording "New Ford Car," a tribute to the newer, more comfortable Model A that succeeded the Model T.[30]

As time passed and the new technology became less intimidating, southern songwriters actually found it possible to harness the imagery of technology to moralist-traditionalist ends. The radio, which provided an ever-widening invasion route for mass society influences, also became an agent for indoctrination in Protestant fundamentalism. If you missed church on Sunday, all you had to do, as the title of Albert Brumley's 1937 gospel composition insisted, was "Turn Your Radio On" and "get in touch with God" by listening to "the songs of Zion coming from the land of endless Spring."[31]

That this phenomenon was operating on both sides of the color line is apparent in the lines of songs popular among black sharecroppers in the Mississippi Delta:

> Friend, I'm married unto Jesus
> And we's never been apart
> I've a telephone in my bosom
> I can ring him up from my heart
> I can get him on the air [radio]
> Down on my knees in prayer.[32]

Finally, the trucker songs of the post–World War II era suggested a growing belief in humanity's inherent ability to win not just a stalemate with technology but a victory over it. In the hands of a hard-drivin', pill-poppin', bed-hoppin', smokey-baitin', "Truck Drivin' Son of a Gun," an eighteen-wheel diesel behemoth became as docile as a dutiful and pampered cowpony. Whereas the mysterious but tragic hobo romanticized by Jimmie Rodgers in the 1930s was forever "Waitin' for a Train," the truck driver was always in motion and firmly in control, confident that he was "gonna make it home tonight." "Six Days on the Road" was little more than a joyride, especially if you were perpetually "ratchet-jawing" on your "CB" (citizens band) radio. The latter activity presented a prime example of high technology — harnessed and humanized, southern style. A classic illustration was "Teddy Bear," a phenomenally popular ballad that told the story of a disabled but ever-chipper orphan lad whose deceased trucker father's old CB was his only link to the outside world.[33]

As the pursuit of larger commercial markets intensified in the 1920s, the more rustic country performers like Fiddlin' John Carson gave way to the decidedly more "modern" and innovative Jimmie Rodgers, who took hillbilly music into areas undreamed of a decade earlier, yodeling melodically, incorporating Hawaiian-style steel guitars and even the jazz stylings of Louis Armstrong. Before he died of tuberculosis in 1933, Rodgers sold twelve million records and at one point was earning more money than Babe Ruth. A slick-talking, black-sounding hipster, Rodgers was a romantic, if ultimately tragic figure and also one of the first hillbilly performers to don cowboy costume.[34]

As performers in the depression-ravaged South realized that their audiences preferred the carefree cowboy to the down-and-out plowboy, the Southwest was busily producing yet another strain of country music, western swing, a marvelous synthesis of jazz and hillbilly with a little Cajun, Mexican mariachi, and polka thrown in as well. Almost solely the creation of Bob Wills, western swing stood out as a musical hybrid exhibiting, in Tony Scherman's words, "a tension between big band modernity and folk tradition." Wills's signature song, "San Antonio Rose," was also recorded by Bing Crosby, suggesting that the possibility of taking country music into the mainstream market was not as remote as it once had seemed.[35]

Like Western swing, World War II–era honky-tonk was a music born in the midst of drinking, dancing, and often brawling. Just as the sinful practices associated with it suggested the morally ruinous potential of modernization, so did the lyrical content of honky-tonk music seem a departure from the moralism and Victorian restraint that marked the songs of the Carter Family, Roy Acuff, and many others who are viewed as country music pioneers. Yet, as Scherman rightly notes, "In its sounds and lyrics honky tonk embodies country's great complex of themes: the opposing tugs of country and city; the collapse of traditional supports like family, community, church; rural Americans' hard adjustment to urban life." Despite its controversial beginnings as a threat to the values traditionally upheld in country music, Scherman predicted that "a century from now honky tonk will probably be considered the classic country music."[36]

Scherman's prophecy was, if anything, an understatement. Actually, however, the performer whose emotional songs and tragic life seem most classically "country" today is Hank Williams. Yet Williams's style was, in its day, both innovative and controversial. It combined country, honky-tonk, and black instrumental and vocal influences to develop a distinctive sound whose appeal shows remarkable endurance. Though Williams's music now seems quintessentially "country," his frequent reliance on a heavy beat and his physical gestures and gyrations on stage clearly foreshadowed the style of Elvis Presley, the "King of Rock 'n' Roll."[37]

Like Williams, Presley borrowed freely from black performers. As southern blacks made their way to the city, the smoother amplified stylings of rhythm and blues artists proved more appealing than the old country blues to the dance club audiences in Chicago and Detroit. Ultimately the growing sophistication of young southerners, black and white, encouraged the development of rock 'n' roll as, to recall Pete Daniel, "the rhythm of the land collided with the beat of the city."[38]

Some observers foresaw rock 'n' roll actually killing off its country music ancestor. Country did suffer greatly in the 1950s, but the 1960s saw a resurgence as the "Nashville Sound" or "country pop" offered the easy listening sounds of artists such as Eddy Arnold and Jim Reeves. Patsy Cline, who is widely regarded today as the classic female country vocalist, actually made her enduring reputation as a country pop star who "crossed over" into the popular mass market with hits such as "Walking after Midnight" and "I Fall to Pieces." The Nashville Sound sold big, but so-called purists despised it, and it elicited a sort of "neo-honky-tonk" reaction (the once suspect honky-tonk had actually already become "traditional"), personified first by "The Possum" George Jones and later by the "Bakersfield Sound" of the great Merle Haggard, the "poet of the common man" whose "Okie from Muskogee" seemed to embody the southernization of America.[39]

And so it still goes today in an enduring dialectic wherein country music seems ready to fade completely into the enveloping blandness of the pop music scene only to have a "new traditionalist" movement emerge. Contemporary favorites Emmylou Harris, Ricky Skaggs, Dwight Yoakam, and Randy Travis at one time or another have worn the "new traditionalist" label.[40]

Certainly, liberal America's lamentations about country music's ascendance in the 1970s seem ironic indeed in retrospect as the twentieth century draws to a close amid a flood of concerns about the South's — and country music's — loss of identity. For more than three-quarters of a century both those who listened to country music (many of whom also pretty much lived it) and those who performed it have struggled to reach the mainstream of American life. Having arrived, they must face up — as John Reed, George Tindall, and others have suggested — to the cultural consequences of their accomplishment, especially the loss of identity that total immersion may bring.[41]

Whereas liberal social critics of the 1970s had fretted about country music's reactionary ideological agenda, music critics of the 1990s complain that the music has no agenda at all, ideological or otherwise. Their lament goes something like this: Settled into a comfortable suburban existence, its traditional core constituency, or at least the descendants thereof, no longer needs so desperately to hear songs about suffering, struggle, tragedy, death, and damnation. The once unapologetically gritty, twangy idiom that expressed real struggle and genuine alienation from the unfamiliar urban-industrial environment now serves up little more than mass-produced, smoothed-out suburban escapism. Tony Scherman insists that "contemporary country symbolizes, along with K-mart and McDonald's, the end of regionalism in American life." This is something of an overstatement, but to the extent that it is true, it is surely testimony to country music's origins and development as an evolving product of southern rural society's ongoing interaction with and adaptation to the forces of change.[42]

The parallels between the odysseys of country music and the blues are striking. In his *History of the Blues,* Francis Davis argued that the music owes as much to the marketplace as to folk tradition. In fact, Davis placed the appearance of the blues within the larger context of "an emerging mass culture in which black Americans were to play no small part, and which would eventually render the very notion of folk culture obsolete." As the blues moved northward and urbanward, its musicians adopted amplification and tailored their stylings to the more sophisticated city dwellers who embraced their music. The blues begat rhythm and blues, which in turn begat Motown and Soul, but the actual blues never approached general white mainstream acceptance until the 1980s at the earliest. By the 1990s, however, the blues craze among affluent urban whites had reached surprising proportions.[43]

I observed this phenomenon firsthand a few years back on a visit to a blues club in Chicago to celebrate what the club's promoter had billed as a celebration of Muddy Waters's birthday. The ribs were terrible, the band was mediocre, and the audience was almost entirely white. With all the zeal of new converts, these white blues fans clapped their hands and attempted to dance in ways and at times that simply did not seem appropriate. (In fact, I was reminded of the old one-liner: "Hey buddy, that song you're dancing to . . . they're playing it next!") The occasion also featured a booth selling T-shirts and bumper stickers advertising the Delta Blues Museum in Clarksdale. It was staffed by two women who not only had never been to the museum themselves but seemed less than certain about Clarksdale's exact whereabouts.

My experience in Chicago suggested why, writing in the *New York Times,* Phil Patton would soon be asking, "Who Owns the Blues?" This question seemed especially pertinent as workmen dismantled the Mississippi Delta cotton gin that once employed Muddy Waters and rebuilt it on Sunset Strip in Los Angeles as the centerpiece of the House of Blues, one of several such clubs in a chain established by Isaac Tigrett, the founder of the Hard Rock Cafe empire. With interest in the blues (among whites at least) at an all-time high, Patton pointed out that this blues boom was more complicated than previous urban folk revivals, because "it raises questions of authenticity and commercialization that go beyond the blues — questions that arise where the dirt road of pre-commercial folk arts meets the neon-lined strip of modern American media." Critics of the House of Blues enterprise condemn it as "a major commercialization and rip-off of the African-American culture." Others complain that the clubs seldom feature performances by real blues artists, offering instead performances by pop acts such as Bonnie Raitt or Hootie and the Blowfish. Investors in the effort range from the Harvard Endowment Fund to the Disney Corporation to a number of successful pop music and show business figures.[44]

House of Blues founder Isaac Tigrett insists, however, that "we are respectfully honoring the music" in clubs whose theme is meant to be "a tribute to the blues." Tigrett did, in fact, establish the House of Blues Foundation to encourage students to learn more about the blues, drawing on the resources of both the W. E. B. Du Bois Institute at Harvard and the Center for the Study of Southern Culture at the University of Mississippi. The academic participants in this enterprise generally share a conviction that the blues cannot be understood as a simple folk-derived musical form but as the product of a process of commercialization that has been shaping the blues for nearly a century. They point out that from the very beginning, blues artists sought a wider audience through a variety of gimmicks and stunts. For example, Robert Johnson's reputed "deal with the devil" had its roots in African lore, but it was also a great marketing gimmick for him. The same was true of Charley Patton's outrageous gymnastics with his guitar.[45]

The music of the twentieth-century African American diaspora, the blues was fluid and mobile, always interacting with other musical styles. Robert Johnson performed the cowboy hit, "Tumbling Tumbleweed," and one of the Delta's classic contemporary juke joints, the Purple Rain Lounge, near Duncan, owes its name to the film and the album of the same name by the artist formerly known as Prince. The foregoing surely suggests the difficulty of maintaining a "pure" or even static version of any artistic or cultural form once it has come into contact with the marketplace. Pioneer blues popularizer W. C. Handy made much the same point many years ago when he remarked slyly that once he saw a country blues band showered with silver dollars, he immediately "saw the beauty of primitive music."[46]

Clearly, many observers see the commercially induced changes in the blues and country music leading to a loss of cultural authenticity. Tony Scherman asks, "How far from its social origins can an art form grow before it simply loses meaning?" Scherman might do well to recall Tindall's always timely suggestion that rather than simply rob us of our identity, change may actually allow us to rediscover or reconfigure it. For example, North Carolina–born Mark Kemp reflected recently that the post–Civil Rights era emergence of "southern rock" music personified by bands such as the Allman Brothers and Lynyrd Skynyrd presented his generation of white southerners with the opportunity to "leave behind the burdens of guilt and disgrace, and go home again."[47]

As Kemp explains: "The Allman Brothers . . . charted this course back in 1969. But the trail has been advanced by new generations of Dixie rockers who still grapple with that most precious of Southern possessions: cultural identity. The difference is that today's Southern musicians feel free to tackle issues directly that were once taboo — racial antagonism, expressions of self-respect — rather than dealing with their feelings defensively or addressing them through metaphor."[48]

Contemporary heirs to the southern rock tradition, the Screamin Cheetah Wheelies offer in their "Moses Brown" what Kemp described as "the most powerful song about Southern pride since Skynyrd's 'Sweet Home Alabama.'" At the very least, "Moses Brown" is a song with considerable relevance to those seeking to recover or reconstruct their sense of what southernness is all about: "Moses Brown told the children to sit down, please. He noticed that they had lost their identity." Preaching interracial unity, Moses Brown also recognizes the obstacle presented by the South's divisive past: "You must forget about hard times, they have ended."[49]

In 1991 as I observed the frantic efforts of southern whites to keep their regional identities alive, I wondered "how long any ethnic or cultural identity could survive through simple self-assertion when the larger society neither challenges this identity nor considers it significant." I even went on to warn that "Southerners may continue to dote on their own distinctiveness yet a while, but scholars who pursue this market are not likely to find preaching only to the converted nearly so lucrative as have certain television evangelists within their region."[50]

So much for my credentials as a trends analyst. As the twentieth century draws to an end, the self-indulgent wallowing and thrashing in southernness shows little sign of abating. The success of *Southern Living* and the proliferation of other "regional" publications such as the *Oxford American* are obvious cases in point. Even academic entrepreneurs have seized the opportunity to "sell" southern culture. The University of Mississippi's Center for the Study of Southern Culture does at times seem like "Bubba Central," as Peter Applebome put it. Not only did the center sponsor Mississippi River cruises aboard the Delta Queen, but it staged two controversial conferences on Elvis Presley, described by the center's director, William R. Ferris, as "the most important pop culture figure of the twentieth century" and "a true modernist who eluded definitions like white or black, male or female." The second conference featured a performance by "Elvis Herselvis," the self-styled "Atomic-Powered Lesbian" and her "Straight White Males." The center likewise offered a "Southern Culture Catalog" that sported a possum on the cover and listed a variety of items from Zydeco recordings to praying pigs videos.[51]

No example, however, better illustrates the lengths to which white southerners are willing to go to maintain some sense of a distinctive identity than the remarkable rise to respectability of the once-despised redneck. The term "redneck" had once been the nation's most acceptable ethnic slur, suggesting lynch mobs, incest, and jacked-up pickup trucks with supercharged stereo systems blasting out Hank Jr. loud enough to wake Hank Sr. By the 1990s, however, "redneck" had become something approaching a term of endearment as white southerners embraced the redneck stereotype as part of a countercultural reaction against the homogenizing pressures permeating American mass society. Wearing sweatshirts proclaiming themselves "Absolutely Proud to Be A Redneck" and sipping Redneck Beer ("the taste of America"), they also fueled the phenomenal success of comedian Jeff Foxworthy, whose endless litany of one-liners ("You may be a redneck if . . . you've ever been too drunk to fish. . . . you go to family reunions trying to get a date," etc.) resulted in a series of hot-selling albums and two major network television series.[52]

Not only do many white southerners continue to indulge in outrageous self-caricature and what Freud called the "narcissism of small differences," but black southerners are now getting into the act as well. There is growing evidence that, fed by the region's economic progress and a swelling stream of black migration back to the South, the generally improving socioeconomic circumstances of black southerners may ultimately plunge them into an identity crisis of their own. The romanticization of the "redneck" that captivated so many southern whites already seems to have a counterpart among southern blacks who actively flaunt their southern lifestyles, dialects, and dietary preferences. Many even proudly identify themselves as "bamas," formerly a stereotypical term of derision directed by northern blacks at southern blacks who seemed "backward" and "country."[53]

The growing popularity of drawling, "southern cool" rap artists like "Goodie Mob" and comedians like television's Steve Harvey clearly has strong parallels among white southerners hooked on Redneck Beer and the one-liners of Jeff Foxworthy. The same is true of the concerns expressed by Elizabeth Fortson Arroyo. Educated at Harvard and Columbia, Arroyo insisted, "I feel Southern the same way an Irish American feels Irish. My roots are in the South, and Southern words and ways are a part of me." Arroyo nonetheless termed herself an "asterisk southerner," because although "I take great pride in being a Southerner, I'm just not sure if I am one." Her parents were indisputably southern, but because of her birth in Washington, D.C., and her lack of a pronounced accent, Arroyo could not help but worry, much like her upwardly mobile white contemporaries, "Is it enough to feel Southern, or must others around you (with shinier credentials) also take you to be so?" Although she was "concerned . . . that the very act of my self-analysis on this topic betrays me," Arroyo also noted Drew Faust's observation that "attempts at self-interpretation have become one of the region's most characteristic cultural products," and she posed a question appropriate for many contemporary southerners, white and black, when she asked, "What could be more Southern than to obsess about being Southern?"[54]

Arroyo's question was altogether appropriate and had actually been so for quite some time. In 1964 as he reviewed a volume titled *The Idea of the South,* Edwin Yoder described the South as an "increasingly homogenized" society that, in the act of "dying," both "gropes for and fondles its fading distinctions." Yoder's metaphoric portrait of white southerners engaging in what amounted to cultural masturbation was racy stuff in 1964, but to respond to his Freudian imagery in kind, his insistence that the South was "dying" also affirmed the susceptibility of Dixie's pundits to premature eulogization of their region's identity.[55]

Thirty-five years after Yoder's pronouncement, the continuing obsession of southerners with their identity must be understood in terms not only of a South still dying but of a North already dead and gone. In 1972 John Shelton Reed's *The Enduring South* documented the persistence of a distinctive southern identity characterized by intense localism, acceptance of violence, and extreme religiosity, all of which, he wrote, were "plausible responses for a minority group surrounded by a culture which is viewed as powerful, hostile, and unresponsive."[56]

Armed with more recent data, in his 1986 update of *The Enduring South,* Reed found that "cultural differences that were largely due to Southerners' lower incomes and educational levels, to their concentration in agricultural and low-level industrial occupations — those differences already diminishing in the 1960s were smaller still in the 1980s," and a few had even vanished altogether. Meanwhile, regional differences and tendencies toward localism and the acceptance of violence were also converging. This trend, however, was primarily the result of the changes in nonsouthern attitudes that had emerged as the late 1960s and 1970s confronted nonsoutherners (courtesy of Vietnam and Watergate) with the experiences of frustration, embarrassment, and defeat, and thus imbued them with the southerners' traditional sense that the world is a hostile place from which it is perhaps wiser to expect the worst than the best.[57]

Reed's explanation for the southernization of America was convincing enough. In 1972 as he looked ahead, however, he had suggested that "if their culture serves Southerners for better or worse, in dealing with a hostile 'outside,' it will probably continue to serve as long as the outside seems hostile." But, Reed added perceptively and prophetically, "the traditional outside has been the North, and the occasion for sectional animosity has usually been the South's racial institutions (although other issues have served at times): if the South's race relations improve or the North's deteriorate, white Southerners may yet realize their ancient wish to be 'let alone.'" Clearly both of the regional racial trends suggested by Reed have emerged and continued, while economic stagnation, urban decay, and a host of other difficulties elsewhere in the nation have also helped to insure that white southerners have, for better or worse, realized their dream of being "left alone."[58] Indeed, having endured more than a generation of premature eulogies for their supposedly moribund southern cultural identity, white southerners were witness within hardly more than a decade (late 1960s–early 1980s) to the decline, disintegration, and virtual disappearance of their figurative regional nemesis, the old morally and economically superior North. The North's demise may have been the cause of smugness and celebration among Dixieites at large, but the tensions between an ostensibly superior North and an envious but proud and often defiant South had fueled southern self-analysis in much the same way as the challenge of Westernization had forced writers and intellectuals in "developing" nations to reexamine their own cultures. In fact, the South owed a good part of its entire regional identity to the existence of an intimidating and antithetical North — affluent, confident, and rational.[59]

Thus, in the wake of the Civil Rights movement as southerners sought to make sense of what remained of southern life after Jim Crow, they found this task complicated immensely by the disappearance of the negative northern reference point that fed their sense of who they were by constantly reminding them of who they were not. If anyone might have anticipated this decidedly ironic outcome, it would be C. Vann Woodward, the supreme ironist himself, who pointed out on several occasions, as early as the 1950s, that the South's experience seemed distinctive only when compared to that of the rest of the United States, especially that of the North.[60]

As those of us who write and talk about the region for a living agonize about its — and our — future, we might actually take heart in Woodward's observation that the South's experience is, after all, far more relevant to the rest of the world than it is to that of the rest of our nation. Perhaps that is why as interest in the post-North South appears to wane among Americans at large, southern studies has become such a popular pursuit in Europe and other areas of the world. The Southern Studies Forum is an outgrowth of the European American Studies Association and the only such adjunct group dedicated to a subnational or regional component of American life and culture. Southern literature is a very big deal among Japanese scholars, and from Vienna to Bonn, from Cambridge to Genoa, from Denmark to the Czech Republic, European universities boast accomplished scholars whose principal interests are the history, literature, and culture of the American South.

Writing in 1958, Woodward pointed out that the South's history as a region, which includes large components of "frustration, failure and defeat," constituted "a heritage that is far more closely in line with the common lot of mankind than the national legends of success and innocence." Four decades later Michael O'Brien explained, "War, failure, prejudice, these are European things. Europeans see themselves in Southern writing and history. . . . By contrast, Europeans can find much in the history of the North that is a puzzle, for having such peace, such success, such want of incident." O'Brien also made an excellent point when he explained that "Columbia, South Carolina, which was burned to the ground by Sherman, makes more sense to someone who, like me, grew in a Plymouth flattened by the Luftwaffe."[61]

O'Brien's words suggest that the fixation of southerners with their past — even in its most tragic aspects — is far less unusual than many nonsoutherners seem to appreciate. After working for years as a correspondent in places such as Bosnia, Iraq, and Northern Ireland, where "memories were elephantine," Tony Horwitz found the refusal of some white southerners to let go of the Civil War far less unusual than the rest of America's "amnesia about its past." In his *Confederates in the Attic,* Horwitz noted that "Serbs spoke bitterly of their defeat by Muslim armies at Kosovo as though the battle had occurred yesterday, not in 1389," while "Protestants in Belfast referred fondly to 'King Billy' as if he were a family friend rather than the English monarch who led Orangemen to victory in 1690." [62]

The history-burdened South clearly has much in common with nations such as Japan and Germany, where the most unpleasant aspects of the past have at times been either revised beyond recognition or consciously ignored. Several scholars have shown the benefits of comparing the racial experiences of South Africa and the American South, but perhaps the most striking contemporary commonality here is the extent to which efforts at interracial cooperation seem to require that the past be pushed aside.

Not all of the South's relevance is rooted in its past. There are more contemporary parallels as well. For example, the South's simultaneous desire for and resistance to the Americanization of its culture is noteworthy for any society that has experienced Western or American cultural imperialism (the latter is sometimes described these days as simply "Disneyfication"). Roy Blount Jr. insisted recently that "They don't have live bait / video stores in the North." Perhaps not, but I wouldn't bet against finding them in small towns all over Europe. Frequent travelers to other parts of the world encounter such adaptations of past to present everywhere they turn. On a recent visit to France, we stayed in a sixteenth-century inn with a satellite dish on the roof and miniature golf course in the courtyard. (I perhaps should at least admit that this was in the South of France.) As John Shelton Reed has pointed out: "We often see, elsewhere in the world, that economic development simply provides new ways to do old things, or ways to do what would have been old things if they hadn't been impossible. Japanese use modern birth control to avoid births in unlucky years; Orthodox Jews ride automated elevators on Shabbat; Muslims are summoned to prayer from unbelievable distances by electronic muezzins." [63]

David Cohn identified the cultural and geographic poles of the region where he was "born and raised" with both precision and flair when he explained that "the Mississippi Delta begins in the lobby of the Peabody Hotel in Memphis and ends on Catfish Row in Vicksburg." A genial globetrotter extraordinaire, Cohn was always fascinated by the many exotic cultures, customs, and traditions he encountered. While no place on earth intrigued him more than his own native region, Cohn's far-flung meanderings and his keen powers of observation made him a "cosmopolitan provincial" who realized that "whatever happened from dawn to dawn in Baghdad on the Tigris, happened to us in Greenville on the Mississippi."[64]

Although I have spent nearly a quarter century writing and talking about the South's distinctiveness, I am increasingly convinced that southernologists of every disciplinary stripe should channel their provincial curiosities toward more cosmopolitan ends. I still believe that there is much that we can learn by asking why the South developed differently from the North. Yet, I also feel that when we ask this question we should do so as part of a broader inquiry that requires us to see both the South and the nation in a global perspective. In the century that lies ahead, dedicating so much attention to the lower right corner of the United States will be increasingly difficult to justify unless we realize that for future generations the value in studying the South's experience may actually lie not in what seems unique about it but in what seems universal.

Notes

INTRODUCTION

1. Reinhard Bendix, "Tradition and Modernity Reconsidered," *Comparative Studies in Society and History* 9 (April 1967): 292.
2. James C. Cobb, *Industrialization and Southern Society, 1877–1984* (Lexington, Ky., 1984), 136–64.
3. C. Vann Woodward, "The Irony of Southern History," *Journal of Southern History* 19 (February 1953): 3–6.

BEYOND PLANTERS AND INDUSTRIALISTS: A NEW PERSPECTIVE ON THE NEW SOUTH

1. The idea of the Civil War as a conflict between an agrarian and an industrial society is most often associated with the work of Charles A. Beard. See Charles A. Beard and Mary R. Beard, *The Rise of American Civilization*, 2 vols., rev. ed. (New York, 1940). See also Barrington Moore Jr., *Social Origins of Dictatorship and Democracy: Lord and Peasant in the Making of the Modern World* (Boston, 1966), 111–58. For an evaluation of the agrarian versus industrial dichotomy as applied to the study of Civil War causation in more recent works, see Eric Foner, "The Causes of the American Civil War: Recent Interpretations and New Directions," *Civil War History* 20 (September 1974): 197–214. On the South as a colony see for example Joe Persky, "Regional Colonialism and the Southern Economy," *Review of Radical Political Economics* 4 (Fall 1972): 70–79. The debate over the question of colonialism is surveyed in Clarence H. Danhof, "Four Decades of Thought on the South's Economic Problems," in Melvin L. Greenhut and W. Tate Whitman, eds., *Essays in Southern Economic Development* (Chapel Hill, 1964), 7–68. On agrarian tradition as a barrier to progress see William H. Nicholls, *Southern Tradition and Regional Progress* (Chapel Hill, 1960); and I. A. Newby, *The South: A History* (New York, 1978), 297–98. Newby also cited the "growing colonization" (p. 298) of the South's postbellum economy. This article is a revised version of a paper delivered at the annual meeting of the Southern Historical Association in Houston in November 1985. I am grateful to David L. Carlton and Robert C. McMath for their comments and suggestions.

2. Woodward, *Origins of the New South, 1877–1913* (Baton Rouge, 1951), 140–74; idem., "The Elusive Mind of the South," in *American Counterpoint: Slavery and Racism in the North-South Dialogue* (Boston, 1971), 281 (first quoted phrase); Cash, *The Mind of the South* (New York, 1941), 109, 153–54. The quotation concerning Cash is from Richard H. King, *A Southern Renaissance: The Cultural Awakening of the American South, 1930–1955* (New York, 1980), 267.

3. See Cash, *Mind of the South,* 224; Woodward, "The Search for Southern Identity," in *The Burden of Southern History* (Baton Rouge, 1968), 6, 10. For the tendency to identify studies according to the planter-industrialist dichotomy, see Gavin Wright, "Rethinking the Postbellum Southern Political Economy: A Review Essay," *Business History Review* 58 (Autumn 1984): 409–16. In this article Wright discusses David L. Carlton, *Mill and Town in South Carolina, 1880–1920* (Baton Rouge, 1982); Ronald D. Eller, *Miners, Millhands, and Mountaineers: Industrialization of the Appalachian South, 1880–1930* (Knoxville, 1982); Crandall A. Shifflett, *Patronage and Poverty in the Tobacco South: Louisa County, Virginia, 1860–1900* (Knoxville, 1982); and Michael S. Wayne, *The Reshaping of Plantation Society: The Natchez District, 1860–1880* (Baton Rouge, 1983). See also Russell S. Kirby's review of James C. Cobb, *The Selling of the South: The Southern Crusade for Industrial Development, 1936–1980,* in *Wisconsin Magazine of History* 68 (Autumn 1984): 63–64.

4. Sheldon Hackney, "*Origins of the New South* in Retrospect," *Journal of Southern History* 38 (May 1972): 191. The literature challenging Woodward's conclusion is summarized in Carl N. Degler, "Rethinking Post–Civil War History," *Virginia Quarterly Review* 62 (Spring 1981): 250–67; and Numan V. Bartley, "In Search of the New South: Southern Politics after Reconstruction," *Reviews in American History* 10 (December 1982): 150–63. See also Dan T. Carter, "From the Old South to the New: Another Look at the Theme of Change and Continuity," in Walter J. Fraser Jr. and Winfred B. Moore Jr., eds., *From the Old South to the New: Essays on the Transitional South* (Westport, Conn., 1981), 23–32. Quotation is from Newby, *South,* 239.

5. Woodward, "The Irony of Southern History," in *Burden of Southern History,* 187–211.

6. Wiener, *Social Origins of the New South: Alabama, 1860–1885* (Baton Rouge, 1978); Billings, *Planters and the Making of a "New South": Class, Politics, and Development in North Carolina, 1865–1900* (Chapel Hill, 1979). Both Wiener and Billings drew on Moore's *Social Origins of Dictatorship and Democracy.* On the differences between the Prussian experience and that of the American South as described by Wiener, see Harold D. Woodman, "Comments," *American Historical Review* 84 (October 1979): 998.

7. Salamon, "Protest, Politics, and Modernization in the American South: Mis-

sissippi as a 'Developing Society'" (Ph.D. dissertation, Harvard University, 1971). Jay R. Mandle, *The Roots of Black Poverty: The Southern Economy after the Civil War* (Durham, N.C., 1978), xi.

8. Wayne, *Reshaping of Plantation Society,* 102 (first quotation), 2 (second and third quoted phrases), 201, 203 (fourth quoted phrase); Fields, *Slavery and Freedom on the Middle Ground: Maryland During the Nineteenth Century* (New Haven, 1985).

9. Carlton, "'Builders of a New State' — The Town Classes and Early Industrialization of South Carolina, 1880–1907," in Fraser and Moore, *From the Old South to the New,* 57; Ford, "Rednecks and Merchants: Economic Development and Social Tensions in the South Carolina Upcountry, 1865–1900," *Journal of American History* 71 (September 1984): 317. See also Carlton's *Mill and Town in South Carolina,* 17.

10. On planter-merchant conflict see Wiener, *Social Origins of the New South,* 106–7.

11. James Tice Moore, "Redeemers Reconsidered: Change and Continuity in the Democratic South, 1870–1900," *Journal of Southern History* 44 (August 1978): 363–64.

12. Woodward, *Thinking Back: The Perils of Writing History* (Baton Rouge, 1986), 74; Wright, *Old South, New South: Revolutions in the Southern Economy Since the Civil War* (New York, 1986), 49.

13. Wright, *Old South, New South,* 48–49 (quotation on p. 49).

14. Genovese, *The Political Economy of Slavery: Studies in the Economy and Society of the Slave South* (New York, 1965); and Genovese, *The World the Slaveholders Made: Two Essays in Interpretation* (New York, 1969). For dissenting views see Shearer Davis Bowman, "Antebellum Planters and *Vormärz* Junkers in Comparative Perspective," *American Historical Review* 85 (October 1980): 779–808; Edward Pessen, "How Different from Each Other Were the Antebellum North and South?" *American Historical Review* 85 (December 1980): 1119–49; Degler, "Rethinking Post–Civil War History," 264. For an analysis of the reasons behind the antebellum South's failure to develop a larger manufacturing sector, see Bateman and Weiss, *A Deplorable Scarcity: The Failure of Industrialization in the Slave Economy* (Chapel Hill, 1981), 161–63.

15. Wiener, *Social Origins of the New South,* 182.

16. Bartley, *The Creation of Modern Georgia* (Athens, Ga., 1983); Moore, "Redeemers Reconsidered," 373.

17. Bartley, "In Search of the New South," 154; Wiener, *Social Origins of the New South,* 152; Ford, "Rednecks and Merchants," 314; Carlton, *Mill and Town in South Carolina,* 66.

18. Thornton, "Fiscal Policy and the Failure of Radical Reconstruction in the Lower South," in J. Morgan Kousser and James M. McPherson, eds., *Region, Race, and Reconstruction: Essays in Honor of C. Vann Woodward* (New York and

Oxford, 1982), 349–94; Robert L. Brandfon, *Cotton Kingdom of the New South: A History of the Yazoo Mississippi Delta from Reconstruction to the Twentieth Century* (Cambridge, Mass., 1967), 197.

19. James C. Cobb, *The Selling of the South: The Southern Crusade for Industrial Development, 1936–1980* (Baton Rouge, 1982), 63.

20. Wiener, "Class Structure and Economic Development in the American South," *American Historical Review* 84 (October 1979): 985; in the same issue of the *American Historical Review* see Woodman, "Comments," 997–1001; O'Brien, "The Nineteenth-Century American South," *Historical Journal* 24 (September 1981): 762; Bowman, "Antebellum Planters and *Vomärz* Junkers," 808; Fields, "The Advent of Capitalist Agriculture: The New South in a Bourgeois World," in Thavolia Glymph and John J. Kushma, eds., *Essays on the Postbellum Southern Economy* (College Station, Tex., 1985), 85–87.

21. Carlton, *Mill and Town in South Carolina,* 63; Wiener, *Social Origins of the New South,* 184. See also James C. Cobb, *Industrialization and Southern Society, 1877–1984* (Lexington, Ky., 1984), 24; and Wright, *Old South, New South,* 152, 172–73.

22. Parker, "The South in the National Economy, 1865–1970," *Southern Economic Journal* 46 (April 1980): 1045.

23. Bendix, "Tradition and Modernity Reconsidered," *Comparative Studies in Society and History* 9 (April 1967): 336.

24. Woodward, "New South Fraud Is Papered by Old South Myth," *Washington Post,* 9 July 1961.

25. Bartley, "In Search of the New South," 154.

26. Woodward, "New South Fraud."

27. On the literature of Populism see Bartley, "In Search of the New South," 155–56. See especially Steven Hahn, *The Roots of Southern Populism: Yeoman Farmers and the Transformation of the Georgia Upcountry, 1850–1890* (New York and Oxford, 1983); and Hahn's review essay, "Wool Hats and Mean Spirits," *Georgia Historical Quarterly* 68 (Winter 1984): 537–50. In this essay Hahn discusses Charles L. Flynn Jr., *White Land, Black Labor: Caste and Class in Late Nineteenth-Century Georgia* (Baton Rouge, 1983); and Barton C. Shaw, *The Wool-Hat Boys: Georgia's Populist Party* (Baton Rouge, 1984).

28. Bendix, "Tradition and Modernity Reconsidered," 334–35; Grantham, *Southern Progressivism: The Reconciliation of Progress and Tradition* (Knoxville, 1983), 258; James A. Caporaso, "The State's Role in Third World Economic Growth," *Annals of the American Academy of Political and Social Science* 459 (January 1982): 103–11. For recent treatments of southern Progressivism in addition to Grantham's *Southern Progressivism,* see J. Morgan Kousser, *The Shaping of Southern Politics: Suffrage Restriction and the Establishment of the One-Party South, 1880–1910* (New Haven, 1974), 229–31.

29. Wright, *Old South, New South,* 79; Grantham, *Southern Progressivism,* 257–61; J. Morgan Kousser, "Progressivism — For Middle-Class Whites Only: North Carolina Education, 1880–1910," *Journal of Southern History* 46 (May 1980): 169–94.

30. Wright, *Old South, New South,* 78; Carlton, *Mill and Town in South Carolina,* 172; James L. Leloudis II, "School Reform in the New South: The Woman's Association for the Betterment of Public School Houses in North Carolina, 1902–1919," *Journal of American History* 69 (March 1983): 887–88.

31. Tindall, "Business Progressivism: Southern Politics in the Twenties," *South Atlantic Quarterly* 62 (Winter 1963): 96.

32. Ibid., 106.

33. Ibid.

34. Hodding Carter III, "The Hegira of Alexander Smith," *Sales Management,* 15 February 1956, p. 36; idem., *Where Main Street Meets the River* (New York, 1953), 208 (first quotation); T. H. Baker, transcript of interview with Hodding Carter, 8 November 1968, Lyndon B. Johnson Library Oral History Collection, copy in Mississippi Department of Archives and History, Jackson, Miss. (second quotation); Jack Edward Prince, "History and Development of the Mississippi Balance Agriculture with Industry Program, 1936–1958" (Ph.D. dissertation, Ohio State University, 1961), 184–85. For other examples of liberal faith in industrial development, see J. Milton Yinger and George E. Simpson, "Can Segregation Survive in an Industrial Society?" *Antioch Review* 43 (Spring 1958): 15–24; and Nicholls, *Southern Tradition,* 9–15. On liberal journalists and the virtues of industrial development, see John T. Kneebone, *Southern Liberal Journalists and the Issue of Race, 1920–1944* (Chapel Hill, 1985), 229. For a brief explanation of this phenomenon see Woodward, "New South Fraud," and Wright, *Old South, New South,* 158, 177.

35. Numan V. Bartley and Hugh D. Graham, *Southern Politics and the Second Reconstruction* (Baltimore, 1975), 72. H. L. Mitchell, "Behind the White Citizens Councils: The Challenge to Labor in the South," *Socialist Call* (January 1956): 9; Dan Pollitt to H. L. Mitchell, 8 February 1956, both in A. E. Cox Collection, Mitchell Memorial Library, Mississippi State University, Starkville.

36. Howard H. Quint, *Profile in Black and White: A Frank Portrait of South Carolina* (Washington, D.C., 1958), 163–64 (first quotation on p. 163); Numan V. Bartley, *The Rise of Massive Resistance: Race and Politics in the South During the 1950's* (Baton Rouge, 1969), 244 (second quotation). Gerschenkron is quoted in Ford, "Rednecks and Merchants," 317.

37. Woodman, "Sequel to Slavery: The New History Views the Postbellum South," *Journal of Southern History* 43 (November 1977): 549.

38. Joseph T. Hill, FBI Report, 2 February 1945, Classified Subject Files, Central

Files, Correspondence, General Records of the Department of Justice, RG 60, National Archives, Washington, D.C. (quotation). Mandle noted that the preference of northern industrial employers for immigrant labor limited black employment opportunities outside the region in the late nineteenth century. He also cited the slow growth of industry in the Deep South, pointing out that "even if no discrimination in hiring was practiced — an assumption of heroic proportions — it is clear that southern industrialization provided only a limited opportunity at best for blacks to escape the confines of plantation life" (p. 21); Mandle, *Roots of Black Poverty,* 21–22. The competition among planters for labor in the late nineteenth century is discussed by Stephen J. DeCanio in *Agriculture in the Postbellum South: The Economics of Production and Supply* (Cambridge, Mass., 1974), 54–61. See also William Cohen, "Negro Involuntary Servitude in the South, 1865–1940: A Preliminary Analysis," *Journal of Southern History* 42 (February 1976): 37.

39. Allison Davis, Burleigh B. Gardner, and Mary R. Gardner, *Deep South: A Social Anthropological Study of Caste and Class* (Chicago, 1941), 260–65. In his study of the Yazoo Delta in the late nineteenth century, Robert L. Brandfon asserted that "the demands for more Negro labor for the Delta's cotton fields were meeting stiff competition from other areas of the South's economy" (p. 142). Brandfon cited the growth of cotton mills, phosphate mines, railroads, and other enterprises in the South at large, but he offered little specific evidence of significant competition between planters and industrialists for black labor. In fact, in explaining the motives for attempts to introduce Italian immigrant labor into the Delta, he noted that "greater than the complaints over inadequate numbers was planter frustration and disgust with Negro labor in general" (p. 143). Brandfon, *Cotton Kingdom of the New South,* 142–43.

40. Gavin Wright, "The Strange Career of the New Southern Economic History," *Reviews in American History* 10 (December 1982): 178 (first and second quotations); Wright, *Old South, New South,* 236 (third quotation).

41. Robert Daryl Lewis, "Delta Council: Transformer of an Agrarian Mind" (M.Ed. thesis, Delta State University, 1984); Don A. Newton, "Industry and the Delta," *Delta Review* 1 (Spring 1964): 29–31, 62.

42. Prince, "History and Development," 73–74; S. G. Laub to Harry O. Hoffman, 4 September 1937, Mississippi Industrial Commission, RG 13, Mississippi Department of Archives and History (quotation). The Delta's "super planter," Oscar Johnston, president of the Delta and Pine Land Company, objected to the subsidization of industries but accepted the goal of industrialization, announcing his desire to see "the South take advantage of its natural resources to develop industry." Oscar Johnston to F. W. Williams, 11 November

1937, Delta and Pine Land Company Records, Oscar Johnston Series, General Correspondence, Mitchell Memorial Library, Mississippi State University, Starkville.

43. Cobb, *Selling of the South,* 115–19. For a detailed analysis of black employment in southern industry see Herbert R. Northrup and Richard L. Rowan, *Negro Employment in Southern Industry* (Philadelphia, 1970); *New York Times,* 15 February 1983; Donna Dyer and Frank Adams, "The Lost Colony of North Carolina," *Southern Changes* 4 (June/July 1982): 7. According to a recent study, between 1977 and 1982 southern counties "with less than 25 percent minority population grew more than twice as fast as those with more than 50 percent minority population" (p. 27); Stuart A. Rosenfeld and Edward M. Bergman, *After the Factories: Changing Employment Patterns in the Rural South* (Research Triangle, N.C., 1985).

44. *Raleigh News and Observer,* 11 September 1977; *Wall Street Journal,* 10 February 1978; Cliff Sloan and Bob Hall, "'It's Good to Be Home in Greenville'... But It's Better If You Hate Unions," *Southern Exposure* 7 (Spring 1979): 83–93; Paul Luebke, Bob McMahon, and Jeff Risberg, "Selective Recruitment in North Carolina," *Working Papers for a New Society* 6 (March/April 1979): 19; Cobb, *Selling of the South,* 254–56.

45. In 1969 nearly 40 percent of the South's manufacturing plants were in rural areas or small towns. See Richard E. Lonsdale and Clyde B. Browning, "Rural-Urban Locational Preferences of Southern Manufacturers," *Annals of the Association of American Geographers* 61 (June 1971): 262; John Hekman and Alan Smith, "Behind the Sunbelt's Growth: Industrial Decentralization," *Federal Reserve Bank of Atlanta, Economic Review* 67 (March 1982): 8. The quotation is from William D. Barnard, *Dixiecrats and Democrats: Alabama Politics, 1942–1950* (University, Ala., 1974), 49.

46. Numan V. Bartley, "The Era of the New Deal as a Turning Point in Southern History," in James C. Cobb and Michael V. Namorato, eds., *The New Deal and the South* (Jackson, Miss., 1984), 135–46; Bartley, "Another New South?" *Georgia Historical Quarterly* 65 (Summer 1981): 119–37; Cobb, *Selling of the South,* 156, 159–60; Cobb, *Industrialization and Southern Society,* 51–53, 153–56; Wright, *Old South, New South,* 270.

47. Cobb, *Selling of the South,* 122–50; Elizabeth Jacoway and David R. Colburn, eds., *Southern Businessmen and Desegregation* (Baton Rouge, 1982); Paul Luebke and Joseph Schneider, "Economic and Racial Ideology in the North Carolina Elite," in James C. Cobb and Charles R. Wilson, eds., *Perspectives on the American South: An Annual Review of Society, Politics and Culture,* vol. 4 (New York, 1987), 129–43.

48. "Warmer Climates: Southern Tier Rated Best for Business," *Industry Week*, 8 July 1985, pp. 21–22.

49. Alfred J. Watkins, "'Good Business Climates': The Second War Between the States," *Dissent* 27 (Fall 1980): 476–85; Tina Rosenberg, "States at War: Going Broke on Tax Breaks," *New Republic*, 3 October 1983, p. 20; Donald H. Trautlein, "Where Have All the Factories Gone?" *Industry Week*, 19 August 1985, p. 28; "When the Bubble Burst in Alabama," *U.S. News and World Report*, 19 April 1982, p. 104; "Textile Industry Faces Struggle for Survival," *Southern Exposure* 13 (February 1985): 4–5; Caporaso, "State's Role in Third World Economic Growth," 103–11. In January 1986 the average manufacturing wage for production workers was $8.37 per hour in the eleven former Confederate states and $9.77 for the remainder of the nation. U.S. Department of Labor, Bureau of Labor Statistics, *Employment and Earnings* 33 (March 1986): 102–6. On wage differentials see Charles Hirschman and Kim Blankenship, "The North-South Earnings Gap: Changes during the 1960s and 1970s," *American Journal of Sociology* 87 (September 1981): 388–403; and Robert S. Goldfarb, Anthony M. J. Yezer, and Sebastian Crewe, "Some New Evidence: Have Regional Wage Differentials Really Disappeared?" *Growth and Change* 14 (January 1983): 48–51.

50. Woodward, "New South Fraud"; Caporaso, "State's Role in Third World Economic Growth," 103–11; George M. Fredrickson, "South Africa and the American South," *Inquiry*, 21 November 1977, p. 16; Richard L. Rudolph, "Agricultural Structure and Proto-Industrialization in Russia: Economic Development with Unfree Labor," *Journal of Economic History* 45 (March 1985): 47–69; Wright, *Old South, New South*, 273.

51. Gavin Wright appeared to be making a similar point when he argued that if the South fails to become "highly unionized," it will be "a sign of the late twentieth-century American times, not the persistence of the Old South" (p. 264); Wright, *Old South, New South*.

WORLD WAR II AND THE MIND OF THE MODERN SOUTH

1. Wilbur J. Cash, *The Mind of the South* (New York, 1991), 96, 429; see also James C. Cobb, "Does 'Mind' No Longer Matter? The South, the Nation, and the Mind of the South, 1941–1991," *Journal of Southern History* (November 1991): 681–718.

2. Bruce Clayton, *W. J. Cash: A Life* (Baton Rouge, 1991), 3, 187.

3. Morton Sosna, "More Important than the Civil War? The Impact of World War II on the South," in James C. Cobb and Charles R. Wilson, eds., *Perspectives*

on the *American South: An Annual Review of Society, Politics, and Culture,* vol. 4 (New York, 1987), 145–61.

4. John Ray Skates Jr., "World War II as a Watershed in Mississippi History," *Journal of Mississippi History* (May 1975): 135.

5. William R. Parker, "The South in the National Economy, 1865–1970," *Southern Economic Journal* 46 (April 1980): 1045–46.

6. Numan V. Bartley, "The Era of the New Deal as a Turning Point in Southern History," in James C. Cobb and Michael V. Namorato, eds., *The New Deal and the South* (Jackson, Miss., 1984), 138. See also George B. Tindall, *The Emergence of the New South, 1913–1945* (Baton Rouge, 1967). For recent examples of the emerging historiographical focus on World War II, see Bartley, *The New South, 1945–1980: The Story of the South's Transformation* (Baton Rouge, 1995). See also Allen Cronenberg, *Forth to the Mighty Conflict: Alabama and World War Two* (Tuscaloosa, Ala., 1995), and C. Calvin Smith, *War and Wartime Change: The Transformation of Arkansas, 1940–1945* (Fayetteville, Ark., 1986).

7. Dewey W. Grantham, *The South in Modern America: A Region at Odds* (New York, 1994) 175; James C. Cobb, *The Selling of the South: The Southern Crusade for Industrial Development, 1936–1990* (Urbana, Ill., 1993), 13–28.

8. Frank E. Smith, *Congressman from Mississippi* (New York, 1964), 64; James C. Cobb, *The Most Southern Place on Earth: The Mississippi Delta and the Roots of Regional Identity* (New York and Oxford, 1992), 210.

9. Jennifer E. Brooks, "From Fighting Nazism to Fighting Bossism: Southern World War II Veterans and the Assault on Southern Political Traditions," and Craig S. Pascoe, "The Monroe Rifle Club: Finding Justice in an Ungodly and Social Jungle Called 'Dixie,'" both unpublished papers presented at the 1996 Southern Historical Association meeting in New Orleans, La.

10. John Egerton, *Speak Now Against the Day: The Generation before the Civil Rights Movement in the South* (New York, 1994), 326.

11. Ibid., 327.

12. Smith, *Congressman,* 101.

13. Ibid., 55; Adam Nossiter, *Of Long Memory: Mississippi and the Murder of Medgar Evers* (Reading, Mass., 1994), 117.

14. Editorial, *Montgomery (Ala.) Advertiser,* 21 May 1946, cited in Brooks, "Fighting Nazism."

15. Pete Daniel, "Going Among Strangers: Southern Reactions to World War II," *Journal of American History* 77 (December 1990): 893–94; Egerton, *Speak Now,* 366–69.

16. John Egerton, interview with Sid McMath, 8 September 1990, A-302, Southern Oral History Program, Southern Historical Collection, University of North

Carolina, Chapel Hill; James C. Cobb, "Colonel Effingham Crushes the Crackers: Political Reform in Postwar Augusta," *South Atlantic Quarterly* 89 (Autumn 1979): 507–19; Cobb, *Selling of the South,* 156.

17. Brooks, "Fighting Nazism."

18. Ibid.

19. The three governors controversy is outlined in detail in James C. Cobb's "Georgia Odyssey," in *The New Georgia Guide* (Athens, Ga., 1996). See also, Numan V. Bartley, *The Creation of Modern Georgia* (Athens, Ga., 1983), 187–91. Herman E. Talmadge, interview with Harold Henderson, 17 July 1987, cited in Brooks, "Fighting Nazism."

20. Katharine DuPre Lumpkin, *The Making of a Southerner* (Athens, Ga., 1991), 233–34; Bartley, *Creation of Modern Georgia,* 187.

21. See James C. Cobb, "Introduction," in Cobb and Namorato, *New Deal and the South,* 3–15.

22. Bruce J. Schulman, *From Cotton Belt to Sunbelt: Federal Policy, Economic Development, and the Transformation of the South, 1938–1980* (New York and Oxford, 1991), 72–87.

23. Ibid., 72; Sosna, "More Important than the Civil War," 149–50.

24. Jacqueline Jones, *The Dispossessed: America's Underclass from the Civil War to the Present* (New York, 1992), 226, 228; Harry L. Wright to George Mitchell, 23 February 1946, cited in Brooks, "Fighting Nazism."

25. Jones, *Dispossessed,* 226–27; *U.S. Bureau of the Census, Census of Population, 1950,* vol. 2, *Characteristics of the Population,* pt. 24, Mississippi, 188.

26. *Atlanta Constitution,* 13 August 1995; Schulman, *From Cotton Belt to Sun Belt,* 81–82.

27. Bill C. Malone, *Southern Music, American Music* (Lexington, Ky., 1979), 88–93; Tony Scherman, "Country," *American Heritage* 45 (November 1994): 40–50.

28. Curtis W. Ellison, *Country Music Culture: From Hard Times to Heaven* (Jackson, Miss., 1995), 33; Bill C. Malone, *Country Music, U.S.A.: A Fifty-Year History* (Austin, 1974), 128, 313–16, 323–24; Cobb, *Most Southern Place,* 284, 299, 302.

29. Samuel C. Adams Jr., "The Acculturation of the Delta Negro," *Social Forces* 26 (December 1947): 202–5; Peter Guralnick, *Sweet Soul Music: Rhythm and Blues and the Southern Dream of Freedom* (New York, 1986), 32–37.

30. Pete Daniel, "Rhythm of the Land," *Agricultural History* 68 (Fall 1994): 22; see also George Lipsitz, *Class and Culture in Cold War America: A Rainbow at Midnight* (New York, 1981), 205.

31. David L. Cohn, *Where I Was Born and Raised* (Cambridge, Mass., 1948), 41, x.

32. Sosna, "More Important than the Civil War," 154. Faulkner is quoted in David Minter, *William Faulkner: His Life and Work* (Baltimore, 1980), 199–200; see

also Frederick R. Karl, *William Faulkner: American Writer* (New York, 1989), 711.

33. Morton Sosna, "The G.I.'s South and the North-South Dialogue during World War II," in Winfred B. Moore Jr., Joseph F. Tripp, and Lyon G. Tyler Jr., eds., *Developing Dixie: Modernization in a Traditional Society* (Westport, Conn., 1988), 813, 322; William Faulkner, *Intruder in the Dust* (New York, 1948), 153.

34. C. Vann Woodward, *Thinking Back: The Perils of Writing History* (Baton Rouge, 1986), 88; idem., *The Origins of the New South, 1877–1913* (Baton Rouge, 1951); idem., *The Strange Career of Jim Crow* (New York and Oxford, 1955).

35. John Hope Franklin, "John Hope Franklin: A Life of Learning," in *Race and Southern History: Selected Essays, 1938–1988* (Baton Rouge, 1989), 287–90.

36. Arnold Rampersad, *The Life of Langston Hughes,* vol. 2: *I Dream a World* (New York and Oxford, 1988), 36, 46, 50.

37. Michel Fabre, *The Unfinished Quest of Richard Wright,* 2nd ed. (Urbana and Chicago, 1993), 223, 227.

38. Robert E. Hemenway, *Zora Neale Hurston: A Literary Biography* (Urbana, Ill., 1977), 287, 288, 294, 295.

39. Lillian Smith, *Strange Fruit* (New York, 1944); Morton Sosna, *In Search of the Silent South: Southern Liberals and the Race Issue* (New York, 1977), 186, 191.

40. *Smith v. Allwright,* 321 U.S. 664; Sosna, *In Search of the Silent South,* 198–211; Bartley, *New South.*

41. Hollinger F. Barnard, ed., *Outside the Magic Circle: The Autobiography of Virginia Foster Durr* (Tuscaloosa, Ala., 1985), 171–72, 191.

42. Walker Percy, interview with Jan Nordby Gretlund, 2 January 1981, *South Carolina Review* (Spring 1981): 12. See also, James C. Cobb, "Southern Writers and the Challenge of Regional Convergence," *Georgia Historical Quarterly* 73 (Spring 1989): 3–9; Faulkner, *Intruder in the Dust,* 119–20; Cohn, *Where I Was Born and Raised,* 299–300; Adams, "Acculturation of the Delta Negro," 203.

43. Flannery O'Connor, "The Displaced Person," in *Flannery O'Connor: The Complete Stories* (New York, 1971), 405–20.

44. Terry Kay, *The Year the Lights Came On* (Athens, Ga., 1989), 11, 12.

45. Flannery O'Connor, "The Fiction Writer and His Country," in Granville Hicks, ed., *The Living Novel: A Symposium* (New York, 1957), 159; Walker Percy, "The Southern Moderate" and "A Southern View," in Patrick Samway, ed., *Signposts in a Strange Land* (New York, 1991), 101 (first quote), 91 (second quote); Percy, "Southern Comfort," *Harper's,* January 1979, p. 83. On Percy's influence, see Fred Hobson, *The Southern Writer in the Post-Modern World* (Athens, Ga., 1991), 57–72. See also Richard Ford, *The Sportswriter* (New York, 1986), and Josephine Humphreys, *Dreams of Sleep* (New York, 1984).

46. John Egerton, *The Americanization of Dixie: The Southernization of America* (New York, 1974); idem., *Speak Now Against the Day,* 327–28.

47. Bertram Wyatt-Brown, "The Mind of W. J. Cash," introduction to 1991 Vintage Press edition of Cash, *Mind of the South,* vii-viii.

48. James C. Cobb, "Oh, Lord, Won't You Buy Me a Mercedes Plant?" *Reckon* 1 (Fall 1995): 20–21.

49. Charlayne Hunter-Gault, *In My Place* (New York, 1992), 253. See the *Atlanta Journal-Constitution* Poll, *Atlanta-Journal Constitution,* 16 February 1992.

50. Sosna, "G.I.'s South," 322.

DOES "MIND" STILL MATTER? THE SOUTH, THE NATION,
AND *THE MIND OF THE SOUTH,* 1941–1991

1. For a recent analysis of Cash's life and his book, which was published in New York in 1941 by Alfred A. Knopf, Inc., see Bruce Clayton, *W. J. Cash: A Life* (Baton Rouge, 1991). The author wishes to acknowledge the comments of Numan V. Bartley, William F. Holmes, and Harvey H. Jackson. This article is an expanded version of a paper presented at the annual meeting of the Southern Historical Association in Fort Worth, Texas, on 13 November 1991.

2. Clement Eaton, review of *The Mind of the South,* in the *American Historical Review* 47 (January 1942): 374–75; C. Vann Woodward, review of *The Mind of the South, Journal of Southern History* 7 (August 1941): 400–401 (quotations); and Arthur S. Link and Rembert W. Patrick, eds., *Writing Southern History: Essays in Honor of Fletcher M. Green* (Baton Rouge, 1965) (quotations in order are on pp. 442, 384, 201). *The Mind of the South* is cited nine times in this volume.

3. Michael O'Brien, "W. J. Cash, Hegel, and the South," *Journal of Southern History* 44 (August 1978): 381; and Bertram Wyatt-Brown, "W. J. Cash and Southern Culture," in Walter J. Fraser Jr. and Winfred B. Moore Jr., eds., *From the Old South to the New: Essays on the Transitional South* (Westport, Conn., 1981), 195.

4. John B. Boles and Evelyn Thomas Nolen, eds., *Interpreting Southern History: Historiographical Essays in Honor of Sanford W. Higginbotham* (Baton Rouge, 1987), 399, 401, 511; O'Brien, "A Private Passion: W. J. Cash" (revised version of O'Brien's article with the same title cited in note 3 above), in *Rethinking the South: Essays in Intellectual History* (Baltimore, 1988), 180.

5. O'Brien, "Private Passion," 179.

6. C. Vann Woodward, *Thinking Back: The Perils of Writing History* (Baton Rouge, 1986), quotations in order, 23 (first, third, and fourth quotations), 22, 27; and Joel Williamson, *The Crucible of Race: Black-White Relations in the American South Since Emancipation* (New York, 1984), 459.

7. Bertram Wyatt-Brown, "W. J. Cash and Southern Culture" (revised version of Wyatt-Brown's article with the same title cited in note 3 above), in *Yankee Saints and Southern Sinners* (Baton Rouge, 1985), 139; Woodward, *Thinking Back,* 23; Bruce Clayton, "A Southern Modernist: The Mind of W. J. Cash," in Clayton and John A. Salmond, eds., *The South Is Another Land: Essays on the Twentieth-Century South* (Westport, Conn., 1987), 171; Daniel Joseph Singal, *The War Within: From Victorian to Modernist Thought in the South, 1919–1945* (Chapel Hill, 1982), 373; Richard H. King, *A Southern Renaissance: The Cultural Awakening of the American South, 1930–1955* (New York, 1980), 146.

8. King, *Southern Renaissance,* 154, 263–65 (quoted material on pp. 263, 154); Singal, *War Within,* 373–74.

9. Jack Temple Kirby, *Media-Made Dixie: The South in the American Imagination,* rev. ed. (Athens, Ga., 1986), 58–60 (quotation on p. 60); Howard W. Odum, *Southern Regions of the United States* (Chapel Hill, 1936); Rupert B. Vance, *Human Geography of the South: A Study in Regional Resources and Human Adequacy* (Chapel Hill, 1932); Arthur F. Raper, *Preface to Peasantry: A Tale of Two Black Belt Counties* (Chapel Hill, 1936); John Dollard, *Caste and Class in a Southern Town* (New Haven, 1937); Hortense Powdermaker, *After Freedom: A Cultural Study in the Deep South* (New York, 1939); Dorothea Lange and Paul S. Taylor, *An American Exodus: A Record of Human Erosion in the Thirties,* rev. ed. (New Haven, 1969); Erskine Caldwell and Margaret Bourke-White, *You Have Seen Their Faces* (New York, 1937); William J. Cooper Jr. and Thomas E. Terrill, *The American South: A History* (New York, 1991), 654.

10. Woodward, *Thinking Back,* 102; Immanuel Wallerstein, "What Can One Mean by Southern Culture?" in Numan V. Bartley, ed., *The Evolution of Southern Culture* (Athens, Ga., 1988), 11–12.

11. Fred Hobson, *Tell about the South: The Southern Rage to Explain* (Baton Rouge, 1983), 300, 315, 301 (quotations in order); Lillian Smith, *Killers of the Dream* (New York, 1949); Stetson Kennedy, *Southern Exposure* (Garden City, N.Y., 1946).

12. Paul M. Gaston, *The New South Creed: A Study in Southern Mythmaking* (New York, 1970), 232; V. O. Key Jr., *Southern Politics in State and Nation* (New York, 1949); C. Vann Woodward, *Origins of the New South, 1877–1913* (Baton Rouge, 1951); Numan V. Bartley, "In Search of the New South: Southern Politics after Reconstruction," in Stanley I. Kutler and Stanley N. Katz, eds., *The Promise of American History* (Baltimore, 1982), 150 (quotation); Hugh Davis Graham, "Southern Politics Since World War II," in Boles and Nolen, *Interpreting Southern History,* 391.

13. Graham, "Southern Politics," 391; King, *Southern Renaissance,* 271, 277; Kirby, *Media-Made Dixie,* 113–14; Kenneth M. Stampp, *The Peculiar Institution: Slavery*

in the Antebellum South (New York, 1956); John Hope Franklin, *Reconstruction after the Civil War* (Chicago, 1961); Stampp, *The Era of Reconstruction, 1865–1877* (New York, 1965).

14. Wyatt-Brown, "W. J. Cash and Southern Culture," in Fraser and Moore, *From the Old South to the New,* 196; Kirby, *Media-Made Dixie,* 112–14; Cash, *The Mind of the South* (New York, 1960) (paper).

15. Bob Smith, "A Prisoner in Time," *Red Clay Reader* 4 (1967): 16.

16. C. Vann Woodward, "White Man, White Mind," *New Republic,* 9 December 1967, p. 28; Wyatt-Brown, "W. J. Cash and Southern Culture," in Fraser and Moore, *From the Old South to the New,* 196.

17. Kirby, *Media-Made Dixie,* 87, 83 (first two quotations); C. Vann Woodward, *The Strange Career of Jim Crow* (New York, 1955); idem., "The Search for Southern Identity," in *The Burden of Southern History,* rev. ed. (Baton Rouge, 1968), 6, 4.

18. Clayton, "Southern Modernist," 182; King, *Southern Renaissance,* 150.

19. O'Brien, "From a Chase to a View: C. Vann Woodward," in *Rethinking the South,* 195–96.

20. Woodward, "White Man, White Mind," 28–29. Echoing Woodward on this point, David Hackett Fischer subsequently charged Cash with falling victim to "the fallacy of composition" by "reasoning improperly from a property of a member of a group to a property of the group itself." For Fischer the consequences of this error on Cash's part were that when "Cash studied a low-country Nabob, he saw a hillbilly in disguise." David Hackett Fischer, *Historians' Fallacies: Toward a Logic of Historical Thought* (New York, 1970), 219–20.

21. Woodward, "White Man, White Mind," 29; King, *Southern Renaissance,* 264.

22. Woodward, "White Man, White Mind," 30; program of the 35th annual meeting of the Southern Historical Association, Washington, D.C., 29, 30, 31 October, and 1 November 1969, p. 68; Woodward, "W. J. Cash Reconsidered," *New York Review of Books,* 4 December 1969, pp. 28–34. Woodward, "The Elusive Mind of the South," in *American Counterpoint: Slavery and Racism in the North-South Dialogue* (Boston, 1971), 261–83 (quotations are on pp. 265, 269, 276).

23. Gaston, *New South Creed,* 11–12; Sheldon Hackney, "*Origins of the New South* in Retrospect," *Journal of Southern History* 38 (May 1972): 201.

24. Eugene D. Genovese, *The World the Slaveholders Made: Two Essays in Interpretation* (New York, 1969), 144 (first quoted phrase), 140 (other quotations). For an up-to-date review of the "guiltomania" debate, see Gaines M. Foster, "Guilt Over Slavery: A Historiographical Analysis," *Journal of Southern History* 56 (November 1990): 665–94.

25. O'Brien, "W. J. Cash, Hegel, and the South," 381; O'Brien, "Private Passion," 179–80.

26. Cash, *Mind of the South,* 23 (first Cash quotation), 115 (second Cash quotation); J. Mills Thornton III, *Politics and Power in a Slave Society: Alabama, 1800–1860* (Baton Rouge, 1978); Michael P. Johnson, *Toward a Patriarchal Republic: The Secession of Georgia* (Baton Rouge, 1977); Steven Hahn, *The Roots of Southern Populism: Yeoman Farmers and the Transformation of the Georgia Upcountry, 1850–1890* (New York and Oxford, 1983), 10.

27. James Oakes, *The Ruling Race: A History of American Slaveholders* (New York, 1982), 67–68, 229–32 (quotations 67, 229); Lacy K. Ford Jr., *Origins of Southern Radicalism: The South Carolina Upcountry, 1800–1860* (New York and Oxford, 1988); Cash, *Mind of the South,* 15.

28. O'Brien, "Private Passion," 179; Wyatt-Brown, "W. J. Cash and Southern Culture," in *Yankee Saints and Southern Sinners,* 139.

29. O'Brien, "Private Passion," 180; Clayton, *W. J. Cash,* 220.

30. Wyatt-Brown, "W. J. Cash and Southern Culture," in Yankee *Saints and Southern Sinners,* 154; Woodward, *Thinking Back.*

31. Hobson, *Tell about the South,* 264–66.

32. Ibid., 264; David L. Cohn, "Tissues of Southern Culture," *Saturday Review,* 22 February 1941, pp. 7, 16–17; Cohn, *Where I Was Born and Raised* (Notre Dame, 1967), 15, 105; Cash, *Mind of the South,* 439–40. Cash's assessment of antebellum society seemed generally in accord with memoirs and travelers' accounts of the Alabama Black Belt. Harvey H. Jackson, "Time, Frontier, and the Alabama Black Belt: Searching for W. J. Cash's Planter," unpublished manuscript in possession of the author.

33. Kirby, *Media-Made Dixie,* 83–84; Hahn, *Roots of Southern Populism;* David L. Carlton, *Mill and Town in South Carolina, 1880–1920* (Baton Rouge, 1982); Ford, *Origins of Southern Radicalism.* On the broad significance of Ford's book see William J. Cooper's review, *Journal of Southern History* 56 (August 1990): 525–27. Ironically, Cash's view of the Piedmont textile belt he ostensibly knew so well has been challenged significantly in recent years. See for example Carlton, *Mill and Town in South Carolina;* Jacquelyn Dowd Hall et al., *Like a Family: The Making of a Southern Cotton Mill World* (Chapel Hill, 1987); and Allen Tullos, *Habits of Industry: White Culture and the Transformation of the Carolina Piedmont* (Chapel Hill, 1989).

34. Williamson, *Crucible of Race,* 1–2; King, *Southern Renaissance,* 163, 162.

35. Richard Wright, *Black Boy: A Record of Childhood and Youth* (New York, 1969), 283; Hobson, *Tell about the South,* 264; Cash, *Mind of the South,* 327; Clayton, "The Proto-Dorian Convention: W. J. Cash and the Race Question," in Jeffrey J. Crow, Paul D. Escott, and Charles L. Flynn Jr., eds., *Race, Class, and Politics in Southern History: Essays in Honor of Robert F. Durden* (Baton Rouge, 1989), 287.

36. Clayton, " Proto-Dorian Convention," 287 (quotation) and *W. J. Cash,* 202–6; O'Brien, "Cash, W. J.," in Charles R. Wilson and William R. Ferris, eds., *Encyclopedia of Southern Culture* (Chapel Hill, 1989), 1130–31.

37. King, *Southern Renaissance,* 272; Howard N. Rabinowitz, "More than the Woodward Thesis: Assessing *The Strange Career of Jim Crow,*" *Journal of American History* 75 (December 1988): 855. For Woodward's response see "Strange Career Critics: Long May They Persevere," *Journal of American History* 75 (December 1988): 857–68.

38. Hobson, *Tell about the South,* 264; Kirby, *Media-Made Dixie,* 81; George M. Fredrickson, *The Black Image in the White Mind: The Debate on Afro-American Character and Destiny, 1817–1914* (New York, 1971), 61.

39. Jacquelyn Dowd Hall and Anne Firor Scott, "Women in the South," in Boles and Nolen, *Interpreting Southern History,* 454; Winthrop D. Jordan, *White over Black: American Attitudes Toward the Negro, 1550–1812* (Chapel Hill, 1968); King, *Southern Renaissance,* 165; Cash, *Mind of the South,* 118–19; Wyatt-Brown, "W. J. Cash and Southern Culture," in Fraser and Moore, *From the Old South to the New,* 209; Dollard, *Caste and Class,* 381; Seth Cagin and Philip Dray, *We Are Not Afraid: The Story of Goodman, Schwerner, and Chaney and the Civil Rights Campaign for Mississippi* (New York, 1988), 157. On Cash's treatment of women see also Clayton, *W. J. Cash,* 208–10.

40. King, *Southern Renaissance,* 166; Wyatt-Brown, "W. J. Cash and Southern Culture," in Fraser and Moore, *From the Old South to the New,* 199; Wyatt-Brown, "W. J. Cash and Southern Culture," in *Yankee Saints and Southern Sinners,* 141.

41. Genovese, *World the Slaveholders Made,* 141–42; Genovese, "Yeomen Farmers in a Slaveholders' Democracy," *Agricultural History* 49 (April 1975): 331–42; and Wyatt-Brown, "W. J. Cash and Southern Culture," in *Yankee Saints and Southern Sinners,* 150–51; idem., "W. J. Cash and Southern Culture," in Fraser and Moore, *From the Old South to the New,* 205–7 (final three quotations).

42. Wyatt-Brown, "W. J. Cash and Southern Culture," in *Yankee Saints and Southern Sinners,* 151, 153.

43. Woodward, *Origins of the New South,* vii (preface to the 1971 edition); Graham, "Southern Politics, " 401. See also James C. Cobb, "Beyond Planters and Industrialists: A New Perspective on the New South," *Journal of Southern History* 54 (February 1988): 45–68.

44. James Tice Moore, "Redeemers Reconsidered: Change and Continuity in the Democratic South, 1870–1900," *Journal of Southern History* 44 (August 1978): 378; Dwight B. Billings Jr., *Planters and the Making of a "New South": Class, Politics, and Development in North Carolina, 1865–1900* (Chapel Hill, 1979), 217.

45. Carlton, "'Builders of a New State' — The Town Classes and Early Industrialization of South Carolina, 1880–1907," in Fraser and Moore, eds., *From the Old*

South to the New, 57; Ford, "Rednecks and Merchants: Economic Development and Social Tensions in the South Carolina Upcountry, 1865–1900," *Journal of American History* 71 (September 1984): 317; Michael S. Wayne, *The Reshaping of Plantation Society: The Natchez District, 1860–1880* (Baton Rouge, 1983); Gavin Wright, *Old South, New South: Revolutions in the Southern Economy Since the Civil War* (New York, 1986), 49; James C. Cobb, "Making Sense of Southern Economic History," *Georgia Historical Quarterly* 71 (Spring 1987): 66. If spectators sometimes found it difficult to identify all the participants in the great Cash-Woodward continuity-discontinuity debate without a scorecard, it was also true that not every scorecard read the same. Woodward claimed Wright for his discontinuity squad, asserting that Wright "leaves no doubt about his views" in *The Political Economy of the Cotton South* as he emphasized "not only the massiveness but the suddenness of change as well." Dan T. Carter, on the other hand, saw the same book emphasizing "the basic coherence and continuity of Southern economic history over the nineteenth century as a whole." Woodward, *Thinking Back,* 77; Carter, "From the Old South to the New: Another Look at the Theme of Change and Continuity," in Fraser and Moore, *From the Old South to the New,* 25; Wright's *Old South, New South* proved similarly difficult to categorize. As Cobb noted, because the value of land in the postbellum South remained so dependent on the availability of an ample supply of cheap labor, the "new mission" of Wright's landlords "depended on nothing so much as the maintenance of the 'old' condition of labor market isolation. So long as this was the case, the overall direction of the South's postbellum economy seems to have been influenced less by the new ends that the landlords pursued than the old means which that pursuit entailed." Cobb, "Making Sense of Southern Economic History," 66–67.

46. Carlton, "The Revolution from Above: The National Market and the Beginnings of Industrialization in North Carolina," *Journal of American History* 77 (September 1990): 474; Cobb, "Beyond Planters and Industrialists," 68; Wright, *Old South, New South,* 264.

47. Bartley and Graham, *Southern Politics and the Second Reconstruction* (Baltimore, 1975), 200; Earl Black and Merle Black, *Politics and Society in the South* (Cambridge, Mass., 1987), 316.

48. Cash, *Mind of the South,* x; Carl Degler, *Place Over Time: The Continuity of Southern Distinctiveness* (Baton Rouge, 1977), 132.

49. John Shelton Reed, *Southerners: The Social Psychology of Sectionalism* (Chapel Hill, 1983), 111, 114; Woodward, "Search for Southern Identity," 4–5.

50. Clayton, *W. J. Cash,* 219; King, *Southern Renaissance,* 267.

51. For a general review of the criticisms of *Origins of the New South* and Woodward's response, see Woodward, *Thinking Back,* 66–79. On Woodward's argu-

ment for the demise of the planter see Moore, "Redeemers Reconsidered," 357–78; Carter, "From the Old South to the New," 24; and Cobb, "Beyond Planters and Industrialists," 47. On Woodward's treatment of New South politics see Carl V. Harris, "Right Fork or Left Fork? The Section-Party Alignments of Southern Democrats in Congress, 1873–1897," *Journal of Southern History* 42 (November 1976): 471–506. On Woodward's analysis of the origins of segregation see John W. Cell, *The Highest Stage of White Supremacy: The Origins of Segregation in South Africa and the American South* (Cambridge, 1982), 82–102. On disfranchisement see J. Morgan Kousser, *The Shaping of Southern Politics: Suffrage, Restriction, and the Establishment of the One-Party South, 1880–1910* (New Haven, Conn., 1974), 5–6, 238, 250, and Cell, *Highest Stage of White Supremacy,* 119–23. On the lack of attention to women in *Origins,* see Hall and Scott, "Women in the South," 454–55 (first two quoted phrases). On Woodward's treatment of blacks in *Origins,* see King, *Southern Renaissance,* 272. On Woodward's analysis of the New South economy see Wright, *Old South, New South,* 62, 156–57. For an appraisal of the overall effect of criticism on Woodward's synthesis of the New South, see John Herbert Roper, *C. Vann Woodward, Southerner* (Athens, Ga., 1987), 145–49, and Michael O'Brien, "From a Chase to a View," 204–5.

52. Wyatt-Brown, "W. J. Cash and Southern Culture," in *Yankee Saints and Southern Sinners,* 131; Williamson, *Crucible of Race,* 3; Grantham, "Mr. Cash Writes a Book," *Progressive* 25 (1961): 41; Wyatt-Brown, "W. J. Cash and Southern Culture," in *Yankee Saints and Southern Sinners,* 136; and Williams, *Crucible of Race,* 3. For example, neither John Hope Franklin's *The Militant South, 1800–1861* (Cambridge, Mass., 1956) nor William R. Taylor's *Cavalier and Yankee: The Old South and American National Character* (New York, 1961) used Cash either as a "takeoff" point or "destination," although he had discussed extensively the topics they explored.

53. Kirby, *Media-Made Dixie,* 80; Fischer, *Historians' Fallacies,* 220.

54. William Faulkner, *Intruder in the Dust* (New York, 1948), 152–53; Fischer, *Historians' Fallacies,* 220; and Singal, *War Within,* 373–74.

55. Kirby, *Media-Made Dixie,* 83; Louis D. Rubin Jr., "The Mind of the South," *Sewanee Review* 62 (Autumn 1954): 684.

56. James W. Silver, *Mississippi: The Closed Society* (New York, 1964), 68.

57. Ibid., 119–20; Walker Percy, "Mississippi: The Fallen Paradise," *Harper's,* April 1965, p. 171. For a sampling of the behavior of die-hard segregationists throughout the Deep South, see Numan V. Bartley, *The Rise of Massive Resistance: Race and Politics in the South During the 1950's* (Baton Rouge, 1969), and Howard H. Quint, *Profile in Black and White* (Westport, Conn., 1958).

58. Edwin M. Yoder, "W. J. Cash after a Quarter Century," in Willie Morris, ed., *The South Today: 100 Years after Appomattox* (New York, 1965), 92.

59. Wyatt-Brown, "W. J. Cash and Southern Culture," in Fraser and Moore, *From the Old South to the New,* 198.

60. Wyatt-Brown, "W. J. Cash and Southern Culture," in *Yankee Saints and Southern Sinners,* 144.

61. Woodward, "Irony of Southern History" and "Second Look at the Theme of Irony," in *The Burden of Southern History* (Baton Rouge, 1968), 190, 214.

62. Yoder, "W. J. Cash," 94; Lewis Chester, Godfrey Hodgson, and Bruce Page, *An American Melodrama: The Presidential Campaign of 1968* (New York, 1969), 652.

63. Kirby, *Media-Made Dixie,* 134.

64. Ibid., 150–51 (quotation on p. 151).

65. Ibid., 142–46.

66. William L. Miller, *Yankee from Georgia: The Emergence of Jimmy Carter* (New York, 1978).

67. Cash, *Mind of the South,* 102; Black and Black, *Politics and Society in the South,* 315.

68. Cooper and Terrill, *American South,* 778; Woodward, "New South Fraud Is Papered by Old South Myth," *Washington Post,* 9 July 1961.

69. *Atlanta Constitution,* 11 December 1990.

70. Sidney Blumenthal, "Duke's Duds," *New Republic,* 15 October 1990, p. 198; Michael Oreskes, "Texas in Black and White," *New York Times Book Review,* 16 December 1990, p. 23.

71. King, *Southern Renaissance,* 255.

72. Howard Zinn, *The Southern Mystique* (New York, 1964), 218, 257, 262.

73. Ibid., 263.

74. Cohn, "Tissues of Southern Culture," 75; F. Gavin Davenport Jr., *The Myth of Southern History: Historical Consciousness in Twentieth-Century Southern Literature* (Nashville, 1970), 112.

75. Cash, *Mind of the South,* 440; Ted Ownby, *Subduing Satan: Religion, Recreation, and Manhood in the Rural South, 1865–1920* (Chapel Hill, 1990), 211; Tony Dunbar, *Delta Time: A Journey Through Mississippi* (New York, 1990), 98; V. S. Naipaul, *A Turn in the South* (New York, 1989), 233. Reviewer John Shelton Reed noted that "it is interesting when Naipaul sounds like W. J. Cash, but he seems unaware that some of his conclusions are recycled." See Reed's review of Naipaul, *A Turn in the South,* in the *Journal of Southern History* 56 (August 1990): 567.

76. Yoder, "W. J. Cash," 98–99; idem., "Thoughts on the Dixiefication of Dixie," in John B. Boles, ed., *Dixie Dateline: A Journalistic Portrait of the Contemporary South* (Houston, 1983), 161, 160.

77. Reed, *One South: An Ethnic Approach to Regional Culture* (Baton Rouge, 1982), 122; Reed, *Whistling Dixie: Dispatches from the South* (Columbia, Mo., 1990), 67; Wilson and Ferris, *Encyclopedia of Southern Culture,* xi. Carter is quoted in "Southern Fried Encyclopedia," *Atlanta Journal-Constitution,* 30 December 1990. See also

"Elvis Encore for Southern Culture Kings?" *Atlanta Journal-Constitution,* 30 December 1990, and Louis D. Rubin Jr., review, *Encyclopedia of Southern Culture,* in the *Journal of Southern History* 57 (February 1991): 85–87.

78. Cash is cited forty times in the index to Wilson and Ferris, *Encyclopedia of Southern Culture;* see 1130–31, 1599. Edwin M. Yoder Jr., "Keeping Southerners Awake," *Anniston Star,* 26 February 1991 (first quotation), "W. J. Cash," 98 (second quotation), and "Thoughts on the Dixiefication of Dixie," 164.

79. John Egerton, *The Americanization of Dixie: The Southernization of America* (New York, 1974), xx.

80. *Columbia (S.C.) State,* 13 January 1991; Cash, *Mind of the South,* 440.

FROM MUSKOGEE TO LUCKENBACH: COUNTRY MUSIC
AND THE "SOUTHERNIZATION" OF AMERICA

1. John Egerton, *The Americanization of Dixie: The Southernization of America* (New York, 1974).

2. George B. Tindall, *The Emergence of the New South, 1913–1945* (Baton Rouge, 1967), 184–218.

3. Tindall, *Emergence,* 210; H. L. Mencken, "The Sahara of the Bozart," *Prejudices: Second Series* (New York, 1920), 140–42.

4. Bill C. Malone, *Southern Music, American Music* (Lexington, 1979), 62. For an excellent survey of the evolution of country music, see Bill C. Malone, *Country Music, U.S.A.: A Fifty-Year History* (Austin, 1974).

5. Jens Lund, "Fundamentalism, Racism, and Political Reaction in Country Music," in R. Serge Denisoff and Richard A. Peterson, *The Sounds of Social Change* (Chicago, 1972), 80–83; Malone, *Southern Music,* 28–37.

6. Malone, *Southern Music,* 70–87.

7. Malone, *Country Music,* 206.

8. Malone, *Southern Music,* 93; Roger M. Williams, *Sing a Sad Song: The Life of Hank Williams* (Garden City, N.J., 1970).

9. Malone, *Southern Music,* 140–44.

10. Paul Hemphill, "Merle Haggard," in Bill C. Malone and Judith McCulloh, eds., *Stars of Country Music* (Urbana, 1975), 331.

11. C. Vann Woodward, "The South Tomorrow," *Time,* 22 September 1976, p. 98.

12. Ibid.

13. Jack Temple Kirby, *Media-Made Dixie: The South in the American Imagination* (Baton Rouge, 1978), 137–38.

14. William Lee Miller, *Yankee from Georgia: The Emergence of Jimmy Carter* (New York, 1978).

15. Reg Murphy, "The South as the New America," *Saturday Review,* 4 September 1976, pp. 8–11; *New York Times,* 11 February 1976, p. 1; Larry L. King, "We Ain't Trash No More," *Esquire,* November 1976, pp. 88–90, 152–56.

16. Sheldon Hackney, "The South as a Counterculture," *American Scholar* 42 (Spring 1973): 283–93.

17. "Those Good Ole Boys," *Time,* 27 September 1976, p. 47; Kirby, *Media-Made Dixie,* 142–46, 151–53.

18. Gurney Breckenfield, "Business Loves the Sunbelt and Vice Versa," *Fortune,* June 1977, p. 133; "Surging to Prosperity," *Time,* 27 September 1976, pp. 72–73; *New York Times,* 9 January 1977, p. 42; Marshall Frady, "Gone with the Wind," *Newsweek,* 28 July 1975, p. 11.

19. "Lord, They've Done It Again," *Time,* 6 May 1974, p. 51.

20. Bill C. Malone, "A Shower of Stars: Country Music Since World War II," in Malone and McCulloh, *Stars of Country Music,* 416–19, 433–34.

21. Ibid., 438–41.

22. Ibid., 429, 434–35, 442; Frye Gailliard, *Watermelon Wine: The Spirit of Country Music* (New York, 1978), 147–70; Malone, *Southern Music,* 112.

23. Malone, "Shower," 434.

24. Katie Letcher Lyle, "Southern Country Music: A Brief Eulogy," in Louis D. Rubin Jr., *The American South: Portrait of a Culture* (Baton Rouge, 1980), 143.

25. Dorothy A. Horstman, "Loretta Lynn," in Malone and McCulloh, *Stars of Country Music,* 318–21.

26. Richard Goldstein, "My Country Music Problem — and Yours," *Mademoiselle,* June 1973, p. 115.

27. Bob McDill, Wayland Holyfield, and Church Neese, copyright 1974, Jack Music, Inc.; Florence King, "Red Necks, White Socks, and Blue Ribbon Fear," *Harper's,* July 1974, p. 31; *New York Times,* 18 November 1979, p. 31-D.

28. Bobby Braddock, copyright 1973, Tree Publishing Company.

29. Howard Zinn, *The Southern Mystique* (New York, 1964), 217–18.

30. Kirby, *Media-Made Dixie,* 156, 158–59.

31. Lyle, "Southern Country Music," 140.

32. Tony Scherman, "Country," *American Heritage,* November 1994, p. 55.

THE BLUES IS A LOWDOWN SHAKIN' CHILL

1. W. C. Handy, *Father of the Blues: An Autobiography* (London, 1957), 76–77.

2. David Evans, "Blues," in Charles Reagan Wilson and William Ferris, eds., *Encyclopedia of Southern Culture* (Chapel Hill, 1989), 959–98.

3. Evans, "Blues," 995.

4. Michele Bernardinelli, "Report on Italian Peonage Matters in Mississippi, March 1909," in Department of Justice, Central Files, Classified Subject File Correspondence, RG 60, Box 10803, National Archives, Washington, D.C.; Lawrence Levine, *Black Culture and Black Consciousness: Afro-American Folk Thought from Slavery to Freedom* (New York and Oxford, 1978), 223–24

5. Levine, *Black Culture and Black Consciousness,* 221; David Evans, *Big Road Blues: Tradition and Creativity in the Folk Blues* (Berkeley, 1982), 43.

6. Evans, *Big Road Blues,* 43; idem., "Blues," 996; Levine, *Black Culture and Black Consciousness,* 218.

7. Levine, *Black Culture and Black Consciousness,* 222.

8. William Barlow, *Looking Up at Down: The Emergence of Blues Culture* (Philadelphia, 1989), 33–35; Robert Palmer; *Deep Blues: A Musical and Cultural History of the Mississippi Delta* (New York, 1982), 48–50.

9. Palmer, *Deep Blues,* 50–53; Barlow, *Looking Up at Down,* 35.

10. Barlow, *Looking Up at Down,* 35–46; Palmer, *Deep Blues,* 62–63.

11. Palmer, *Deep Blues,* 62; Pete Daniel to the author, 28 May 1991.

12. Handy, *Father of the Blues,* 77.

13. Palmer, *Deep Blues,* 61–62.

14. Peter Guralnick, *Feel Like Going Home: Portraits in Blues and Rock 'n' Roll* (New York, 1989), 50.

15. Palmer, *Deep Blues,* 44.

16. Levine, *Black Culture and Black Consciousness,* 221.

17. Evans, *Big Road Blues,* 40.

18. Barlow, *Looking Up at Down,* 6.

19. Gavin Wright, *Old South, New South: Revolutions in the Southern Economy Since the Civil War* (New York, 1986), 66.

20. Houston A. Baker Jr., *Blues, Ideology, and Afro-American Literature: A Vernacular Theory* (Chicago, 1984), 11; Paul Oliver, *Blues Fell This Morning: The Meaning of the Blues* (London, 1960), 70.

21. Barlow, *Looking Up at Down,* 6; Neil R. McMillen, *Dark Journey: Black Mississippians in the Age of Jim Crow* (Urbana, 1989), 271–72.

22. Sydney Nathans, "Got a Mind to Move, a Mind to Settle Down: Afro-Americans and the Plantation Frontier," in William J. Cooper et al., eds., *A Master's Due: Essays in Honor of David Herbert Donald* (Baton Rouge, 1985), 220.

23. Guralnick, *Feel Like Going Home,* 67; Evans, *Big Road Blues,* 19.

24. Joel Williamson, *The Crucible of Race: Black-White Relations in the American South since Emancipation* (New York, 1984), 213.

25. Charley Patton, "Bird Nest Bound," quoted in Evans, *Big Road Blues,* 19.

26. Levine, *Black Culture and Black Consciousness,* 237.

27. Ibid.; Larry Neal, "The Ethos of the Blues," *Black Scholar* 3 (Summer 1972): 45. See also Giles Oakley, *The Devil's Music: A History of the Blues* (New York, 1978), 50–51.

28. Levine, *Black Culture and Black Consciousness,* 154–89, 261, 326–30, 519; Steve West, "The Devil Visits the Delta: A View of His Role in the Blues," *Mississippi Folklore Register* 19 (Spring 1985): 12; Robert Johnson, "If I Had Possession over Judgment Day," in Michael Taft, *Blues Lyric Poetry: An Anthology* (New York, 1983), 148; Son House, "Preachin' the Blues," in Eric Sackheim, comp., *The Blues Line: A Collection of Blues Lyrics* (New York, 1969), 212.

29. Jeff Todd Titon, *Early Downhome Blues* (Urbana, 1977), 33; Clifton Taulbert, *Once upon a Time When We Were Colored* (Tulsa, Okla., 1980), 45–46.

30. Levine, *Black Culture and Black Consciousness,* 234.

31. Frederick Jay Hay, "The Delta Blues and Black Society: An Examination of Change (1900–1960) in Style and Community" (M.A. thesis, University of Virginia, 1981), 119.

32. Palmer, *Deep Blues,* 59; Barlow, *Looking Up at Down,* 39.

33. Hay, "Delta Blues," 129–30.

34. Barry Lee Pearson, *"Sounds So Good to Me": The Bluesman's Story* (Philadelphia, 1984), 66; Palmer, *Deep Blues,* 59–60.

35. Palmer, *Deep Blues,* 59–60.

36. Samuel Charters, *Robert Johnson* (New York, 1973), 17.

37. Ibid., 18.

38. Palmer, *Deep Blues,* 113, 111.

39. Peetie Wheatstraw, "Peetie Wheatstraw Stomp" and "Peetie Wheatstraw Stomp No. 2," in Taft, *Blues Lyric Poetry,* 298. See also West, "Devil Visits the Delta," 18–20; Ralph Ellison, *Invisible Man* (New York, 1972), 134.

40. Palmer, *Deep Blues,* 59–60; West, "Devil Visits the Delta," 13.

41. Barlow, *Looking Up at Down,* 50, 21.

42. Pearson, "Sounds So Good to Me," 67.

43. Charley Patton, "Mississippi Bo Weavil Blues," in Taft, *Blues Lyric Poetry,* 210. See also Oakley, *Devil's Music,* 58–59.

44. Oliver, *Blues Fell This Morning,* 70.

45. Handy, *Father of the Blues,* 74; Oliver, *Blues Fell This Morning,* 74.

46. Charley Patton, "Pea Vine Blues," in Taft, *Blues Lyric Poetry,* 211–12.

47. Robert Johnson, "Ramblin' on My Mind," in Taft, *Blues Lyric Poetry,* 146; Palmer, *Deep Blues,* 117–18.

48. Evans, *Big Road Blues,* 189.

49. Robert Johnson, "Terraplane Blues," in Taft, *Blues Lyric Poetry,* 147.

50. Paul Oliver, *Screening the Blues: Aspects of the Blues Tradition* (London, 1968), 199.

51. William R. Ferris, "The Blues Family," *Southern Exposure* 5 (Summer/Fall 1977): 22; Robert Johnson, "Come On in My Kitchen" and "Stones in My Passway," in Taft, *Blues Lyric Poetry,* 149.

52. Alan Lomax, "The Land Where the Blues Began: A Transcript and Study Guide to the Film" (Jackson, Miss., 1982), 11.

53. Liner notes, "Robert Johnson/King of the Delta Blues Singers," Columbia Records, CL1654.

54. Levine, *Black Culture and Black Consciousness,* 338.

55. James "Son" Thomas Exhibition of Clay Sculpture, 17 January–22 February 1985, University Art Gallery, New Mexico State University, Las Cruces, N.M.

56. Ibid.

57. Russell J. Linnemann, "Country Blues: Mirror of Southern Society," *Western Journal of Black Studies* 9 (1985): 185.

58. Lomax, "Land Where the Blues Began," 18.

59. Powdermaker, *After Freedom: A Cultural Study in the Deep South* (New York, 1968), 192–93.

60. Richard Wright, "Long Black Song," in *Uncle Tom's Children* (New York, 1965), 126.

61. Furry Lewis, "Furry's Blues," in Taft, *Blues Lyric Poetry,* 169; Barlow, *Looking Up at Down,* 22.

62. Lonnie Johnson, "Low Land Moon" and Robert Johnson, "Me and the Devil Blues," in Taft, *Blues Lyric Poetry,* 140, 150.

63. Wright, "Long Black Song," 118–19, 125.

64. Louise Johnson, "On the Wall" and Mattie Delaney, "Down the Big Road Blues," in Taft, *Blues Lyric Poetry,* 144, 76.

65. Robert Johnson, "I'm a Steady Rollin' Man" and "From Four Until Late"; Louise Johnson, "All Night Long Blues"; and Mattie Delaney, "Down the Big Road Blues," all in Taft, *Blues Lyric Poetry,* 149, 144, 76.

66. Son House, "Dry Spell Blues — Part 1," in Taft, *Blues Lyric Poetry,* 112–13; Muddy Waters, "Flood," quoted in Palmer, *Deep Blues,* 168–69.

67. Robert Johnson, "Preachin' Blues," in Taft, *Blues Lyric Poetry,* 148.

68. Lonnie Johnson, "Devil's Got the Blues," in Taft, *Blues Lyric Poetry,* 143.

69. Lomax, "Land Where the Blues Began," 6; Lawrence Goodwyn, *The Populist Moment: A Short History of the Agrarian Revolt in America* (New York and Oxford, 1978), 320; Levine, *Black Culture and Black Consciousness,* 283.

70. Ralph Ellison, "Richard Wright's Blues," in Ellison, *Shadow and Act* (New York, 1972), 88–89; Lomax, "Land Where the Blues Began," 11.

71. Levine, *Black Culture and Black Consciousness,* 226–28; Bill C. Malone, *Southern Music,* American Music (Lexington, Ky., 1979), 97–98.

72. Malone, *Southern Music,* 97–98.

73. Ibid.; Palmer, *Deep Blues,* 222–23.

74. Palmer, *Deep Blues,* 223–25.

75. Ibid., 224–25; Malone, *Southern Music,* 101–2; Nick Tosches, *Country: Living Legends and Dying Metaphors in America's Biggest Music* (New York, 1985), 45.

76. Charlie Gillett, *The Sound of the City: The Rise of Rock and Roll,* rev. ed. (New York, 1983), 28.

77. Dave McGee, "Carl Perkins," *Rolling Stone,* 19 April 1990, p. 75.

78. For a thorough discussion of the themes of country music see Bill C. Malone, *Country Music, U.S.A.: A Fifty-Year History* (Austin, 1975).

79. Patrick Carr, "Killer Verite," *Southern* 3 (July/August 1989): 75; Malone, *Southern Music,* 103.

80. Gillett, *Sound of the City,* 8; Robert Palmer, "The 50s," *Rolling Stone,* 19 April 1990, p. 46.

81. Barlow, *Looking Up at Down,* 336.

82. Malone, *Southern Music,* 105.

83. Barlow, *Looking Up at Down,* 337.

84. Jim Curtis, *Rock Eras: Interpretations of Music and Society, 1954–1984* (Bowling Green, Ohio, 1987), 39; Tosches, *Country,* 100, 73; Gillett, *Sound of the City,* 17–18.

85. Richard Petersen, "Why 1955? Explaining the Advent of Rock Music," *Popular Music* 9 (January 1990): 113.

86. Palmer, "50s," 48; Barlow, *Looking Up at Down,* 336–37; Gillett, *Sound of the City,* 168.

87. Malone, *Southern Music,* 99.

88. The Rolling Stones to Muddy Waters, 4 April 1975, in *Muddy Waters* (pamphlet accompanying "Muddy Waters: The Chess Box," recordings, 1990), 24; Palmer, *Deep Blues,* 259–60.

89. Palmer, *Deep Blues,* 262–63; Guralnick, *Feel Like Going Home,* 28.

90. *Robert Johnson: The Complete Recordings* (pamphlet accompanying "Robert Johnson: The Complete Recordings." 1990), 21, 23; "There's Blues in the News," *Newsweek,* 12 November 1990, pp. 72–74; Guralnick, *Feel Like Going Home,* 61.

SEARCHING FOR SOUTHERNNESS: COMMUNITY
AND IDENTITY IN THE CONTEMPORARY SOUTH

1. Charlayne Hunter-Gault, *In My Place* (New York, 1993), 178–79.

2. *New York Times,* 31 July 1994.

3. Hunter-Gault, *In My Place,* 248, 253.

4. W. J. Cash, *The Mind of the South* (New York, 1941), 429.

5. Ibid., 49–50.

6. Thadious M. Davis, "Expanding the Limits: The Intersection of Race and Region," *Southern Literary Journal* 20 (Spring 1988): 6.

7. C. Vann Woodward, "Look Away, Look Away," *Journal of Southern History* 59 (August 1993): 496; Harry Crews, *A Childhood: A Biography of a Place* (New York, 1978); Hunter-Gault, *In My Place,* 232. For further discussion of the role of "place" in the South's autobiographical tradition, see J. Bill Berry, ed., *Located Lives: Place and Idea in Southern Autobiography* (Athens, Ga., 1990).

8. Nikki Giovanni, *Gemini: An Extended Autobiographical Statement on My First Twenty-Five Years of Being a Black Poet* (New York, 1980), 12; idem., *Black Feeling, Black Talk/Black Judgment* (New York, 1970), 58; idem., *Knoxville, Tennessee* (New York, 1994).

9. Maya Angelou, *I Know Why the Caged Bird Sings* (New York, 1993), 6–7.

10. David R. Goldfield, *Black, White, and Southern: Race Relations and Southern Culture, 1940 to the Present* (Baton Rouge, 1990), 170; Alice Walker, *In Search of Our Mother's Gardens* (New York, 1983), 143.

11. Walker, *In Search,* 144–45.

12. Ibid., 20–21.

13. Ibid., 21.

14. Alice Walker, "Everyday Use," *Harper's,* April 1973, p. 81.

15. Alice Walker, *The Color Purple* (New York, 1985); Endesha Ida Mae Holland, "Memories of the Mississippi Delta," *Michigan Quarterly Review* 26 (Winter 1987): 246–47; Tina McElroy Ansa, *Ugly Ways* (New York, 1993).

16. Walker, *In Search,* 17.

17. Clifton L. Taulbert, *Once Upon a Time When We Were Colored* (Tulsa, Okla., 1989), 5–6.

18. *New York Times,* 31 July 1994.

19. Belle Gayle Chevigny, "Mississippi Stories I: The Fruits of Freedom Summer," *Nation,* 8/15 August 1994, p. 157.

20. Willie Morris, *North Toward Home* (Oxford, Miss., 1982), 140.

21. Ibid., 141.

22. Melany Neilson, *Even Mississippi* (Tuscaloosa, Ala., 1986), 36.

23. Chalmers Archer Jr., *Growing Up Black in Rural Mississippi: Memories of a Family, Heritage of a Place* (New York, 1992), 147, 139.

24. Crews, *Childhood,* 40; idem., "The Mythic Mule," *Southern Magazine,* 25 January 1987, p. 22; Dorothy Allison, *Bastard Out of Carolina* (New York, 1993), 17.

25. Will D. Campbell, *Brother to a Dragonfly* (New York, 1977), 148.

26. Robert Coles, "Introduction," in Tony Dunbar, *Our Land, Too* (New York, 1969), x.

27. Douglas Lederman, "Old Times Not Forgotten," *Chronicle of Higher Education,* 20 October 1993, p. A51.

28. *Richmond Times Dispatch,* 26 April 1992; *Boston Globe,* 10 April 1991.

29. *Dallas Times-Herald,* 19 May 1991; *Daily (Oklahoma City, Okla.) Oklahoman,* 10 June 1989; *Sarasota Herald-Tribune,* 1 May 1988; *(Columbia, S.C.) State,* 30 May 1993; *Birmingham News,* 25 April 1993; *Jackson Clarion-Ledger,* 9 November 1989; *Atlanta Journal-Constitution* 17 January and 7 March 1993.

30. *Atlanta Journal-Constitution,* 29 January 1994.

31. Ibid., 2 August and 29 March 1992.

32. Ibid., 29 and 13 January 1993; Richard Hyatt, *Zell, the Governor Who Gave Georgia Hope* (Macon, Ga., 1997), 132.

33. *Atlanta Journal-Constitution,* 7 March 1993; John Shelton Reed, "Capture the Flag," manuscript transmitted via e-mail, copy in possession of the author; Roy Blount Jr., *Now Where Were We?* (New York, 1988), 161.

34. John Shelton Reed, "South Polls" and "Confederate Agents in the Ivy League," manuscript transmitted via e-mail, both copies in possession of the author.

35. *Atlanta Journal-Constitution,* 18 March 1994.

36. Lederman, "Old Times Not Forgotten," A51.

37. *Atlanta Journal-Constitution,* 16 February 1992, 18 March and 3 April 1994; Walter Shapiro, "The Glory and the Glitz," *Time,* 5 August 1991, p. 56; William Zinsser, "I Realized Her Tears Were Becoming Part of the Memorial," *Smithsonian,* September 1991, pp. 33–43; *Memphis Commercial Appeal,* 5 July 1991; *Birmingham News,* 28 March 1993.

38. *Atlanta Journal-Constitution,* 21 March 1993.

39. Ibid., 21 July 1991.

40. Woodward, "Look Away," 504; Hodding Carter III, "The End of the South," *Time,* 6 August 1990, p. 82; Melton A. McLaurin, *Separate Pasts* (Athens, Ga., 1987).

41. James Morgan, "Going Home," *American Way,* 15 September 1993, p. 106.

42. John Shelton Reed, *Southerners: The Social Psychology of Sectionalism* (Chapel Hill, 1983), 111, 114.

43. John Shelton Reed, *One South: An Ethnic Approach to Regional Culture* (Baton Rouge, 1982), 122; Beth Arnold Graves, "What I Love about the South, A to Z: An Alphabetical Appreciation of the Reasons We Live in Dixie," *Southern Magazine,* August 1987, p. 32–39; Charles R. Wilson and William R. Ferris, eds., *The Encyclopedia of Southern Culture* (Chapel Hill, 1989); James C. Cobb, "Does 'Mind' No Longer Matter?: The South, the Nation, and *The Mind of the South,* 1941–1991," *Journal of Southern History* 57 (November 1991): 716. For a description of *Reckon,* see *Southern Register* (Spring 1994): 3.

44. Edwin M. Yoder, "Thoughts on the Dixiefication of Dixie," in John B. Boles, ed., *Dixie Dateline: A Journalistic Portrait of the Contemporary South* (Houston, 1983), 161; "W. J. Cash after a Quarter Century," in Willie Morris, ed., *The South Today: 100 Years after Appomattox* (New York, 1965), 98–99; Jim and Susan Erskine, *The Southerner's Instruction Book* (Gretna, La., 1994), n.p.

45. Robert Kelly, "Redneck Chic: A New Honky-Tonk Craze Sweeps the City," *Highpoint,* 4–17 December 1992, pp. 1, 8.

46. Crews is quoted in "A Stubborn Sense of Place," *Harper's,* August 1986, pp. 40–41; Carter, "End of the South."

47. W. Hampton Sides, "Interview, Richard Ford: Debunking the Mystique of the Southern Writer," *Memphis,* February 1986, pp. 42, 49; Fred Hobson, *Tell about the South: The Southern Rage to Explain* (Baton Rouge, 1983); Walker Percy, "Southern Comfort," *Harper's,* January 1979, p. 8. See also, James C. Cobb, "Southern Writers and the Challenge of Regional Convergence: A Comparative Perspective," *Georgia Historical Quarterly* 73 (Spring 1989): 1–25.

48. *Atlanta Journal-Constitution,* 24 October 1993.

49. Ibid.

50. Ibid., 2 April and 30 October 1993; Reed, "Capture the Flag."

51. *New York Times,* 9 February and 6 October 1993; Reed, "Capture the Flag."

52. George B. Tindall, *The Ethnic Southerners* (Baton Rouge, 1976), 21.

53. "Lewis Grizzard Live! The Goodwill Tour: From Moreland to Moscow," Southern Tracks Records, 1986.

54. Lewis Grizzard, *I Haven't Understood Anything Since 1962 (And Other Nekkid Truths)* (New York, 1992), 152–53, 31–32.

55. See Johnson's columns in the *Atlanta Journal-Constitution,* 19, 20, 26 June and 11 July 1994.

56. Jimmie L. Franklin, "Black Southerners, Shared Experience and Place: A Reflection," *Journal of Southern History* 59 (February 1994): 4; idem., "A Southern Sense of Place: Notes of a Native Son," an address delivered on the occasion of the Seventh Annual Author's Dinner at the University of Alabama, 13 April 1993; Ellison is quoted in David Remnick, "Visible Man," *New Yorker,* 14 March 1994, p. 38; *Birmingham Post-Herald,* 11 March 1993.

57. Weaver's observation is quoted on the jacket of J. Bill Berry, ed., *Home Ground: Southern Autobiography* (Columbia, Mo., 1991).

58. Woodward, "Look Away," 504.

59. Yoder, "Thoughts," 164.

1. John Shelton Reed and Dale Volberg Reed, *1001 Things Everyone Should Know About the South* (New York, 1966), 294 (first quote); Fred C. Hobson, *Tell About the South: The Southern Rage to Explain* (Baton Rouge, 1983), 114 (second quote); Paul M. Gaston, *The New South Creed: A Study in Southern Mythmaking* (Baton Rouge, 1971); W. J. Cash, *The Mind of the South* (New York, 1991), xlvii (fourth quote).

2. Daniel J. Singal, *The War Within: From Victorian to Modernist Thought in the South, 1919–1945* (Chapel Hill, 1982), 8–9; Frank L. Owsley, "The Old South and the New," *American Review* 6 (February 1936): 482 (first quote); Richard H. King, *A Southern Renaissance: The Cultural Awakening of the American South, 1930–1955* (New York, 1980), 146 (second quote).

3. Singal, *War Within*, 374 (first quote); Cash, *Mind of the South*, 65–66 (second quote), 134–41, 184 (third and fourth quotes). Writing in 1919 Holland Thompson had tied the effort to create an industrialized New South to the widespread belief among white southerners that the South had lost the Civil War because it lacked sufficient capacity to "manufacture goods for its own needs" or "build a navy to defend its ports." Holland Thompson, *The New South: A Chronicle of Social and Industrial Evolution* (New York, 1919), 3.

4. Cash, *Mind of the South*, xlviii (first quote); Gaston, *New South Creed*, 7 (second quote); Benedict Anderson, *Imagined Communities: Reflections on the Origins and Spread of Nationalism* (London and New York, 1995), 6 (third quote); Ernest Gellner, *Nations and Nationalism* (Ithaca, N.Y., 1983), 49; Eric Hobsbawm, "Mass-Producing Traditions: Europe, 1870–1914," in Eric Hobsbawm and Terence Ranger, eds., *The Invention of Tradition* (Cambridge, 1983), 269–80; Eric Hobsbawm, "The New Threat to History," *New York Review of Books*, 16 December 1993, p. 62.

5. Anderson, *Imagined Communities*, xiv; Eric Hobsbawm, "Introduction: Inventing Traditions," in Hobsbawm and Ranger, *Invention of Tradition*, 14.

6. Gaston, *New South Creed*, 186 (first quote), 174 (third quote); King, *Southern Renaissance*, 30 (second quote); Hobson, *Tell About the South*, 144 (fourth quote). See also Daniel J. Singal, *William Faulkner: The Making of a Modernist* (Chapel Hill, 1997), 67.

7. William R. Taylor, *Cavalier and Yankee: The Old South and the American National Character* (Garden City, N.Y., 1963); Drew Gilpin Faust, *The Creation of Confederate Nationalism: Ideology and Identity in the Civil War South* (Baton Rouge, 1988), 21 (quotes).

8. Thomas Nelson Page, *The Old South: Essays Social and Political* (Chautauqua, N.Y., 1919), 6 (first quote); Wayne Mixon, *Southern Writers and the New South Movement, 1865–1913* (Chapel Hill, 1980), 33 (second quote); Gaines M. Foster, *Ghosts of the Confederacy: Defeat, the Lost Cause, and the Emergence of the New South, 1865 to 1913* (New York, 1987), 84 (third quote).

9. Anwar Sadat, *In Search of Identity: An Autobiography* (New York, 1978), 313 (quote). On the relationship between nationalism and modernity, see Liah Greenfeld, *Nationalism: Five Roads to Modernity* (Cambridge, Mass., 1992).

10. Gaston, *New South Creed,* 194.

11. Hobsbawm, "Inventing Traditions," 4 (first quote); Gellner, *Nationalism,* 49; Charles Reagan Wilson, "The Invention of Southern Tradition: The Writing and Ritualization of Southern History, 1880–1940," in Lothar Honninghausen and Valeria Gennardo Lerda, eds., *Rewriting the South: History and Fiction* (Tubingen, 1993), 13–15 (15, second quote).

12. John W. Cell, *The Highest Stage of White Supremacy: The Origins of Segregation in South Africa and the American South* (Cambridge, 1982), 181. On segregation as an invented tradition see also Wilson, "Invention of Southern Tradition," 4–5.

13. Cell, *Highest Stage of White Supremacy,* 182.

14. Wayne Mixon, *Southern Writers and the New South Movement, 1865–1913* (Chapel Hill, 1980), 48–51.

15. J. Morgan Kousser, *The Shaping of Southern Politics: Suffrage Restriction and the Establishment of the One-Party South, 1880–1910* (New Haven, 1974).

16. Anderson, *Imagined Communities,* 5 (first quote), 7 (second quote); E. J. Hobsbawm, *Nations and Nationalism Since 1780: Programme, Myth, Reality,* 2nd ed. (Cambridge, 1982), 12 (third quote).

17. Burton J. Hendrick, *The Training of An American: The Earlier Life and Letters of Walter Hines Page, 1855–1913* (Boston, 1928), 168 (first quote), 176 (second quote); Bruce Clayton, *The Savage Ideal: Intolerance and Intellectual Leadership in the South, 1890–1914* (Baltimore, 1972), 48; Hobson, *Tell About the South,* 164–65 (third quote), 179 (fourth quote), 158 (fifth quote).

18. Mixon, *Southern Writers,* 110 (first quote); Charles W. Chesnutt, "The March of Progress," *Century Magazine,* January 1901, p. 424 (remaining quotes).

19. Chesnutt, "March of Progress," 428.

20. Charles W. Chesnutt, *The Colonel's Dream* (New York, 1905), 115–16.

21. Hobson, *Tell About the South,* 106; George W. Cable, "The Silent South," *Century* 30 (September 1885): 674–91.

22. Gaston, *New South Creed,* 94.

23. George W. Cable, *John March, Southerner* (New York, 1894).

24. Cable, *John March,* 121 (first quote), 326 (third quote); William Faulkner, *Absalom, Absalom!* (New York, 1972), 361 (second quote).

25. Hobson, *Tell About the South,* 119, 114 (quote).

26. King, *Southern Renaissance,* 31 (first quote); Gaston, *New South Creed,* 224 (second quote).

27. Frank Tannenbaum, *The Darker Phases of the South* (New York, 1924); William H. Skaggs, *The Southern Oligarchy: An Appeal in Behalf of the Silent Masses of Our Country Against the Despotic Rule of the Few* (New York, 1924), quoted in Hobson, *Tell About the South,* 185 (first quote); see also, page 184; H. L. Mencken, "The Sahara of the Bozart," in James T. Farrell, ed., *H. L. Mencken, Prejudices: A Selection* (New York, 1958), 70 (second quote), 73 (third quote).

28. Allen Tate, "The New Provincialism," in *Essays of Four Decades* (New York, 1970), 545–46 (first quote); idem., "The Profession of Letters in the South," *Virginia Quarterly Review* 11 (April 1925): 175–76 (second quote).

29. C. Vann Woodward, "Why the Southern Renaissance," in *The Future of the Past* (New York, 1989), 217 (quote); Michael O'Brien, "A Heterodox Note on the Southern Renaissance," in James C. Cobb and Charles R. Wilson, eds., *Perspectives on the American South,* vol. 4 (New York, 1987), 1–18; Singal, *War Within,* xii.

30. Reinhard Bendix, "Tradition and Modernity Reconsidered," *Comparative Studies in Society and History* 9 (1967): 293 (first quote); Richard H. King, "Victorian to Modernist Thought," *Southern Literary Journal* 15 (1983): 127 (second quote); Thomas Wolfe to his Mother, May 1923, in John Skally Terry, ed., *Thomas Wolfe's Letters to His Mother, Julia Elizabeth Wolfe* (New York, 1943), 50 (remaining quotes).

31. Clarence Cason, "Alabama Goes Industrial," *Virginia Quarterly Review* 6 (April 1930): 164, 166, 170, 167.

32. William Faulkner, "An Introduction to *The Sound and the Fury,*" *Mississippi Quarterly* 16 (Summer 1973): 411.

33. Robert A. Nisbet, *Emile Durkheim* (Englewood Cliffs, 1965), 20 (first quote); Dewey W. Grantham, *Southern Progressivism: The Reconciliation of Progress and Tradition* (Knoxville, 1983), 411 (second quote). See also James C. Cobb, "Southern Writers and the Challenge of Regional Convergence: A Comparative Perspective," *Georgia Historical Quarterly* 63 (Spring 1989): 1–25.

34. Fred Hobson, *Serpent in Eden: H. L. Mencken and the South* (Chapel Hill, 1974), 148 (first quote); Edwin Mims, *The Advancing South: Stories of Progress and Reaction* (Port Washington, 1969), 315–16 (second quote).

35. Hobson, *Tell About the South,* 187–88 (first and second quotes); idem., *Serpent in Eden,* 73 (second quote), 148–49; Louis D. Rubin Jr., "The Historical Image of Modern Southern Writing," *Journal of Southern History* 22 (May 1956): 157–58 (third quote).

36. "Twelve Southerners," *I'll Take My Stand: The South and the Agrarian Tradition* (New York, 1930).

37. Hobson, *Serpent in Eden,* 157.

38. John Shelton Reed, "For Dixieland: The Sectionalism of I'll Take My Stand," in William C. Harvard and Walter Sullivan, eds., *A Band of Prophets: The Vanderbilt Agrarians After Fifty Years* (Baton Rouge, 1982), 45.

39. Ibid., 45, 47 (first quote); Mary Matossian, "Ideologies of Delayed Industrialization," in Jason L. Finkle and Richard W. Gable, eds., *Political Development and Social Change* (New York, 1966), 178 (second quote).

40. For a survey of criticism of the Agrarians, see Hobson, *Tell About the South,* 215–17.

41. Bendix, "Tradition and Modernity Reconsidered," 334; George B. Tindall, "Business Progressivism: Southern Politics in the Twenties," *South Atlantic Quarterly* 62 (Winter 1963): 92–106; Grantham, *Southern Progressivism,* 258; William J. Cooper Jr. and Thomas E. Terrell, *The American South: A History* (New York, 1990), 560–61.

42. Bendix, "Tradition and Modernity Reconsidered," 344 (first quote); Reed, "For Dixieland," 61 (second quote).

43. Cason, "Alabama Goes Industrial," 168.

44. Singal, *War Within,* 125 (first quote); Hobson, *Serpent in Eden,* 90–94 (94, second quote); H. L. Mencken, "The South Astir," *Virginia Quarterly Review* 11 (January 1935): 50.

45. Matossian, "Ideologies of Delayed Industrialization," 175 (first quote); Bendix, "Tradition and Modernity Reconsidered," 45 (second quote).

46. Hobson, *Tell About the South,* 192 (first quote), 193; Howard W. Odum, *American Epoch: Southern Portraiture in the National Picture* (New York, 1930), x (first and second quotes), 30–52 (52, third quote).

47. Wayne D. Brazil, *Howard W. Odum: The Building Years, 1884–1930* (New York, 1988), 596 (first quote); Hobson, *Tell About the South,* 193; Singal, *War Within,* 153 (second quote).

48. Hobson, *Serpent in Eden,* 3 (first quote); Mencken, "Sahara of the Bozart," in Farrell, *H. L. Mencken,* 82 (second quote).

49. Wilbur J. Cash, "The Mind of the South," *American Mercury* 18 (October 1929): 185 (first quote), 191 (second-seventh quotes), 192 (eighth quote).

50. Mencken, "Sahara of the Bozart," in Farrell, *H. L. Mencken,* 77; W. J. Cash to Howard Odum, 13 November 1929 (first quote); Howard W. Odum to W. J. Cash, 20 November 1929 (second quote); Cash to Odum, 22 November 1929 (third quote), all in Howard Washington Odum Papers, Southern Historical Collection, University of North Carolina, Chapel Hill.

51. William E. Dodd, "Some Difficulties of the History Teacher in the South," *South Atlantic Quarterly* 3 (April 1904): 119.

52. Ibid.

53. Gaston, "The New South," in Arthur S. Link and Rembert W. Patrick, eds., *Writing Southern History: Essays in Historiography in Honor of Fletcher M. Green* (Baton Rouge, 1965), 321 (first quote); Philip Alexander Bruce, *The Rise of the New South* (Philadelphia, 1905), v–vii (second quote).

54. Broadus Mitchell, *The Rise of the Cotton Mills in the South* (Baltimore, 1921), vii (first quote); Gaston, *New South Creed,* 321; Singal, *War Within,* 66 (second quote), 81 (third quote).

55. Hobsbawm, "New Threat to History," 63 (quote). See also Gellner, *Nations and Nationalism,* 44; Rubin, "Historical Image," 156.

56. Donald Davidson, *The Attack on Leviathan: Regionalism and Nationalism in the United States* (Chapel Hill, 1938), 323.

57. Rupert B. Vance, *Human Geography of the South: A Study in Regional Resources and Human Adequacy,* 2nd ed. (Chapel Hill, 1935), 76 (first quote), 312 (third quote); Howard W. Odum, *Southern Regions of the United States* (Chapel Hill, 1936), 227 (second quote).

58. Vance, *Human Geography* (1935 ed.), 22; Rupert Vance to C. Vann Woodward, 1, 9 August, 20 September 1949 (Folder 12); Vance to Woodward, 21 September 1954 (Folder 28), in Rupert B. Vance Papers, Southern Historical Collection, University of North Carolina, Chapel Hill; George B. Tindall et al., "Rupert Bayless Vance, March 15, 1899–August 25, 1975," a memorial presented to the Faculty Council of the University of North Carolina, 17 October 1975 (copy in possession of the author).

59. C. Vann Woodward, *Thinking Back: The Perils of Writing History* (Baton Rouge, 1986), 22 (first and third quote), 23 (second quote).

60. King, *Southern Renaissance,* 257 (first quote); Woodward, *Thinking Back,* 29 (second quote).

61. Woodward, *Thinking Back,* 31–32.

62. C. Vann Woodward, *Origins of the New South, 1877–1913* (Baton Rouge, 1951); idem., *Thinking Back,* 63 (quote).

63. C. Vann Woodward, *The Strange Career of Jim Crow* (New York, 1955); idem., *Thinking Back,* 82–83 (first quote); King, *Southern Renaissance,* 271 (second quote).

64. Woodward, *Thinking Back,* 23 (first quote); Rubin, "Historical Image," 159 (second quote).

65. Singal, *War Within,* 93; Ellen Glasgow, *Romance of a Plain Man* (New York, 1909); idem., *Virginia* (New York, 1913).

66. Glasgow, *Virginia,* 13 (first quote), 73 (second quote), 12–13 (third quote), 65 (fourth quote).

67. Ibid., 65 (first quote); Ellen Glasgow, "The Novel in the South," *Harper's,* December 1928, p. 98 (second quote).

68. Ellen Glasgow, *A Certain Measure: An Interpretation of Prose Fiction* (New York, 1943), 147; Darden Asbury Pyron, *Southern Daughter: The Life of Margaret Mitchell* (New York, 1992), 315 (quote).

69. Margaret Mitchell, *Gone with the Wind* (New York, 1993), 46 (first quote), 48 (second quote), 47 (third quote), 51 (fourth quote), 53 (fifth quote).

70. Ibid., 600 (first quote), 602 (second quote), 605.

71. Ibid., 607 (first quote), 621 (second quote), 611 (third quote), 631 (fourth quote), 632 (fifth quote), 654 (sixth quote).

72. Singal, *War Within,* 165; Frederick R. Karl, *William Faulkner: American Writer, A Biography* (New York, 1989), 413–414, 788; Joel Williamson, *William Faulkner and Southern History* (New York, 1993), 327–28, 333–34.

73. William Faulkner, *Sartoris* (New York: Harcourt Brace Jovanovich, Inc., 1929); idem., *The Sound and the Fury* (New York, 1929), 17 (quote); Singal, *William Faulkner,* 135–38.

74. Faulkner, *Absalom, Absalom!;* Irving Howe, *William Faulkner: A Critical Study* (Chicago, 1975), 74.

75. William Faulkner, *The Hamlet* (New York, 1940); Rubin, "Historical Image," 159.

76. David Herbert Donald, "Look Homeward: Thomas Wolfe and the South," *Southern Review* 23 (April 1987): 246–47.

77. David Herbert Donald, *Look Homeward: A Life of Thomas Wolfe* (Boston and Toronto, 1987), 79 (first quote); Thomas Wolfe, *Look Homeward, Angel* (New York, 1929), 230 (second quote), 233 (third, fourth, and fifth quotes), 548 (sixth quote).

78. Donald, "Look Homeward," 250, 252 (first and second quotes); Thomas Wolfe, *The Web and the Rock* (New York, 1939), 15. See also King, *Southern Renaissance,* 200.

79. Cash, *Mind of the South,* xlviii.

80. Clarence Cason, *90 Degrees in the Shade* (Chapel Hill, 1935); David L. Cohn, *God Shakes Creation* (Boston, 1935); William Alexander Percy, *Lanterns on the Levee: Recollections of A Planter's Son* (New York, 1941); Ben Robertson, *Red Hills and Cotton: An Upcountry Memory* (New York, 1942); W. J. Cash, "Genesis of the Southern Cracker," *American Mercury* 35 (May 1935): 108.

81. Ibid., xlix (first quote), 8 (second quote), 9 (third quote).

82. Ibid., 14–17 (14, first quote; 15, second and third quotes; 17, fourth quote).

83. Ibid., 17 (first quote), 19 (second quote).

84. Ibid., 92.

85. Ibid., 95–96.

86. Glasgow, "Novel in the South," 94.

87. Cash, *Mind of the South,* 38–39.

88. Ibid., 106, 171–78, 198–99, 198 (quote).

89. Singal, *War Within,* 373 (first quote). Reviews are quoted in Bruce Clayton, *W. J. Cash: A Life* (Baton Rouge, 1991), 166.

90. Singal, *War Within,* 373.

91. King, *Southern Renaissance,* 3–4; Gaston, *New South Creed,* 228–29; James C. Cobb, "World War II and the Mind of the Modern South," in Neil R. McMillen, ed., *Remaking Dixie: The Impact of World War II on the American South* (Jackson, Miss., 1997), 15–16; Numan V. Bartley, *The New South, 1945–1980* (Baton Rouge, 1995), 65; see Ralph Ellison, "In a Strange Country," "Flying Home," in John F. Callahan, ed., *Flying Home and Other Stories* (New York, 1996), 137–146, 147–73; "Black Boy: A Negro Writes a Bitter Autobiography," *Life,* 4 June 1945, p. 87 (quote); Singal, *War Within,* 373.

92. Walker Percy, "Red, White, and Blue Gray," in Patrick Sammway, ed., *Signposts in a Strange Land* (New York, 1991), 80 (first quote); Hobson, *Tell About the South,* 300 (second quote), 309; Lillian Smith, "The Right Way Is Not the Moderate Way," in Michelle Cliff, ed., *The Winner Names the Age* (New York, 1978), 68 (third quote).

93. William H. Nicholls, *Southern Tradition and Regional Progress* (Chapel Hill, 1960), 5 (first quote); Frank E. Smith, *Look Away from Dixie* (Baton Rouge, 1965), 88 (second quote), 9 (fifth quote); Harry S. Ashmore, *An Epitaph for Dixie* (New York, 1958), 25 (third and fourth quotes).

94. Hodding Carter III, "The End of the South," *Time,* 6 August 1990, p. 82.

95. Bartley, *New South,* xii.

96. Leslie W. Dunbar, "The Final New South?" *Virginia Quarterly Review* 74 (Winter 198): 58.

97. On the current effort to redefine southern identity, see James C. Cobb, "Community and Identity: Redefining Southern Culture," *Georgia Review* 50 (Spring 1996), 9–24.

98. Carter, "End of the South," 82 (first quote); Hobsbawm, "New Threat to History," 64 (second quote); Hobsbawm, *Nations and Nationalism,* 12 (third quote); William Pfaff, *The Wrath of Nations: Civilization and the Furies of Nationalism* (New York, 1993), 58 (fourth quote).

99. C. Vann Woodward, "New South Fraud Is Papered by Old South Myth," *Washington Post,* 9 July 1961 (quote). See also Numan V. Bartley, "Social Change and Sectional Identity," *Journal of Southern History* 61 (February 1995): 16.

MODERNIZATION AND THE MIND OF THE SOUTH

1. Bertram Wyatt-Brown, "Introduction: The Mind of W. J. Cash," in W. J. Cash, *The Mind of the South* (New York, 1991), vii–viii (Cash's quote, xlviii). Wyatt-

Brown's contention that the South Cash knew has largely disappeared is a more debatable proposition, because Cash readily acknowledged the physical and institutional changes that had occurred between Appomattox and the eve of Pearl Harbor. It was the cultural continuities that persisted in the face of these changes that interested and concerned him.

2. Edward L. Ayers, "W. J. Cash, the New South, and the Rhetoric of History," in Charles W. Eagles, ed., *The Mind of the South: Fifty Years Later* (Jackson, Miss., and London, 1992), 126. See also James C. Cobb, *Industrialization and Southern Society, 1877–1984* (Lexington, Ky., 1964), 136–64.

3. C. Vann Woodward, *The Origins of the New South, 1877–1913* (Baton Rouge, 1951).

4. Jonathan M. Wiener, *Social Origins of the New South: Alabama, 1860–1885* (Baton Rouge and London, 1978), 4. See also Dwight B. Billings Jr., *Planters and the Making of a "New South": Class, Politics, and Development in North Carolina, 1865–1900* (Chapel Hill, 1979), and James C. Cobb, "Beyond Planters and Industrialists: A New Perspective on the New South," *Journal of Southern History* 54 (February 1988), 45–68.

5. William H. Nicholls, *Southern Tradition and Regional Progress* (Chapel Hill, 1960), 162; Gavin Wright, "The Strange Career of the New Southern Economic History," *Reviews in American History* 10 (December 1982): 120; David L. Carlton, "The Revolution from Above: The National Market and the Beginnings of Industrialization in North Carolina," *Journal of American History* 77 (September 1990): 474.

6. Reinhard Bendix, "Tradition and Modernity Reconsidered," *Comparative Studies in Society and History* 9 (April 1967): 312, 316.

7. David L. Cohn, "The American Temperament," *Atlantic Monthly,* September 1951, p. 65.

8. David L. Carlton and Peter A. Coclanis, "The Uninventive South: A Quantitative Look at Region and American Inventiveness," *Technology and Culture* 36 (April 1995): 325.

9. David L. Carlton and Peter A. Coclanis, "Capital Mobilization and Southern Industry, 1880–1905: The Case of Carolina Piedmont," *Journal of Economic History* 49 (March 1989): 73, 91.

10. Louis Wirth, "Urbanism as a Way of Life," *American Journal of Sociology* 64 (July 1938): 1–24; James C. Cobb, "Urbanization and the Changing South: A Review of Literature," *South Atlantic Urban Studies* (1977): 254.

11. Bendix, "Tradition and Modernity Reconsidered," 341–42.

12. Nicholls, *Southern Tradition,* 34, 58–59.

13. James C. Cobb, "The Sunbelt South: Industrialization in Regional, National, and International Perspective," in Raymond A. Mohl, ed., *Searching of the Sun-*

belt: *Historical Perspectives on a Region* (Athens, Ga., 1993), 37–38; Richard E. Lonsdale and Clyde E. Browning, "Rural-Urban Locational Preferences of Southern Manufacturers," *Annals of the Association of American Geographers* 61 (June 1971): 262.

14. On mill workers see Jacquelyn Dowd Hall et al., *Like a Family: The Making of a Southern Cotton Mill World* (Chapel Hill, 1987); Ben Robertson, *Red Hills and Cotton: An Upcountry Memory* (New York, 1942), 280–81.

15. *Bureau of the Census, County and City Data Book* (Washington, D.C., 1983), lvii.

16. C. Vann Woodward, "The Search for Southern Identity," in *The Burden of Southern History*, 3rd ed. (Baton Rouge and London, 1993), 9–10.

17. William H. Nicholls, *Southern Tradition and Regional Progress* (Chapel Hill, 1960), 5, 163, 162, 6.

18. Lawrence Levine, *Black Culture and Black Consciousness: Afro-American Folk Thought from Slavery to Freedom* (Oxford, London, and New York, 1978), 5.

19. Daniel J. Singal, review of Bruce Clayton, *W. J. Cash: A Life, Journal of Southern History* 59 (February 1993): 166.

20. Marshall Frady, "Gone with the Wind," *Newsweek*, 28 July 1975, p. 11.

21. James C. Cobb, *Georgia Odyssey* (Athens, Ga., 1997), 84–85.

22. Ibid., 85; Peter Applebome, *Dixie Rising: How the South Is Shaping American Values, Politics, and Culture* (New York, 1996), 194.

23. Cobb, *Georgia Odyssey*, 88–89, 129–30.

24. Mary Hood, "Of Water and Wal-Mart: The Demographics of Progress in a Georgia Community," *Southern Magazine*, January 1987, p. 22.

25. Ibid.

26. Ibid., 22–23.

27. Francis Davis, *The History of the Blues: The Roots, the Music, the People from Charley Patton to Robert Cray* (New York, 1995), 169; Edward L. Ayers, *The Promise of the New South: Life After Reconstruction* (New York and Oxford, 1992), 385, 377, 373.

28. Bill C. Malone, *Country Music, U.S.A.: A Fifty Year History* (Austin, Texas, and London, 1968), 65; Dorothy Horstman, *Sing Your Heart Out, Country Boy* (New York, 1975), 83.

29. Horstman, *Sing Your Heart Out*, 88–89.

30. Charles Wolfe, "Uncle Dave Macon," in Bill C. Malone and Judith McCulloh, eds., *Stars of Country Music: Uncle Dave Macon to Johnny Rodrigues* (Urbana, Chicago, and London, 1975), 42, 59–60.

31. Horstman, *Sing Your Heart Out*, 61.

32. Samuel C. Adams Jr., "The Acculturation of the Delta Negro," *Social Forces*, December 1947, p. 203.

33. James C. Cobb, "From Rocky Top to Detroit City: Country Music and the

Economic Transformation of the South," in Melton A. McLaurin and Richard A. Peterson, eds., *You Wrote My Life: Lyrical Themes in Country Music* (London, 1992), 71.

34. Malone, *Country Music,* 93–99; Tony Scherman, "Country," *American Heritage* 45 (November 1994): 42.

35. Scherman, "Country," 55.

36. Ibid., 47–48.

37. Charlie Gillett, *The Sound of the City: The Rise of Rock and Roll,* rev. ed. (New York, 1983), 8.

38. Pete Daniel, "Rhythm of the Land," *Agricultural History* 68 (Fall 1994): 22.

39. Malone, *Country Music,* 254; Scherman, "Country," 52.

40. Scherman, "Country," 55.

41. John Shelton Reed, *Southerners: The Social Psychology of Sectionalism* (Chapel Hill, 1983); George B. Tindall, *The Ethnic Southerners* (Baton Rouge, 1976); Scherman, "Country," 55.

42. Scherman, "Country," 55.

43. Davis, *History of the Blues,* 2; James C. Cobb, *The Most Southern Place on Earth: The Mississippi Delta and the Roots of Regional Identity* (New York and London, 1992), 289–90, 304–5.

44. Phil Patton, "Who Owns the Blues?" *New York Times,* 26 November 1995.

45. Ibid.; Cobb, *Most Southern Place,* 289–90, 304–5.

46. Patton, "Who Owns the Blues?"; Cobb, *Most Southern Place on Earth,* 284.

47. Tindall, *Ethnic Southerners,* 21; Mark Kemp, "Coming Home to a New Strain of Southern Rock," *New York Times,* 5 July 1998.

48. Kemp, "Coming Home."

49. Ibid.

50. James C. Cobb, "Tomorrow Seems Like Yesterday: The South's Future in the Nation and the World," in Joe P. Dunn and Howard L. Preston, eds., *The Future South: A Historical Perspective for the Twenty-First Century* (Urbana and Chicago, 1991), 229–30.

51. Applebome, *Dixie Rising,* 286–88; *New Orleans Times-Picayune,* 13 August 1995; *New York Times,* 5 August 1995.

52. Jack Temple Kirby, *The Countercultural South* (Athens, Ga., and London, 1995), 73; *Atlanta Journal-Constitution,* 17 September 1995.

53. *Washington Post,* 5 January 1997.

54. Ibid.; Elizabeth Fortson Arroyo, "The Asterisk Southerner," *Oxford American* (August/September 1996): 26, 28.

55. Edwin M. Yoder, "A Dixieland Reverie," *Saturday Review,* 30 May 1964, p. 40.

56. John Shelton Reed, *The Enduring South* (Chapel Hill and London, 1986), 89.

57. Ibid., 91.

58. Ibid., 90.

59. James C. Cobb, "Southern Writers and the Challenge of Regional Convergence: A Comparative Perspective," *Georgia Historical Quarterly* 73 (Spring 1989): 25.

60. Woodward, "Search for Southern Identity," 19; idem., "Irony of Southern History," 187–90.

61. Woodward, "Search for Southern Identity," 19, 25; Michael O'Brien, "The Apprehension of the South in Modern Culture," unpublished paper in possession of the author.

62. Tony Horwitz, *Confederates in the Attic: Dispatches from the Unfinished Civil War* (New York, 1998), 5–6; O'Brien, "Apprehension of the South."

63. Diane Young, "South Watchers," *Southern Living*, April 1998, p. 129; John Shelton Reed, *One South: An Ethnic Approach to Regional Culture* (Baton Rouge, 1982), 186.

64. David L. Cohn, *Where I was Born and Raised* (Cambridge, Mass., 1948), 12; idem., "Growing Up in Greenville," in James C. Cobb, ed., *The Mississippi Delta and the World: The Memoirs of David L. Cohn* (Baton Rouge and London, 1995), 2.